Measuring
the Success of
Learning Through
Technology

A Step-by-Step Guide for Measuring Impact and ROI
on E-Learning, Blended Learning, and Mobile Learning

 es, PhD

Patricia Pulliam Phillips, PhD

Jack J. Phillips, PhD

ASTD
PRESS

ROI INSTITUTE™

ASTD Press is an internationally renowned source of insightful and practical information on workplace learning, training, and professional development.

ASTD Press
1640 King Street Box 1443
Alexandria, VA 22314 USA

Ordering information: Books published by ASTD Press can be purchased by visiting ASTD's website at store.astd.org or by calling 800.628.2783 or 703.683.8100.

Library of Congress Control Number: 2014943562

ISBN-10: 1-56286-950-2
ISBN-13: 978-1-56286-950-2
e-ISBN: 978-1-60728-425-3

ASTD Press Editorial Staff:
Director: Glenn Saltzman
Manager and Editor, ASTD Press: Ashley McDonald
Community of Practice Manager, Learning Technologies: Justin Brusino
Editorial Assistant: Ashley Slade
Cover Design: Lon Levy
Interior Design: Marisa Kelly
Printed by Versa Press, East Peoria, IL, www.versapress.com

Table of Contents

Preface vii

Part I: **The ROI Methodology: A Credible Approach to Evaluating Your Learning Through Technology Programs** 1

Chapter 1   Learning Through Technology: Trends and Issues 3
The Evolution of Learning Techniques 4
Concerns About Technology-Based Learning. 8
Final Thoughts 13

Chapter 2   Measuring ROI: The Basics 15
ROI Defined. 16
The ROI Methodology. 17
ROI Process. 23
Benefits of ROI 24
Final Thoughts 26

Chapter 3   Evaluation Planning and Data Collection 27
Achieving Business Alignment. 28
Developing the Evaluation Plans 34
Considerations for Collecting Data 38
Methods for Collecting Data 41
Generating High Response Rates 44
Identifying the Source. 44
Determining the Timing of Data Collection 47
Final Thoughts 48

Chapter 4   Data Analysis. 49
Isolating the Effects of Learning. 49
Techniques to Isolate the Effects of Learning 50
Selecting Isolation Techniques. 60
Types of Data. 60
Data Conversion Methods. 62
Five Steps to Data Conversion 66
Fully Loaded Costs 67
ROI Calculation. 69
Intangible Benefits 70
Final Thoughts 71

Chapter 5   Reporting and Using the Results 73
             The Importance of Reporting Results 73
             Identify the Needs 74
             Identify the Audience 75
             Select the Media 76
             Develop the Report 78
             Communicate Results and Evaluate the Results of Communication 83
             Delivering Bad News 83
             Using the Data 84
             Final Thoughts 85

Chapter 6   Designing for Results 87
             Communication With Results in Mind 87
             Changing the Role of Participants 88
             Creating Expectations 90
             Design for Relevance 92
             Design for Results 93
             Built-In Application Tools 94
             Use Transfer Tools 97
             Involving the Participant's Manager 99
             Final Thoughts 102

Part II: Evaluation in Action: Case Studies Describing the
             Evaluation of Learning Through Technology Programs   103

Chapter 7   Measuring ROI in Work Engagement: A Blended
             Learning Solution 105
             John Kmiec, Sandra Dugas, Cyndi Gaudet,Heather Annulis,
             Mary Nell McNeese, and Susan Bush

Chapter 8   Measuring ROI in Sales Training: A Game-Based Program   125
             Claude MacDonald, CRP and Louis Larochelle, CRP

Chapter 9   Measuring ROI in a Sales Program: A Web-Based
             Learning Solution 149
             Lizette Zuniga

Chapter 10   Measuring ROI in an English-as-a-Second-Language
             Program: An Online Learning Solution 161
             Edward P. Nathan

Chapter 11 Measuring ROI in an Upgrade Selling Program:
A Mobile Learning Solution 177
Jack J. Phillips and Patti P. Phillips

Chapter 12 Measuring ROI in a Sales Program: An
E-Learning Solutions 195
Patrick Whalen

About the ROI Institute 209
Index 211
About the Authors 217

Preface

Few would dispute the convenience, cost, and efficiency of learning through technology. Whether e-learning, blended learning, or mobile learning, it's usually just in time, just enough, and just for the user, which is the ideal form of customization and convenience for participants. At the same time, for large audiences, e-learning represents a tremendous cost savings. Learning through technology allows large numbers of people to learn at the same time without ever leaving the workplace. What executive wouldn't love that? The problem is that the results are not always apparent. Based on dozens of ROI studies at the ROI Institute, the results at the application and impact levels usually don't measure up to traditional facilitator-led versions.

Some professionals measure the ROI for e-learning on the basis of cost savings alone, comparing e-learning to its facilitator-led counterpart. When large numbers of participants are involved, this cost savings is dramatic. This is acceptable only if the outcome would be the same when comparing both processes. Unfortunately, that's not often the case.

According to ASTD, technology-based learning accounts for about 40 percent of all learning delivery in organizations, representing about $50 billion per year. With that level of investment, executives are interested in the impact and ROI.

ROI for learning through technology can be an elusive number, but it doesn't have to be. Unfortunately, many technology-based learning evaluations are revealing deficiencies with on-the-job success, making it difficult to convince management that e-learning and mobile learning add significant value. Despite the timeliness and low cost of e-learning, executives need assurance that it will drive application and impact. Thus, ASTD and the ROI Institute developed this book to tackle the issue.

By following steps prescribed in this book, designers and developers can significantly affect the success of e-learning at the application and impact levels, ultimately making the ROI easy to develop.

TWO BOOKS IN ONE

While measuring ROI in technology-based learning is not new, no book exists that describes how to apply the ROI Methodology specifically to it. In addition, with the number of case studies available describing its application to technology, we could not pass up the opportunity to share a few. With ASTD's support, we decided to develop two books in one. First we describe the steps that make up the logical approach to evaluation using the ROI Methodology. We outline the step-by-step process that has been used to measure the success of all types of programs and projects in organizations worldwide. The ROI Methodology is the most widely used process to account for noncapital investments. But more importantly, it is an approach to accountability through which program owners collect data that can be used to improve their processes as well. Chapter 1 begins with a brief definition of learning through technology and why ROI is an important part of its accountability story. Chapter 2 outlines the step-by-step ROI Methodology, and chapter 3 discusses evaluation planning and data collection. Chapter 4 presents an overview of the steps required to calculate the ROI: convert data money, tabulate costs, and calculate the ROI. Chapter 5 works as the "how-to" part of the book, with tips on reporting results. Chapter 6 focuses on designing technology-based learning programs to deliver results.

The second part of the book describes how the ROI Methodology has been applied in specific situations. These case studies represent a variety of industries and applications. Table 1 summarizes the case studies in terms of industry, application, and target audience involved in the program.

The authors of the case studies are experienced, professional, knowledgeable, and on the leading edge of learning and development, particularly learning through technology. Collectively, they represent practitioners, consultants, researchers, and professors. All of them are—or will be—highly successful in their fields.

SUGGESTIONS

We welcome your input. If you have ideas or recommendations regarding presentation, case selection, or case quality, please send them to us at ROI Institute, Inc., P.O. Box 380637, Birmingham, AL 35238-0637, or send them via email to info@roiinstitute.net.

TARGET AUDIENCE

Practically every organization is implementing learning through technology programs in some way, and companies and employees alike are beginning to see their potential impact. Executives want to use technology, and they want to see the ROI for that implementation. With this book as a guide, these programs can be positioned to drive results important to all stakeholders. For organizations making major improvements in technology, a measurement system that can show the financial ROI of major programs, while at the same time provide a balanced set of measures, is imperative.

The primary audience for this book is anyone directly charged with implementing technology-based learning programs. This could mean designers, developers, project managers, or the evaluator of technology-based learning programs. They are the ones who request a logical, rational, and credible approach to measuring the success of technology-based learning, along with real-world examples.

TABLE 1. Overview of Case Studies by Industry, Program, and Audience

Case Study	Chapter	Industry	Program	Target Audience
Measuring ROI in Work Engagement: A Blended Learning Solution	7	Plastics Manufacturing	Work Engagement	First-Level Managers
Measuring ROI in Sales Training: A Game-Based Program	8	Telecommunications	Sales Training	Sales Professionals
Measuring ROI in a Sales Program: A Web-Based Learning Solution	9	Financial Services	Sales Skills Improvement	Sales Associates
Measuring ROI in an English-as-a-Second-Language Program: An Online Learning Solution	10	Pharmaceutical	Language Skills	All Employes
Measuring ROI in an Upgrade Selling Program: A Mobile Learning Solution	11	Transportation	Sales Training for Software Upgrade	Sales Associates
Measuring ROI in a Sales Program: An E-Learning Solution	12	Petroleum	Sales Training	Sales Engineers

The second audience is professors. Whether they choose this book for university-level students who are pursuing degrees that include courses or modules on design, as a text for internal workshops for professionals interested in developing and implementing technology programs, or for public seminars on technology implementation, this book will be a valuable reference. It can serve as a supplement to a more detailed text on technology-based learning or as a stand-alone book. This combination of text and casebook offers the technical details of the measurement and evaluation process, along with examples of practical applications, which together show participants that the measurement and evaluation process makes a difference.

A third audience is the researchers and consultants who seek new ways to document program results. This book provides additional insight into how to satisfy clients with impressive results. It shows the application of the leading process on ROI evaluation for learning and performance improvement, including technology-based solutions—a process based on sound theory and logical assumptions. The process described in these examples follows a set of standards that ensure reliable, valid results.

The last audience consists of managers and executives who must support technology-based learning in a variety of ways. These may be managers who are requesting programs, who support their employees as they participate in programs, and those who occasionally advise or assist in the development of programs. In these roles, managers must understand the process and appreciate the value of programs, how they are evaluated, and how the results of the evaluation are used to make improvements.

Each audience should find the book interesting and engaging reading. The case studies detail lessons learned and improvements made to the programs. Discussion questions appear at the end of the case studies to stimulate additional thought and discussion. One of the most effective ways to maximize the usefulness of this book is through group discussions, using the questions to develop and dissect the issues, techniques, methodologies, and results.

We hope you find the two-books-in-one format a useful approach to delivering a sound evaluation process and its application through case studies. We look forward to hearing from you with your comments and feedback. As technology-based learning grows and its application expands, we hope to develop even more case study books on the topic.

ACKNOWLEDGMENTS

Tamar Elkeles

This book is dedicated to my daughter, Mia. She always inspires me to be the best I can be. She is my role model, my greatest source of encouragement, my favorite "plus one" and my BFF. Mia, I am very proud to have you as my daughter. I love you—you rock!

My heartfelt thanks go to Jack and Patti Phillips. You are wonderful colleagues, friends, and business partners. I am so grateful to have both of you in my life. You have influenced me and my thinking so much more than you will ever know. You leave a lasting impression on everyone you meet, and I always cherish our time together. I look forward to our continued collaboration.

This book would not be possible without the hard work of my assistant, Laurie Mee. Thank you, Laurie, for all you do to manage my ever-changing schedule and overall hectic life. You are amazing. I don't know how I'd manage my work life without you.

Special thanks to all of my staff at Qualcomm, who consistently ensure we have a leading-edge learning organization and impact the business in all we do. I truly value all your contributions. I am particularly grateful to Geoff Stead, senior director of mobile learning at Qualcomm, for his assistance with chapter 1.

Thank you to my husband, Larry, for your constant support of my career and acceptance of my engagement in professional endeavors like this book. I appreciate all you do and cannot thank you enough.

And finally, thank you to my father, Gidon Elkeles, who taught me to work hard and enjoy life. Your tremendous wisdom and thoughtful advice were invaluable and have shaped who I am. Thanks, Dad. Your memory lives forever within me.

Jack and Patti Phillips

This book is a how-to guide, as well as a casebook containing the collective work of many individuals. Our first acknowledgment goes to all the case authors. We appreciate you for your commitment to your studies and for your interest in furthering the development and implementation of ROI evaluation in your work within your own organizations or within your clients' organizations.

We would like to thank Belinda Keith, who provided editorial assistance for the book, and Rebecca Finally, thanks to Hope Nicholas, director of publications, for her final touches on the manuscript.

We are very excited about authoring another book with Tamar Elkeles. Tamar is an amazing person and is the most respected CLO. She accomplishes much and her influence is extensive. Thanks, Tamar, for your support, friendship, and inspiration.

Part I

The ROI Methodology

A Credible Approach to Evaluating Your
Learning Through Technology Programs

1

Learning Through Technology:
Trends and Issues

I t's hard to imagine a world of learning and development without technology-based solutions. Imagine a U.S.–based technology company with 250 product launches each year and a need to train the sales team to sell the new product. Bringing the sales team into the classroom environment would be prohibitive in terms of cost, time, and convenience. It is unimaginable that we would do that 250 times during the year with the entire sales team. Technology makes learning easy, convenient, and inexpensive. Imagine a logistics company with 300,000 employees and a need to make all employees aware of a new compliance regulation. The regulation requires some evidence that each employee actually knows this information. A live, face-to-face briefing or an email would be out of the question. Technology makes it happen.

Imagine employees in remote locations in Alaska who need job-related learning. The cost of either bringing them to the classroom or bringing the classroom to them would be prohibitive, and it would also be inconvenient and time-consuming. Technology makes it happen. Imagine that women at a university in the Middle East, unable to attend a live class because it is taught by a male instructor, have no opportunity to take the course. With online learning, the same course is possible for women.

These types of situations are multiplied thousands of times throughout the global landscape. It is difficult to imagine a world of learning and development without technology, and investment in technology continues to grow at astonishing rates. These investments attract attention from executives who often want to know if they're working properly. Executives who have sales teams participate in new product training are concerned that the learning translates into new sales. "Does it make a difference? How does it connect to the business? Does it really add the value that we anticipated? Is it as effective as facilitator-led learning?" These questions and others are fully explored and answered in this book. It's all about how to measure the success of learning through technology. This opening chapter describes the trends and issues for technology-based learning and the need for accountability.

THE EVOLUTION OF LEARNING TECHNIQUES

Technology has been integrated into our lives, both at home and at work. It has dramatically changed how we communicate, how we spend our money, how we spend our time, how we work, how we play, and how we find out more about the world in which we live. But what does this mean for corporate learning, training, and development?

Learning technologies have been used in the workplace for more than 20 years, but it is only in the last few years that their impact could be described as a "fundamental change." This book explores some of the more recent evolutions of learning technology and how it can bring significant change in how we grow and develop our current and future employees.

For as long as we can remember, companies have been training and developing employees, helping them master the skills needed to do their work. What originally started as apprenticeships evolved toward more centralized training as companies grew in size and complexity. Experts were brought to classrooms full of employees to teach them the skills needed to do their jobs better. Much of this early training followed the traditional "knowledge broadcast" model, with the expert on the stage presenting what he knows. Early learning technologies such as projectors, digital presentations, and training videos fit this model well.

In the late 1990s, the rise of the Internet gave a huge boost to "digital content." Suddenly, it was much easier to create and share content around the world. This led to the growth of two very different types of stakeholders: content specialists, who developed and sold learning content in their areas of expertise (for example, financial management); and systems specialists, who developed learning platforms or learning management systems (LMS), which allowed companies to deliver online learning to employees around the world at any time.

Broadly, this was a success. Companies were putting more and more of their training online and were able to reach an increasingly diverse group of learners. The next 10 years were vibrant days for learning technologists, with companies investing heavily in e-learning, excited by the potential cost savings of no more face-to-face training. During this time, hundreds of new e-learning companies formed, merged, and were acquired. Digital content became commoditized and was increasingly bought in segments, either by the hour or by an amount of content. There was little regard for the learning quality itself. Unfortunately, as with many new technologies, a large number of overly enthusiastic training departments forged ahead with this technology trend and mistakenly thought that some badly—e-learning courses would somehow be as effective as expert face-to-face training sessions—they were not!

From the mid-2000s the e-learning market started to mature with the addition of three new ideas and associated technologies:

1. **Shift from training delivery to talent management:** Some of the leading LMS vendors started to add enhanced features to their platforms to appeal to HR and training departments. These platforms evolved into "talent management platforms," which included features like employee development plans and talent management tools. Their popularity grew rapidly, since both companies and employees were becoming increasingly dissatisfied with using "course completions" as a meaningful criterion for successful employee development.

2. **Increased use of blended learning:** Digital content and LMS-style platforms don't work just for remote learners. In fact, they are most effective when used in combination with a face-to-face classroom experience. After an initial frenzy of "do it all online," many training professionals discovered that the best use of these new technologies was to enhance traditional training, not replace it. The technologies didn't change much, but how they were used did!

3. **Virtual classrooms, video streaming, collaboration tools:** As the use of social media grew and video tools like Skype and WebCT entered the mainstream, trainers were able to mix more of the benefits of a face-to-face training class with the reach of a web-based learning platform. Students from all over the world could log on together to a live session and participate in online discussions.

These three ideas helped e-learning evolve into a more useful business tool and consolidate a small number of big players, who offer platforms that can deliver on all of these features. But this only gets us to 2010. Who are the learning technology leaders that are prepared to replace these big players? What are the emerging innovations in learning technology?

Mobile Learning

Much hyped but only moderately understood, mobile learning involves mobile devices woven into a learning or training scenario. Often, but not always, the learners themselves are mobile. Mobile learning has found significant success in areas where traditional training or learning are not working that well (such as hard-to-reach learners or traveling employees). It has also triggered a rethink about traditional e-learning modules. Mobile is great for instantaneous lookup, and small, chunk-based learning, but a poor tool for a drawn-out e-learning course.

The most important aspect to bear in mind is that mobile learning isn't just one thing. It is a toolbox of approaches that can be used how and when it's needed. Conversations about mobile learning in schools are likely to be very different from those in the college or work setting.

Mobile learning is already making a huge impact in some industries and in specific areas. It will continue to do so, but don't assume it replaces all face-to-face experiences. Think of it more as an enriching and enhancing aspect of training.

Game-Based Learning

Game-based learning has been described as the next big thing for the past 10 years. Two often repeated disastrous models are:

- An interesting game, often a first-person adventurer/puzzle-solving variety, with corny 2-D content quizzes scattered throughout. A fun game ruined by insufficient learning.
- A linear e-learning-style content course with a series of quizzes and knowledge tests that have been built up into a contest/competition format. The "game" just proves content knowledge.

There is very little evidence that either of these models works. There are a few instances where the latter can work well, such as where mastery of the subject matter required drill and practice (like learning vocabulary or practicing math).

Two interesting and more successful models are:

- Playing a real game, designed for entertainment, but setting challenges within it that build on learning.
- Doing real learning tasks, but using a badging system to show progress and gains. Mozilla's Open Badges framework offers good tools for this.

Mixing play with learning has always been effective and will continue to be so. But low-quality resources aren't magically improved by adding a quiz at the end, a leaderboard, or badges. Get the learning right first, then implement around it.

Bring Your Own Devices (BYOD)

"Bring your own devices" (BYOD) refers to initiatives that allow students or employees to use their own personal mobile technology devices at work or at school as part of their day. Opinions about this technique vary widely, although in most scenarios it is a useful and empowering approach. In colleges, the main concerns are about classroom management and fairness of access. In the workplace, concerns range from privacy of personal data to security of corporate data. BYOD is here to stay. Organizations need to adapt their policies to support it, rather than resisting the use of personal mobile technology devices. Resistance puts them in a race to provide equivalent devices and access.

Open Educational Resources (OER)

Historically, there has been an uncomfortable relationship between publishers and educators. Who owns the rights to the content used during teaching and training? How much should be paid for the books and resources?

Enter the OER movement—open educational resources that can be used, modified, and shared for free. They're mostly used in the context of traditional education (not much in corporate training). Momentum seems to be moving faster in some countries than others, but many heavyweight backers, funders, and institutions are starting to put their money and weight behind the idea that educational resources should be made available for free.

It is still a fairly disconnected movement with many different stakeholders and various definitions of "free" and "open." But a large range of very good resources and publications have already been made available. In some cases, teams of educators are working together to write their own collaborative textbooks as open alternatives to commercial ones.

Of note is Creative Commons, which offers a very simple licensing model to help users understand exactly how free content can be used and reused while still respecting the creator of the content.

Massive Open Online Course (MOOC)

A MOOC is a web-based course, often free, designed to offer learning to many thousands of students at the same time. Although they have been around since 2008, they have received a lot of attention since 2012, thanks to recent backing from some notable schools (Stanford, Princeton, and MIT, for example) and high-profile start-ups. However, the most recent hype is also slightly skewed to one specific genre of MOOC.

Why is everyone suddenly excited about MOOCs? Several schools have started offering free access to their course materials. This is a real-world case of the democratization of learning. A student at an under-resourced school can now access the same content as an MIT graduate. However, the fast pace of change hasn't taken into account some of the unforeseen issues surrounding this broadened access. Once access to education is opened up and notions of paying for courses are removed, is the perceived quality of the course reduced? Should a nonresident student be able to earn a degree from the college offering a course? Is distance learning devoid of a pastoral context equivalent to the full collegiate experience? The debates surrounding MOOCs have compromised the perception of them. Some see them purely as a distribution channel for prerecorded mass learning. Many of the most inspired MOOCs are not modeled on a traditional lecture- or classroom-based experience at all; rather, they're built on learner-centered, connectivist environments where students work together, albeit remotely.

To try to distinguish between these, one of the founders of the MOOC movement has suggested renaming them xMOOC and cMOOC. xMOOCs are modeled on a traditional lecture-based experience, with professors handing over the knowledge; and cMOOCs are collaborative courses, where learners work together the generate their knowledge.

For the purposes of this discussion we have coined a new term, domain MOOCs. These are MOOCs designed for individual access, to teach a specific subject by making the content available for free, to be used in other platforms. Aligned with these are sites offering indexes to all of these courses, styling themselves as MOOC aggregators.

Flipped Classroom

If so much information is available online and quality time with a teacher is hard to find, why waste the time you have together by sitting quietly in your chair and listening to a lecture? Far better, perhaps, to watch the recorded lecture before you come into class and then spend the face-to-face time discussing it, asking questions, and doing activities. This is the idea behind the flipped classroom, and it has some great stories around it.

CONCERNS ABOUT TECHNOLOGY-BASED LEARNING

Technology, with its many forms and features, is here to stay. Its growth is inevitable and its use is predestined. At the same time, some concerns must be addressed about the accountability and success of technology-based learning. Three critical issues create a dilemma: the need for business results, the executive view, and a lack of results.

The Need for Business Results

Most would agree that any large expenditure in an organization should in some way be connected to business success. Even in nonbusiness settings, large investments should connect to organizational measures of output, quality, cost, and time—classic measure categories of hard data that exist in any type of organization. In a review of articles, reports, books, and blogs about learning through technology, the emphasis is on making a business connection. For example, in the book *Learning Everywhere: How Mobile Content Strategies Are Transforming Training* (2012) author Chad Udell makes the case for connecting mobile learning to businesses measures. He starts by listing the important measures that are connected to the business. A sampling is shown in Table 1-1.

Udell goes on to say that mobile learning should connect to any of these, and he takes several measures step-by-step to show how, in practical and logical thinking, a mobile learning solution can drive any or all of these measures. He concludes by suggesting that if an organization is investing in mobile learning or any other type of learning, it needs to connect to these business measures. Otherwise, it shouldn't be pursued. This dramatic call for accountability is not that unusual.

TABLE 1-1. High-Level Business Benefits From Mobile Learning

Decreased Product Returns	Reduced Incidents
Increased Productivity	Decreased Defects
Increased Accuracy	Increased Shipments
Fewer Mistakes	On-Time Shipments
Reduced Rise	Decreased Cycle Time
Increased Sales	Less Downtime
Less Waste	Reduced Operating Cost
Fewer Accidents	Fewer Customer Complaints
Fewer Compliance Discrepancies	Reduced Response Time to Customers

Source: Adapted from Udell, C. (2012). *Learning Everywhere: How Mobile Content Strategies are Transforming Training.* Nashville, TN: Rockbench Publishing (co-published with ASTD Press).

The Executive View

Those who fund budgets are adamant about seeing the connection. Yes, these executives realize that employees must learn through technology, using the devices, while being actively involved in the process and enrolled in the programs. But more importantly, they must use what they've learned and have the business impact. Top executives weighed in on this issue in an important study sponsored by ASTD (*Measuring for Success: What CEOs Really Think About Learning Investment*, 2010). In a study of large company CEOs, particularly the Fortune 500 group, the executives indicated the extent to which they see certain type of metrics connected to learning now, what they would like to see in the future, and the ranking of these measures. Table 1-2 shows the results.

Clearly, this table shows that regardless of what method of learning is used, executives want to see the business connection. In total, 96 percent of them want to see business impact, but only 8 percent see it now. Surprisingly, 74 percent would like to see the ROI on learning, and yet only 4 percent see it now. Even for application, the use of the learning on the job, 61 percent wanted to see this data, and only 11 percent see it now. Clearly, the measures that executives want to see are not being pursued to a significant degree by the learning and development team, regardless of whether learning is technology based or classroom based.

TABLE 1-2. Executive View of Learning Investments

Measure	We Currently Measure This	We Should Measure This in the Future	My Ranking of the Importance of This Measure
Inputs: "Last year, 78,000 employees received formal learning."	94%	85%	6
Efficiency: "Formal learning costs $2.15 per hour of learning consumed."	78%	82%	7
Reaction: "Employees rated our training very high, averaging 4.2 out of 5."	53%	22%	8
Learning: "92% of participants increased knowledge and skills."	32%	28%	5
Application: "At least 78% of employees are using the skills on the job."	11%	61%	4
Impact: "Our programs are driving our top five business measures in the organization."	8%	96%	1
ROI: "Five ROI studies were conducted on major programs, yielding an average of 68% ROI."	4%	74%	2
Awards: "Our learning and development program won an award from the American Society of Training & Development."	40%	44%	3

Results Are Missing

Unfortunately, the majority of results presented in learning through technology case studies are devoid of measurements at the levels needed by executives. Only occasionally are application data presented, measuring what individuals do with what they learn, and rarely do they report a credible connection to the business. Even rarer is the ROI calculation. In a recent review of award-winning e-learning and mobile learning case studies published by several prestigious organizations, the following observations of results were noted.

- No study was evaluated at the ROI level where the monetary value of the impact was compared to the program's cost to calculate the ROI. Only two or three were evaluated on the cost savings of technology-based learning compared to facilitator-led learning. This may not be a credible evaluation.

- The benefits and results sections of the studies mentioned ROI but didn't present it. They used the concept of ROI to mean any value or benefit from the program. Mislabeling or misusing ROI creates some concerns among executives who are accustomed to seeing ROI calculated a very precise way from the finance and accounting team.
- Credible connections to the business were rare. Only one study attempted to show the impact of mobile learning using comparison groups. Even there, the details about how the groups were set up and the actual differences were left out. When the data are vague or missing, it raises a red flag.
- Many of the studies made the connection to the business based on anecdotal comments, often taken from very small samples. Sometimes comments were observations from people far removed from the actual application. For example, a corporate manager suggesting that e-learning is "making a difference in store performance."
- Very few results were provided for application. Although they can be built in, they were rarely reported, usually listed as antidotal comments about the use of the content and the success they are having with its use.
- Learning was measured, but in less than half of the studies. Learning is at the heart of the process, yet it was left out of many of these studies.
- Reaction was typically not addressed in these studies. Reaction measures such as "relevant to my work," "important to my success," "I would recommend it to others," and "I intend to use this" are very powerful predictors, but not measured very frequently in technology solutions.

Clearly, as this review of studies has shown, there is more talk than action when it comes to the value of technology-based learning. So the pressure is on for proponents of technology-based learning to show the value to funders and sponsors, and this accountability should include business impact and maybe even the ROI. Although business impact and ROI are critical for senior executives, they rarely make this level of analysis. Let's explore why.

Reasons for Lack of Data

In our analysis of technology-based learning programs, several major barriers have emerged. These obstacles keep the proponents from developing metrics to the levels desired by executives. Here are eight of the most significant ones.

1. **Fear of results.** Although few will admit it, the number one barrier is that the individuals who design, develop, or own a particular program are concerned about evaluation at the business impact and ROI levels. They have a fear that if the results are not there, the program may be discontinued and it will affect their reputation and performance. They prefer not to know, instead of actually taking the time to make the connection. The

fear can be reduced if process improvement is the goal—not performance evaluation for users, designers, developers, and owners.

2. **This is not necessary.** Some of the designers and developers are suggesting that investments in technology-based learning should be measured on the faith that it will make a difference. Though executives may want results at these levels, there is a concern that technology should not be subjected to that level of accountability. After all, technology is absolutely necessary in the situations outlined in the beginning of this chapter. Although the learning may have to be technology based, this doesn't preclude it from also delivering results.

3. **Measuring at this level is not planned.** When capturing the business impact and developing the ROI, the process starts from the very beginning, at the conception of the project or program. The planning at this point helps facilitate the process and even drive the needed results. Unfortunately, evaluation is not given serious consideration until after the project is implemented—too late for an effective evaluation.

4. **Measurement is too difficult.** Some feel it is too difficult to capture the data or that it's impossible to secure quality information. Data collection was not built into the process, so therefore it takes extra steps to find it. When it's collected, it's difficult to connect the business data to the program and convert to monetary value. The ROI seems to be too complicated to even think about. Using systematic, easy steps helps with this process. Technology proponents tackle some very difficult problems and create marvelous solutions requiring much more knowledge, expertise, and capability than the measurement side of the process. Measurement is easy and doesn't demand high-level mathematics, knowledge of statistics, or expertise in finance and accounting.

5. **Impact and ROI is too expensive.** By the time the evaluation is considered, the investment in technology and development is high and designers are unwilling to invest in measurement. The perception is that this would be too expensive, adding cost to a budget that is already strained. In reality, the cost of evaluation is a very minute part of the cost of the project, often less than 1 percent of the total cost, for an ROI study.

6. **Measurement is not the fun part of the process.** Technology-based learning is amazing, awesome, and impressive. What can be accomplished is exciting for those involved and for those who use it. Gamification is taking hold. People love games. They're fun. Measuring the application, impact, and ROI is not fun. Metrics could be made more interesting and fun at the same time using built-in tools and technology. Designers,

developers, and owners need to step up to the responsibility to show the value of these processes.

7. **Not knowing which programs to evaluate at this level.** Some technology proponents think that if they go down the ROI path, executives will want to see the ROI in every project and program. In that case, the situation seems mind boggling and almost impossible. We agree. The challenge is to select particular projects or programs that will need to be evaluated at this level.

8. **Not prepared for this.** The preparation for designers, developers, implementers, owners, and project managers does not usually include courses in metrics, evaluation, and analytics. Fortunately, things are changing. These issues are now addressed in formal education. Even ROI Certification is available for technology-based learning applications.

Because these barriers are perceived to be real, they inhibit evaluation at the levels desired by executives. But they are myths for the most part. Yes, evaluation will take more time and there will be a need for more planning. But the step-by-step process is logical. Technology owners bear the responsibility to show the value of what they own. The appropriate level of evaluation is achievable within the budget and it is feasible to accomplish. This book shows how it's done in simple, easy processes. The challenge is to take the initiative and be proactive—not wait for executives to force the issue. Owners and developers must build in accountability, measure successes, report results to the proper audiences, and make adjustments and improvements. This brings technology-based learning to the same level of accountability that IT faces in the implementation of its major systems and software packages. IT executives have to show the impact, and often the ROI, of those implementations. Technology-based learning should not escape this level of accountability.

FINAL THOUGHTS

This initial chapter covered the landscape of technology-based learning, revealing some of the trends and issues of this explosive phenomenon in the learning and development field. There is no doubt that learning through technology is the wave of the future. It has to be, with complex and large organizations and an ever increasing need for learning. In a society that is willing to take only small amounts of time for anything, learning through technology is just in time, just enough, and just for the user. However, it must be subjected to accountability guidelines. It must deliver value that is important to all groups, including those who fund it. Executives who fund large amounts of technology-based learning want to see the value of their programs and projects. Their definition of value is often application, impact, and ROI. The challenge is to move forward and accomplish this in the face of several barriers that can easily get in the way. The rest of the book will show how this is accomplished.

2

Measuring ROI: The Basics

Measuring and evaluating learning through technology has earned a place among the critical issues in the learning and development and performance improvement fields. For decades, this topic has been on conference agendas and discussed at professional meetings. Journals and newsletters regularly embrace the concept, dedicating increased print space to it. Even executives have an increased appetite for evaluation data.

Although interest in the topic has heightened and much progress has been made, it is still an issue that challenges even the most sophisticated and progressive learning departments. While some professionals argue that having a successful evaluation process is difficult, others are quietly and deliberately implementing effective evaluation systems. The latter group has gained tremendous support from the senior management team and has made much progress. Regardless of the position taken on the issue, the reasons for measurement and evaluation are intensifying. Almost all technology-based learning professionals share a concern that they must show the results of the investments. Otherwise, funds may be reduced or the function may not be able to maintain or enhance its present status and influence within the organization.

The dilemma surrounding the evaluation of learning through technology is a source of frustration with many senior executives—even within the field itself. Most executives realize that technology-based learning is a basic necessity when organizations experience significant growth or increased competition. They intuitively feel that providing e-learning and mobile learning opportunities is valuable, logically anticipating a payoff in important bottom-line measures, such as productivity improvements, quality enhancements, cost reductions, time savings, and improved customer service. Yet the frustration comes from the lack of evidence to show that programs really work. While results are assumed to exist and programs appear to be necessary, more evidence is needed, or executives may feel forced to adjust funding in the future. A comprehensive measurement and evaluation process represents the most promising, logical, and rational approach to show this accountability. This book shows how to

---

For more detail on this methodology, see *The Value of Learning: How Organizations Capture Value and ROI and Translate Them Into Support, Improvement, Funds* (Phillips and Phillips, 2007, Pfeiffer).

measure the contributions of learning through technology with several case studies. This chapter defines the basic ROI issues and introduces the ROI Methodology.

ROI DEFINED

Return on investment (ROI) is the ultimate measure of accountability. Within the context of measuring learning through technology, it answers the question: For every dollar invested in technology-based learning, how many dollars were returned after the investment is recovered? ROI is an economic indicator that compares earnings (or net benefits) to investment, and is expressed as a percentage. The concept of ROI to measure the success of investment opportunities has been used in business for centuries to measure the return on capital expenditures such as buildings, equipment, or tools. As the need for greater accountability in learning, demonstrated effectiveness, and value increases, ROI is becoming an accepted way to measure the impact and return on investment of all types of programs, including technology-based learning.

The counterpart to ROI, benefit-cost ratio (BCR), has also been used for centuries. Benefit-cost analysis became prominent in the United States in the early 1900s, when it was used to justify projects initiated under the River and Harbor Act of 1902 and the Flood Control Act of 1936. ROI and the BCR provide similar indicators of investment success, although one (ROI) presents the earnings (net benefits) as compared to the cost, while the other (BCR) compares benefits to costs. Here are the basic equations used to calculate the BCR and the ROI:

$$BCR = \frac{\text{Program Benefits}}{\text{Program Costs}}$$

$$ROI\,(\%) = \frac{\text{Program Benefits} - \text{Program Costs}}{\text{Program Costs}} \times 100$$

What is the difference between these two equations? A BCR of 2:1 means that for every $1 invested, $2 in benefits are generated. This translated into an ROI of 100 percent, which says that for every $1 invested, $1 is returned after the costs are covered (the investment is recovered plus $1 extra).

Benefit-cost ratios were used in the past, primarily in public sector settings, while ROI was used mainly by accountants managing capital expenditures in business and industry. Either calculation can be used in both settings, but it is important to understand the difference. In many cases the benefit-cost ratio and the ROI are reported together.

While ROI is the ultimate measure of accountability, basic accounting practice suggests that reporting the ROI metric alone is insufficient. To be meaningful, ROI must be reported with other performance measures. This approach is taken with the ROI Methodology, the basis for the studies in this book.

THE ROI METHODOLOGY

The ROI Methodology is comprised of five key elements that work together to complete the evaluation puzzle. Figure 2-1 illustrates how these elements are interconnected to create a comprehensive evaluation system.

FIGURE 2-1. Key Elements of an Evaluation System

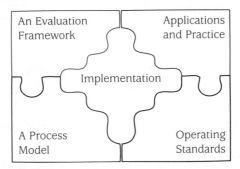

Evaluation Framework

The system begins with the five-level ROI framework, developed in the 1970s and becoming prominent in the 1980s. Today, this framework is used to categorize results for all types of programs and projects.

- *Level 1 Reaction and Planned Action* data represent the reactions to the program and the planned actions from participants. Reactions may include views of the format, ease of use, convenience, and fit. This category must include data that reflect the value of the program content, including measures of relevance, importance, amount of new information, and participants' willingness to recommend the program to others.

- *Level 2 Learning* data represent the extent to which participants have acquired new knowledge about their strengths, development areas, and skills needed to be successful. This category also includes the level of confidence of participants as they plan to apply their newly acquired knowledge and skills on the job.

- *Level 3 Application and Implementation* data determine the extent to which professionals apply their newly acquired knowledge and skills from the learning program. This category of data also includes data that describe the barriers preventing application, as well as any supporting elements (enablers) in the knowledge and skill transfer process.

- *Level 4 Business Impact* data are collected and analyzed to determine the extent to which applications of acquired knowledge and skills positively influenced key measures that were intended to improve as a result of the learning experience. The measures include errors, rejects, new accounts, customer complaints, sales, customer returns, down time, cycle time, job engagement, compliance, absenteeism, and operating costs. When reporting data at this level, a step to isolate the program's effect on these measures is always taken.

- *Level 5 Return on Investment* compares the monetary benefits of the impact measures (as they are converted to monetary value) to the fully loaded program costs. Improvement can occur in sales, for example, but to calculate the ROI, the measure of improvement must be converted to monetary value (profit of the sale) and compared to the cost of the program. If the monetary value of sales improvement exceeds the costs, the calculation is a positive ROI.

Each level of evaluation answers basic questions regarding the success of the program. Table 2-1 presents these questions.

TABLE 2-1. Evaluation Framework and Key Questions

Level of Evaluation	Key Questions
Level 1: Reaction and Planned Action	• Was the learning relevant to the job and role? • Was the learning important to the job and success of the participant? • Did the learning provide the participant with new information? • Do participants intend to use what they learned? • Would they recommend the program or process to others? • Is there room for improvement in duration and format?
Level 2: Learning	• Did participants gain the knowledge and skills identified at the start of the program? • Do participants know how to apply what they learned? • Are participants confident to apply what they learned?
Level 3: Application and Implementation	• How effectively are participants applying what they learned? • How frequently are participants applying what they learned? • Are participants successful with applying what they have learned? • If participants are applying what they learned, what is supporting them? • If participants are not applying what they learned, why not?

Level 4: Business Impact	• So what if the application is successful—what impact will it have on the business? • To what extent did application of knowledge and skills improve the business measures the program was intended to improve? • How did the program affect sales, productivity, operating costs, cycle time, errors, rejects, job engagement, and other measures? • How do you know it was the learning program that improved these measures?
Level 5: ROI	• Do the monetary benefits of the improvement in business impact measures outweigh the cost of the technology-based learning program?

Source: ROI Institute, Inc.

Categorizing evaluation data as levels provides a clear and understandable framework to manage the technology-based learning design and objectives and manage the data collection process. More importantly, however, these five levels present data in a way that makes it easy for the audience to understand the results reported for the program. While each level of evaluation provides important, stand-alone data, when reported together, the five-level ROI framework represents data that tell the complete story of program success or failure. Figure 2-2 presents the chain of impact that occurs as participants react positively to the program; acquire new knowledge, skills, and awareness; apply the new knowledge, skills, and awareness; and, as a consequence, positively affect key business measures. When these measures are converted to monetary value and compared to the fully loaded costs, an ROI is calculated. Along with the ROI and the four other categories of data, intangible benefits are reported. These represent Level 4 measures that are not converted to monetary value.

ROI Process Model

The second part of the evaluation puzzle is the process model. As presented in Figure 2-3, the process model is a step-by-step guide to ensure a consistent approach to evaluating a learning project. Each phase of the four-phase process contains critical steps that must be taken to ensure the output of a credible evaluation. The ROI process is described in more detail in the next section.

FIGURE 2-2. Chain of Impact

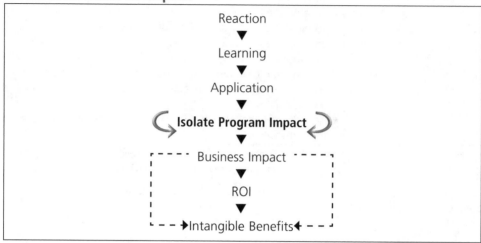

Source: Phillips, P.P., and J.J. Phillips. (2005). *Return on Investment Basics.* Alexandria, VA: ASTD Press.

Operating Standards and Philosophy

The third piece of the evaluation puzzle ensures consistent decision making around the application of the ROI Methodology. These standards, called the 12 Guiding Principles of the ROI Methodology, provide clear guidance about the specific ways to implement the methodology to ensure consistent, reliable practice in evaluating learning through technology. When these guiding principles (shown in Table 2-2) are followed, consistent results can be achieved. Additionally, these principles help maintain a conservative and credible approach to data collection and analysis. They serve as a decision-making tool and influence decisions on the best approach by which to collect data, the best source and timing for data collection, the most appropriate approach for isolation and data conversion, the costs to be included, and the stakeholders to whom results are reported. Adhering to the principles provides credibility when reporting results to executives.

FIGURE 2-3. The ROI Process Model

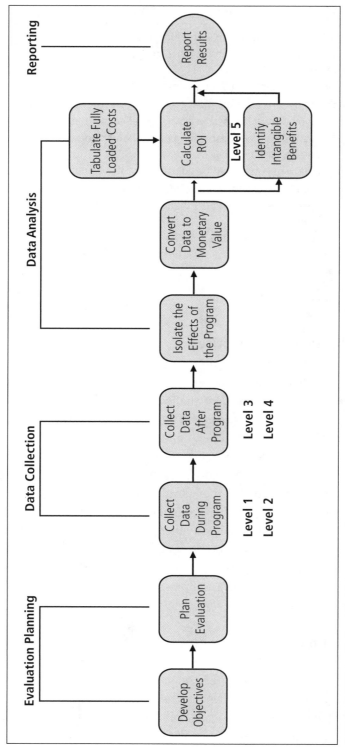

TABLE 2-2. 12 Guiding Principles for Effective ROI Implementation

1. When a higher level of evaluation is conducted, data must be collected at lower levels.
2. When an evaluation is planned for a higher level, the previous level of evaluation does not have to be comprehensive.
3. When collecting and analyzing data, use only the most credible sources.
4. When analyzing data, choose the most conservative alternatives for calculations.
5. At least one method must be used to isolate the effects of the solution/program.
6. If no improvement data are available for a population or from a specific source, it is assumed that no improvement has occurred.
7. Estimates of improvements should be adjusted for the potential error of the estimate.
8. Extreme data items and unsupported claims should not be used in ROI calculations.
9. Only the first year of benefits (annual) should be used in the ROI analysis for short-term solutions/programs.
10. Costs of the solution/program should be fully loaded for ROI analysis.
11. Intangible measures are defined as measures that are purposely not converted to monetary values.
12. The results from the ROI Methodology must be communicated to all key stakeholders.

Source: ROI Institute, Inc.

Case Applications and Practice

The fourth piece of the ROI Methodology evaluation puzzle includes case applications and practice, which allow for a deeper understanding of the ROI Methodology's comprehensive evaluation process. Case studies are a way to provide evidence of a program's success. Thousands of case studies across many industries, including business and industry, healthcare, government, and even community and faith-based initiatives, have been developed, describing the application of the ROI Methodology. The case studies in this book, all based on measuring the ROI in learning through technology, provide excellent examples of application of the ROI Methodology.

Practitioners beginning their pursuit of the ROI Methodology can learn from these case studies, as well as those found in other publications. However, the best learning comes from actual application. Conducting an ROI study around learning through technology will allow participants to see how the framework, process model, and operating standards come together. The first study serves as a starting line for a track record of program success.

Implementation

The last piece of the ROI Methodology evaluation puzzle is implementation. While it is significant to conduct an ROI study, one study alone adds little value to your efforts to continuously improve and account for learning investments. The key to a successful learning function is to sustain the use of ROI. Building the philosophy of the ROI Methodology into everyday decision making is imperative for attaining credibility and consistency in learning effectiveness. Implementing the ROI Methodology requires assessing the organization's culture for accountability and its readiness for evaluating technology-based learning programs at the ROI level. It also requires defining the purpose for pursuing this level of evaluation; building expertise and capability; and creating tools, templates, and standard processes.

ROI PROCESS

To evaluate a technology-based learning program using the ROI Methodology, it is important to follow the step-by-step process to ensure consistent, reliable results. These 10 steps taken during the four phases of an evaluation project make up the evaluation process model.

Evaluation Planning

The first phase of a successful application of the ROI Methodology is planning. The plan addresses the key questions about the evaluation and defines how to know when success has been achieved. The plan begins with developing and reviewing the program objectives to ensure that the application and impact objectives have been defined. Next, the data collection plan is developed, which includes defining the measures for each level of evaluation, selecting the data collection instrument, identifying the source of the data, and determining the timing of data collection. The baseline data for the measures being tracked should be collected during this time. The next step is to develop the ROI analysis plan. Working from the impact data, the most appropriate technique to isolate the effects of the learning initiative is selected. The most credible method for converting data to money is identified along with the cost categories for the program. Intangible benefits are listed and the communication targets for the final report are identified.

Data Collection

Once the planning phase is complete, the data collection phase begins. Level 1 and 2 data are collected as learning takes place, using common instruments such as questionnaires, completion of exercises, demonstrations, and a variety of other techniques. Follow-up data at Levels 3 and 4 are collected after the program is complete, when application of the newly acquired knowledge, skills, attitudes, and awareness becomes routine. After the application the consequences are captured as impact measures.

Data Analysis

Once the data are collected, data analysis begins. As described earlier, the method for data analysis is defined in the planning stage; so data analysis is just a matter of execution. The first step in data analysis is to isolate the effects of the learning program on impact data. Isolation is often overlooked when evaluating the success of technology-based learning programs, yet this step answers the critical question, "How much of the improvement in business measures is due to this particular learning program?"

Moving from Level 4 to Level 5 begins with converting Level 4 impact measures to monetary value. This step is usually easy because most of the important impact data are already converted to money. If not, there are some easy techniques to use. The fully loaded costs are developed during the data analysis phase. These costs include needs assessment (when conducted), design, participants' time, overhead, and evaluation costs.

Intangible benefits are also identified during the data analysis phase. Intangible benefits are the Level 4 measures that are not converted to monetary value. These measures can also represent any unplanned program benefits that were not identified during the planning phase.

The final step of the data analysis phase is the ROI calculation. Using simple addition, subtraction, multiplication, and division, the ROI is calculated.

Reporting

The most important phase in the evaluation process is the final report. Evaluation without communication of results is a worthless endeavor. If the key stakeholders are not aware of the program's progress, it is difficult to improve the process, secure additional funding, and market programs to other participants.

While there are a variety of ways to report data, a micro-level report of the complete ROI impact study is important. This is a record of the success of the learning program. (A macro-level reporting process includes results for all programs, projects, and initiatives, and serves as a scorecard of results for all initiatives.) An important point to remember, however, is regardless of how detailed or brief the report may be, the information in it must be actionable. Otherwise, there is no value in conducting the ROI analysis.

BENEFITS OF ROI

The ultimate use of results generated through the ROI Methodology is to show value of programs, specifically the economic value. However, there are a variety of other uses for ROI data, including justification of spending, improvement of the programs, and gain of support for learning through technology.

Justify Spending

Justifying spending on technology-based learning is becoming critical today. Learning managers are often required to justify investments in existing and new programs, as well as investment in changes or enhancements to existing programs.

For those who are serious about justifying investments in learning through technology, the ROI Methodology described in this book is a valuable tool. For new programs where a preprogram justification is required, there are two approaches: preprogram forecasts and ROI calculated on pilot implementation.

Calculating ROI in existing programs is more common in practice than forecasting success for new programs. Typically, ROI is used to justify continued investments in existing programs. While technology-based learning programs have been routinely conducted, there is sometimes a concern that the value does not justify continuation of the program.

Improve the Learning Program

The most important use of the ROI Methodology is to improve programs. Data are collected along a chain of impact as the results are generated. When there is a lack of success, the causes are pinpointed. These are the barriers. In addition, certain factors that have caused the success are identified. These are the enablers. Together, this information helps to improve the learning program.

Set Priorities

In almost all organizations, the need for learning exceeds available resources. A comprehensive evaluation process, such as the ROI Methodology, can help determine which programs rank as the highest priority. Learning programs with greatest impact (or the potential for greatest impact) are often top priority. Of course, this approach has to be moderated by taking a long view, ensuring that developmental efforts are in place for a long-term payoff.

Eliminate Unsuccessful Programs

While eliminating a learning initiative is rare, it's possible that this action would be taken only if the learning program cannot add the value that was envisioned (it was the wrong solution). Sometimes, a program is no longer needed or necessary, but a new need for a different process emerges. The ROI Methodology can help determine which approach is eliminated and which alternative is selected as a replacement.

Gain Support

Another use for the ROI Methodology is to gain support for learning through technology. A successful program needs support from key executives and administrators. Showing the ROI for programs can alter managers' and executives' perceptions and enhance the respect and credibility of all technology-based learning.

Key executives and administrators are likely the most important group to influence learning programs. They commit resources and show support for learning with the need to achieve results that positively affect business impact. To ensure that effective programs are continued, it is necessary for learning managers to think like business leaders—focusing programs on results in the organization. ROI is one way this focus can occur. ROI evaluation provides the economic justification and value of investing in the technology-based learning program selected to solve a problem or take advantage of an opportunity.

Managers and supervisors of participants can sometimes be antagonistic about learning programs, questioning their value. When this occurs, it is generally because the manager or supervisor has not seen success with a change in behavior from participants. Managers and supervisors aren't interested in what their participants learn; they are interested in what they do with what they learn. Participants also must take learning gained through the programs a step further by showing the effect on the job with outcomes in errors, rejects, sales, new accounts, incidents, down time, operating costs, and engagement. If the programs can show results linked to the business, managers and supervisors will provide increased support for these programs.

Participants and prospective participants should also support the program. Showing the value of programs, including ROI, can enhance their credibility. When a technology-based learning program is achieving serious results, participants will view programs in a value-add way and may be willing to spend time away from their pressing duties. Also, by making adjustments in the learning based on the evaluation findings, participants will see that the evaluation process is not just a superficial attempt to show value.

FINAL THOUGHTS

This chapter introduced the concept of the ROI Methodology, a systematic and logical process with conservative standards that is used by more than 5,000 organizations. The process collects and generates six types of data: reaction, learning, application, impact, ROI, and intangible benefits. It also includes techniques to isolate the effects of the learning on impact data, such as sales, productivity, new accounts, quality, costs, and time. The next three chapters explain this process in more detail and form the basis for the case studies presented in later chapters. Chapter 3 introduces the important steps of evaluation planning and the first major challenge, data collection.

3

Evaluation Planning and Data Collection

As the learning and development profession has matured, accountability of learning has increased. In the past, we could provide learning solutions, including technology-enabled learning, to clients and measure the success of that solution based upon self-reports. But in a complex world of increased scrutiny, less time, and fewer resources, this is no longer enough. Instead, the very real demands for learning require a shift from an activity-based approach to a results-based approach to learning through technology, as outlined in Table 3-1. In some cases, executives want to see the financial ROI.

TABLE 3-1. Activity-Based vs. Results-Based Approach

Activity-Based	Results-Based
Business need is not linked to the learning.	Program is linked to specific business impact measures, such as revenue, productivity, quality, cost, time, and new customers.
No assessment of performance issues that need to change to meet business needs.	There is an assessment of performance that needs to improve to meet business needs.
Smart objectives are not developed for application.	Smart objectives for change and the related business impact are identified.
Participants are not fully prepared to achieve results from the program.	Results expectations are communicated to, and in partnership with, participants.
Work environment is not prepared to support the transfer of learning to application and business impact.	Work environment is prepared to support transfer of learning to application and business impact.
Partnerships with key managers to support the participants have not been identified and developed.	Partnerships are established with key managers prior to learning to ensure participation and support.
Results or ROI analysis in real, tangible, and objective measures—including monetary impact—are not captured.	Results and ROI analysis are measured.
Planning and reporting is input focused.	Planning and reporting is outcome focused.

For more detail on this shift, see *The Value of Learning: How Organizations Capture Value and ROI and Translate Them Into Support, Improvement, Funds* (Phillips and Phillips, 2007, Pfeiffer).

For learning programs to lead to results, they must first be positioned for success. Positioning occurs through the establishment of alignment, the starting point for implementation. Alignment drives objectives, the first step in the ROI process, as shown in Figure 2-3 (found in chapter 2). Objectives drive the design of learning programs by describing how participants should react to the program, what they will learn, what they will do with what they learn, and the impact their behavior change will have on key business measures. A variety of data collection methods are available to collect reaction, learning, application, and impact data. This chapter explores alignment, objectives, evaluation planning, and data collection.

ACHIEVING BUSINESS ALIGNMENT

Objectives are core to business alignment. As shown in Figure 3-1, they evolve from the needs assessment process and drive the evaluation process. Objectives serve as the catalyst between what stakeholders want and need and what they get from a program or initiative. The first step toward developing objectives is clarifying stakeholder needs. First, business alignment starts as the learning program is connected to the business need. Next, alignment continues with impact objectives. Participants focus on the business impact during implementation. Finally, business alignment is validated as the learning program's contribution to the business impact is calculated (isolating the impact of learning).

Clarifying Stakeholder Needs

Technology-based learning programs originate from a need. The ultimate need is in the potential positive payoff of the investment. Several questions should be asked when deciding if and how much to invest in a new initiative:
- Is the program required?
- Is the program worth implementing?
- Is this problem worth pursuing?
- Is this an opportunity?
- Is there likelihood for a positive ROI?

The problem or opportunity can be obvious, such as:
- Sales have decreased 30 percent from last year.
- Compliance discrepancies have doubled in the last year.
- Sales are flat—no growth.
- Error rate is 0.09; should be less than 0.03 percent.
- Product returns have increased 20 percent in six months.
- Excessive turnover of critical talent has occurred (35 percent above benchmark data).

- Customer service has been inadequate—3.89 on a 10-point customer satisfaction scale.
- Safety record is the worst in the industry.
- This year's out-of-compliance fines totaled $1.2 million, up 82 percent from last year.
- Product returns are excessive—30 percent higher than previous year.
- Absenteeism is excessive in call centers—12.3 percent compared to industry average of 5.4 percent.
- Sexual harassment complaints per 1,000 employees are the highest in the industry.
- Grievances are up 38 percent from last year.
- Upgrade sales are 50 percent of last year.
- Operating costs are 47 percent higher than the industry average.

Or they may be less obvious, such as:
- We want our customers to be more engaged.
- Create a project management office.
- The sales force should be more consultative.
- Develop an "open-book" company.
- Become a technology leader.
- Become fully in compliance.
- Implement a career advancement program.
- Create a wellness and fitness center.
- Build capability for future growth.
- Create an empowered workforce.
- Become a green company.
- Integrate all technology systems.
- Improve branding for all products.
- Implement lean Six Sigma for all professional employees.
- Every sales professional must have negotiation skills.
- We need more just-in-time training.
- Let's organize a virtual business development conference.
- Create a great place to work for the sales team.

In either case, payoff needs are those problems or opportunities that, if addressed, will ultimately help the organization make money, save money, or avoid costs, and deliver a positive ROI. When the payoff need is discussed, the specific business measures that need to improve to address the payoff need are identified. These "business needs" represent hard data, categorized as output, quality, cost, and time; they may also represent soft data such as measures of satisfaction, image, and reputation. Examples of business measures in need of improvement may be sales, errors, waste,

FIGURE 3-1. Business Alignment Process

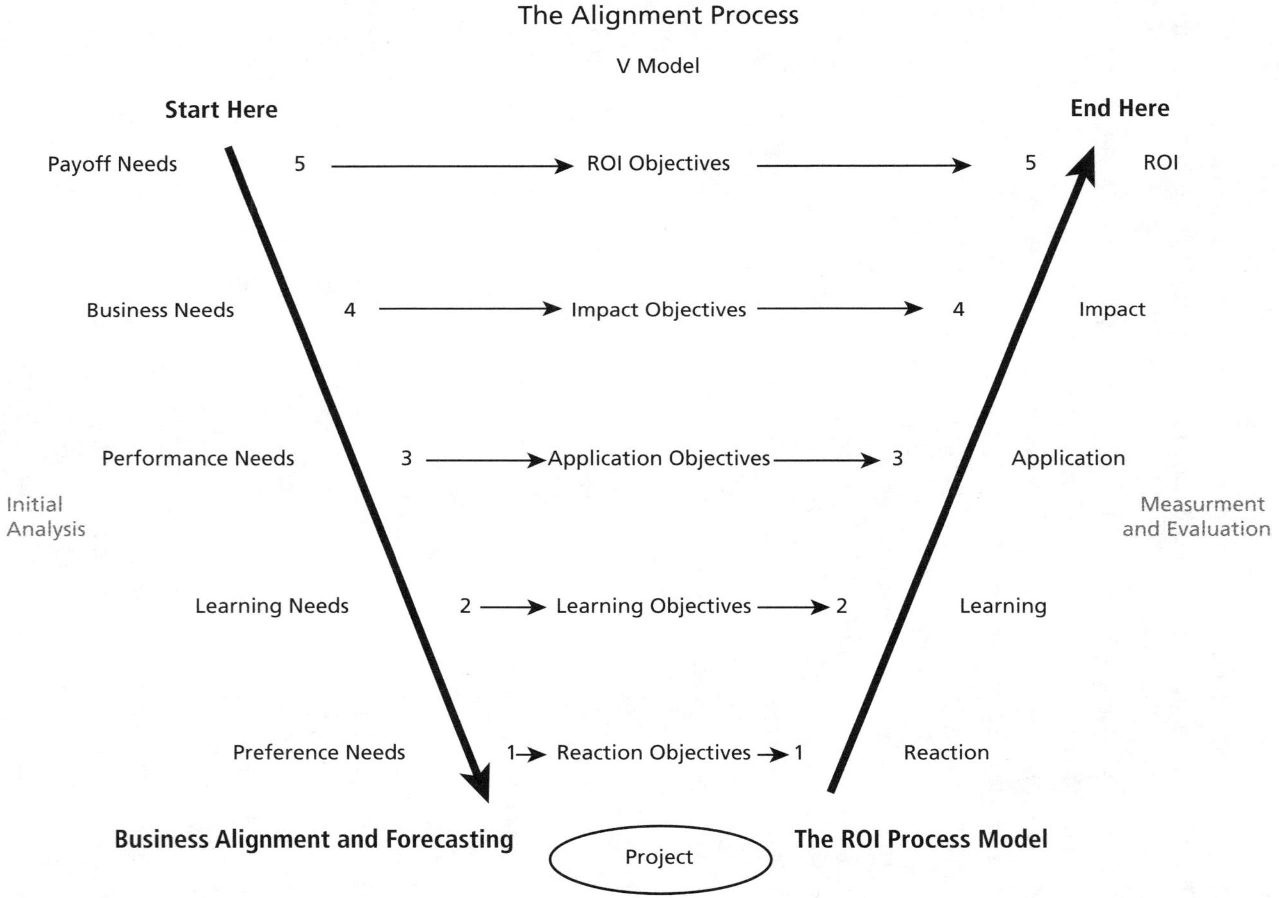

The Alignment Process

V Model

Start Here

End Here

Payoff Needs — 5 — 5 — ROI Objectives — ROI

Business Needs — 4 — 4 — Impact Objectives — Impact

Performance Needs — 3 — 3 — Application Objectives — Application

Learning Needs — 2 — 2 — Learning Objectives — Learning

Preference Needs — 1 — 1 — Reaction Objectives — Reaction

Initial Analysis

Measurment and Evaluation

Project

Business Alignment and Forecasting

The ROI Process Model

Source: ROI Institute, Inc.

rework, accidents, incidents, new accounts, cycle time, downtime, product returns, and customer complaints.

After the business needs are defined, the next step is to clarify performance needs. These are behaviors, actions, or activities that need to change or improve on the job in order to influence the business measures. The needs at this level can vary considerably and might include ineffective behavior, not following a procedure, and incomplete process flows. There are a variety of ways to identify gaps in performance, including questionnaires, interviews, observations, brainstorming, nominal group technique, statistical process control, and other approaches.

When performance needs are identified, the assessment addresses learning needs. When identifying learning needs, the basic question being answered is: What do participants need to know in order to change their behavior or take the desired actions on the job (performance need) to improve business measures (business need)? A variety of techniques are available to uncover learning needs, including task analysis, questionnaires, surveys, interviews, and observations.

Next, preference needs represent the preferred way in which the knowledge, skill, and information are delivered. This addresses the issue of preference for the learning program for the participant, her manager, and other stakeholders. This focuses on issues such as relevance, importance, and intent to use.

Finally, the project team determines the input needs, which simply represent the target audience, required resource investment, timing, duration, and all other aspects of program implementation. With needs analysis complete, the next step is to develop objectives.

Determining Program Objectives

Program objectives reflect the needs of stakeholders. When implementing technology-based learning, it is important to develop objectives at all five levels of evaluation. These objectives tie the learning to meaningful outcomes (reaction, learning, application, impact, and ROI). Program objectives represent the chain of impact, ensuring that designers, developers, participants, supervisors and managers, senior leaders, and evaluators are aware of the potential for success. Objectives should detail specifics about quality, accuracy, and time.

Level 1 reaction objectives describe expected immediate satisfaction with the program. They describe issues that are important to success, including the relevance of the program and importance of the information or content. In addition, these objectives describe expected satisfaction with the logistics of the learning, from delivery to expected use. Table 3-2 shows some typical reaction objectives.

Level 2 learning objectives describe the expected immediate outcomes in terms of knowledge acquisition, skills attainment, and awareness and insights obtained through the learning experience. These objectives set the stage for preparing participants for job performance transformation. It is important to note that even performance support tools (a nonlearning solution) will still have a learning component and thus learning objectives. Table 3-3 shows some typical learning objectives.

TABLE 3-2. Typical Reaction Objectives

At the end of the program, participants should rate each of the following statements at least a 4 or 5 on a 5-point scale:
- The program was organized.
- The delivery of the content was appropriate.
- The program was valuable for my work.
- The program was important to my success.
- I will recommend this program to others.
- The program was motivational for me personally.
- The program had practical content.
- The program contained new information.
- The program represented an excellent use of my time.
- I will use the content from this program.

TABLE 3-3. Typical Learning Objectives

After completing the program, participants will be able to:
- Identify the six features of the new policy in three minutes.
- Demonstrate the use of each software routine in the standard time.
- Use problem-solving skills, given a specific problem statement.
- Determine whether they are eligible for the early retirement program.
- Score 75 or better in 10 minutes on the new-product quiz.
- List all five customer-interaction skills.
- Explain the five categories for the value of diversity in a work group.
- Document suggestions for award consideration.
- Score at least 9 out of 10 on a sexual harassment policy quiz.
- Identify five new technology trends explained at the virtual conference.
- Name the six pillars of the division's new strategy.
- Successfully complete the leadership simulation in 15 minutes.

Level 3 application objectives describe the expected intermediate outcomes in terms of what the participant should do differently as a result of the technology-based learning. Objectives at this level also describe expectations as to the time at which participants should apply knowledge, skills, and insights routinely. Table 3-4 presents some typical application objectives.

Level 4 impact objectives define the specific business measures that should improve as a result of the actions occurring through the learning process. Improvement in these intermediate (and sometimes, long-term) outcomes represent changes in output, quality, costs, and time measures, as well as "softer" measures, such as engagement, satisfaction, and brand. Objectives at this level answer the question, "So what?" as it relates to the investment in learning. They describe to stakeholders the importance of learning through technology. Table 3-5 offers some examples of typical impact objectives.

TABLE 3-4. Typical Application Objectives

When the project is implemented:
- At least 99.1 percent of software users will be following the correct sequences after three weeks of use.
- Within one year, 10 percent of employees will submit documented suggestions for saving costs.
- The average 360-degree leadership assessment score will improve from 3.4 to 4.1 on a 5-point scale in 90 days.
- 95 percent of high-potential employees will complete individual development plans within two years.
- Employees will routinely use problem-solving skills when faced with a quality problem.
- Sexual harassment activity will cease within three months after the zero-tolerance policy is implemented.
- 80 percent of employees will use one or more of the three cost-containment features of the healthcare plan in the next six months.
- By November, pharmaceutical sales reps will communicate adverse effects of a specific prescription drug to all physicians in their territories.
- Managers will initiate three workout projects within 15 days.
- Sales and customer service representatives use all five interaction skills with at least half the customers within the next month.

Last, the Level 5 ROI objective defines for stakeholders the intended financial outcome. This single indicator sets the expectation for how the benefits of learning will relate to the cost. (Will the improvement in impact generated from the program recoup the costs of its implementation?)

An ROI objective is typically expressed as an acceptable return on investment percentage that compares the annual monetary benefits minus the cost, divided by the actual cost, and multiplied by 100. A 0 percent ROI indicates a break-even program. A 50 percent ROI indicates that the cost of the program is recaptured and an additional 50 percent "earnings" (50 cents for every dollar invested) is achieved.

For some programs, the ROI objective is larger than what might be expected from the ROI of other expenditures—such as the purchase of a new company, a new building, or major equipment. However, the two are related, and the calculation is the same for both. For many organizations, the ROI objective for a learning program is set slightly higher than the ROI expected from other "routine investments" because of the relative newness of applying the ROI concept to these types of programs. For example, if the expected ROI from the purchase of a new company is 20 percent, the ROI from a team leader development program might be in the 25 percent range. The important point is that the ROI objective should be established up front and in coordination with the sponsor.

TABLE 3-5. Typical Impact Objectives

After project completion, the following conditions should be met:
- Sales for upgrades should reach $10,000 per associates in 60 days.
- After nine months, grievances should be reduced from three per month to no more than two per month.
- The average number of new accounts should increase from 300 to 350 per month in six months.
- Tardiness should decrease by 20 percent within the next calendar year.
- An across-the-board reduction in overtime of 40 percent should be realized for front-of-house managers in 60 days.
- Employee complaints should be reduced from an average of three per month to an average of one per month.
- By the end of the year, the average number of produce defects should decrease from 214 per month to 153 per month.
- The employee engagement index should rise by one point during the next calendar year.
- Sales expenses should decrease by 10 percent in the fourth quarter.
- A 10 percent increase in brand awareness should occur among physicians during the next two years.
- Customer returns per month should decline by 15 percent in six months.

Evaluating the Program

This final phase of the alignment process is the basis for this book. Evaluation is based on meeting the objectives of the learning program. The more specific the objective, the easier it is to plan the evaluation. From clear objectives, the evaluator can determine what measures to collect during the evaluation process, the sources of the data, the timing of data collection, and the criterion for success. A critical step in the evaluation phase that validates the alignment of the program to the business need is isolating the effects of the program. As you will explore in the next chapter, this step is an imperative to report credible, reliable, and valid results. A variety of techniques are available to isolate the effects of learning.

DEVELOPING THE EVALUATION PLANS

When planning an evaluation, two documents are completed in as much detail as possible. The data collection plan lays the initial groundwork and answers the five key questions outlined in Table 3-6.

Providing detailed answers to these questions up front sets the scope of the data collection process. An example of a completed data collection plan is shown in Figure 3-2. In this program, sales associates are selling an upgrade to an existing product using a mobile device. Level 1 and Level 2 collections are built into the learning program. Level 3 is collected with a web-based questionnaire sent by the sales coordinator. Level 4 data are monitored in the system and tracked by the evaluator and from system records.

TABLE 3-6. Data Collection Plan Key Questions and Descriptions

Key Question	Description
What do you ask?	The answers to this question lie in the program objectives and their respective measures.
How do you ask?	How you ask depends on a variety of issues, including resources available to collect data. For example, Level 2 data may require tests, self-assessments, or exercises.
Whom do you ask?	Use the most credible source; sometimes this includes multiple sources.
When do you ask?	Timing of data collection is critical, particularly for application and impact measures. Select a point in time at which you believe application and impact will occur.
Who does the asking?	Typically, the system collects data at Levels 1 and 2. For the higher levels of evaluation, representatives of the evaluation team may be assigned specific roles.

The second planning document is the ROI analysis plan, which includes the seven key information categories listed in Table 3-7. These seven key areas are addressed in detail in the ROI analysis plan, as shown in Figure 3-3. Two impact measures are monitored—monthly sales and time to first sale. Although the upgrade is released to all sales associates at the same time, not all the sales associates were using the mobile learning program. This provided an opportunity to compare a user group to a nonuser group (experimental versus control group). The profit margin for the upgrade was used to convert to money. The profit of the first sale was not included since it was included in the total sales of the upgrade.

Planning in detail what you are going to ask, how you are going to ask, who you are going to ask, when you are going to ask, and who will do the asking, along with the key steps in the ROI analysis will help ensure successful execution. Additionally, having clients sign off on the plans will ensure support for the evaluation approach when results are presented. These planning documents (Figures 3-2 and 3-3) are explained in more detail in chapter 11.

FIGURE 3-2. Completed Data Collection Plan

Program: Product Upgrade With Mobile Learning   **Responsibility:** _____   **Date:** _____

Level	Broad Program Objective(s)	Measures of Success	Data Collection Method/ Instruments	Data Sources	Timing	Responsibilities
1	REACTION & PLANNED ACTIONS Achieve positive reaction on: • Relevance to my work • Recommend to others • Important to my success • Intent to use	Rating of 4 out of 5 on a composite of four measures	LMS survey, built into program	Participant	End of program	Program manager
2	LEARNING Learn to use five concepts to sell new upgrade: • Rationale for upgrade • Features of upgrade • How upgrade will increase client profit • Pricing options • Implementation and support	Achieve 4 out of 5 correct answers on each module Achieve 20 of 25 total correct answers	True/False quiz	Participant	End of program	Program manager

		Measures	Data Collection Method	Data Sources	Timing	Responsibilities
3	APPLICATION/ IMPLEMENTATION Use of five skills: • Explain rationale for upgrade • Identify key features of upgrade • Describe how upgrade increases client profit • Identify pricing options • Explain implementation and support • Make the first call in 5 days	Rating (4 of 5) on a 1-5 scale System check	Questionnaire, web-based Performance monitoring	Participant Salesforce.com	1 month after program 1 month after program	Evaluator
4	BUSINESS IMPACT • Increase in sales to $10,000 per month • Sell first upgrade in 3 weeks	Monthly sales per associate Actual sale	Business performance monitoring Business performance monitoring	Salesforce.com Salesforce.com	3 months after program 1 month after program	Evaluator
5	ROI 30%	Comments:				

TABLE 3-7. ROI Analysis Plan Key Areas and Description

Key Area	Description
Methods for isolating the effects of the program	Decide the technique you plan to use to isolate the effects of the program on the impact measures.
Methods for converting data to monetary value	Identify the methods to convert impact measures to monetary value.
Cost categories	Include the cost of needs assessment, program design and development, program delivery, evaluation costs, along with some amount representative of overhead and administrative costs for those people and processes that support programs.
Intangible benefits	List those measures you choose not to convert to monetary value are considered intangible benefits.
Communication targets for the results	Identify those audiences to whom results will be communicated.
Other issues that may influence the impact or the evaluation itself	Anticipate any issues that may occur during the learning process that might have a negative effect or no effect on impact measures.
Comments or reminders to the staff managing the program	Place reminder notes of key issues, comments regarding potential success or failure of the program, reminders for specific tasks to be conducted by the evaluation team, etc.

CONSIDERATIONS FOR COLLECTING DATA

A variety of data collection techniques can be used to collect the right data from the right source at the right time. How data are collected depends upon a variety of factors, including accuracy, time, cost, and utility.

Accuracy

The data collection technique that will provide the most accurate results is desired when selecting a data collection method. However, accuracy will have to balance with the cost of data collection. Usually the higher the accuracy, the higher the costs. Never spend more on data collection than the cost of the program. A guideline to keep in mind is that the full cost of an ROI study should not exceed 5 to 10 percent of the fully loaded cost of the learning program. All evaluation costs are included in the denominator of the ROI equation, which means expensive data collection reduces the ROI percentage. It's usually a trade-off.

FIGURE 3-3. Completed ROI Analysis Plan

Program: Product Upgrade With Mobile Learning   **Responsibility:** _____   **Date:** _____

Data Items (Usually Level 4)	Methods for Isolating the Effects of the Program/Process	Methods of Converting Data to Monetary Values	Cost Categories	Intangible Benefits	Communication Targets for Final Report	Other Influences/Issues During Application	Comments
• Monthly sales per associate	• Control group analysis • Participant estimates • (Both measures)	• Direct conversion using standard profit contribution	• Needs assessment • Design • Content development • Mobile device • Participants' salaries plus benefits (time) • Cost of coordination and administration (time) • Project management (time) • Evaluation	• Customer engagement and satisfaction • Job satisfaction of sales associates • Stress reduction • Reputation	• Program participants • Sales managers • Product manager • Senior executives, regional and headquarters • Learning coordinators, designers, and managers • All sales associates	• No communication with control group	
• Time to first sale	• Control group analysis • Participant estimates • (Both measures)	• N/A					

Validity and Reliability

A basic way to look at validity is to ask, "Are you measuring what you intend to measure?" Content validity can be determined using sophisticated modeling approaches; however, the most basic approach to determining the validity of the questions asked is to refer to objectives. Well-written objectives represent the measures to take. Consider the use of subject matter experts, along with additional resources, such as literature reviews and previous case studies to judge validity.

While validity is concerned with ensuring you are measuring the right measures, reliability is concerned with whether the responses are consistent. The most basic test of reliability is repeatability. This is the ability to obtain the same data from several measurements of the same group collected in the same way. A basic example of repeatability is to administer the questionnaire to the same individual repeatedly over a period of time. If the individual responds the same way to the questions every time, there is minimum error, meaning there is high reliability. If, however, the individual has different responses, there would be high error, meaning low reliability.

Time and Cost

When selecting data collection methods, several issues should be considered with regard to time and cost. The time required to complete the instrument is one consideration. Also, consider the time required for managers to complete the instrument if they are involved, or the time in assisting participants through the data collection process. All expenditures for data collection—including time to develop and test the questionnaire, time for the completion of data collection instruments, and the printing costs—are costs to the program. Also, consider the amount of disruption that the data collection will cause employees; interviews and focus groups typically require the greatest disruption, yet provide some of the best data. Balance the accuracy of the data needed to make a decision about the program with what it will cost to obtain that data.

Utility

A final consideration when selecting a data collection method is utility. How useful will the data be, given the type of data collected through the process? Data collected through a questionnaire can be easily coded and put into a database and analyzed. Data collected through focus groups and interviews, however, call for a more challenging approach to analysis. While information can be collected through dialogue and summarized in the report, a more comprehensive analysis should be conducted. This requires developing themes for the data collected and coding those themes. This type of analysis can be quite time-consuming and in some cases frustrating if the data are not collected, compiled, and recorded in a structured way.

Another issue with regard to utility has to do with the use of the data. Avoid asking a lot of questions simply because you can, and instead consider whether you really need to ask a question in order to obtain the data to make decisions about the learning program. Remember, data collected and reported leads to business decisions, regardless of whether the programs are offered through a corporate, government, nonprofit, community, or faith-based organization. How can you best allocate the resources for programs to develop people or improve processes? With these issues in mind, if you can't act on the data, don't ask the question.

METHODS FOR COLLECTING DATA

Given the considerations covered in the previous section, a variety of methods and instruments are available to collect data at the different levels of evaluation. Some techniques are more suited toward some levels of evaluation than others; but in many cases, the approaches to data collection can cut across all levels of evaluation. Table 3-8 lists different data collection methods used to collect data at different levels. The most often used are questionnaires, interviews, focus groups, action plans, and performance records.

TABLE 3-8. Data Collection Methods

Method	Type of Data Level			
	1	2	3	4
Surveys	✓	✓	✓	
Questionnaires	✓	✓	✓	✓
Observation	✓	✓	✓	
Interviews	✓	✓	✓	
Focus Groups	✓	✓	✓	
Tests/Quizzes		✓		
Demonstrations		✓		
Simulations		✓		
Action Planning/Improvement Plans			✓	✓
Performance Contracting			✓	✓
Performance Monitoring				✓

Questionnaires and Surveys

Surveys and questionnaires are the most often used data collection technique when conducting an ROI evaluation. Surveys can collect perception data (such as reaction), and precise data (such as the amount of sales). Questionnaires and surveys are inexpensive, easy to administer, and depending on the length, take very little of respondents' time. Questionnaires can be sent via mail, memo, email, or distributed online (posted on an intranet or via one of any number of survey tools available on the Internet).

Questionnaires also provide versatility in the types of data that can be collected. They are used to collect data at all levels of evaluation: the demographics of participants (Level 0), reaction to the learning program (Level 1), knowledge gained during the program (Level 2), how participants applied that knowledge (Level 3), and the impact of the application (Level 4). You can also ask participants to indicate how much a particular measure is worth, how much that measure has improved, other variables that may have influenced improvements in that measure, and the extent of the influence of those variables.

Questions can be open-ended, closed, or forced-choice. Likert-scale questions are common in questionnaires, as are frequency scales, ordinal scales, and other types of scales, including paired comparison and comparative scales. Periodically, an adjective checklist on a questionnaire gives participants the opportunity to reinforce their perception of the program.

While questionnaires can be quite lengthy and include any number of questions, the best are concise and reflect only questions that allowfor the collection of needed data. Results from brief questionnaires are powerful when describing the impact of a learning program, as well as its monetary benefits.

Interviews

Interviews are an ideal method of data collection when details must be probed from a select number of participants. Interviews allow for gaining more in-depth data than questionnaires, action plans, and focus groups. However, it is important to consider costs and utility, particularly when considering evaluation at Levels 1 and 2. Guiding Principle 2 states, "When evaluating at a higher level, the previous level does not have to be comprehensive." For example, if you plan to evaluate the program to Level 3, it would not be cost effective to use interviews to collect Level 2 learning data.

Interviews can be structured or unstructured. Unstructured interviews allow for greater depth of dialog between the evaluator and the participant. Structured interviews work much like a questionnaire, except that there is a rapport between the evaluator and the participant. The respondent has the opportunity to elaborate on responses and the evaluator can ask follow-up questions for clarification.

Interviews can be conducted in person, over the telephone, or online. Interviews conducted in person have the greatest advantage, because the person conducting the interview can show the participant items that can help clarify questions and response options. In-person interviews also allow for observation of body language that may indicate that the participant is uncomfortable with the question, anxious because of time commitments, or not interested in the interview process. Unlike the situation with an email or web-based questionnaire where the disinterested participant can simply throw away the questionnaire or press the delete key, in an interview setting, the evaluator can change strategies in hopes of motivating participants. Interviews are used when the evaluator needs to ask complex questions or the list of response choices is so long that it becomes confusing if administered through a questionnaire. In-person interviews are often conducted when the information collected is viewed as confidential or when the participant would feel uncomfortable providing this information on paper or over the telephone.

While interviews provide the most in-depth data, they are also the most expensive. Scheduling interviews can be a challenge with busy managers, professionals, and sales staff. If possible, consider using a professional interviewer, who is skilled at interviewing as well as at using the ROI Methodology. The interviewing process can be daunting, especially when asking questions related to Level 4 business impact measures, isolation, and data conversion. A third-party interviewer skilled in these techniques can ensure that the data obtained are accurate and credible when presented to stakeholders during the reporting phase.

Focus Groups

Focus groups are a good approach to collect information from a group of people when dialogue among the group is important. Focus groups work best when the topic is important to the participants. High-quality focus groups produce discussions that address the topics you want to know about. The key to successful focus groups is to keep focused. Serious planning is necessary to design the protocol for a focus group. The conversations that transpire are constructed conversations focusing on a key issue of interest.

Action Plans and Performance Contracts

In many cases, action plans are incorporated into the program. They are used to collect Level 3 and Level 4 data. Prior to the learning program, participants identify specific business measures they need to improve as a result of the program. Through the process they, along with their program leader, identify specific actions to take or behaviors that they will change to target improvement in those measures.

Performance Records

Performance records are organizational records. Data found in performance records represent standard data used throughout the organization in reporting success for a variety of functions; using performance records as a method of data collection can save time and money. Sales records and quality data are generally easy to obtain. However, not all measures in which there is interest are readily available in the record. It would be a wise investment of your time to learn what data are currently housed within the organization and can be utilized or referenced for the program.

GENERATING HIGH RESPONSE RATES

An often asked question when considering the data collection process is, "How many responses do you need to receive to make the data valid and useable?" The answer is, all of it! Guiding Principle 6 states that if no improvement data are available for a population or from a specific source, it is assumed that no improvement has occurred. While it is unlikely that 100 percent of potential respondents will provide data, it is important to collect as many responses as possible. Inference may not be possible to nonrespondents, so if 20 participants are involved and data are only provided by 10, results are only reported for the 10 and all the analysis and ROI is based on the 10 responses. This conservative standard ensures that credible results are reported.

If we report for nonrespondents, then we inflate the results on an assumption for which we have no basis. However, because we also adhere to Guiding Principle 10, costs of the solution or program should be fully loaded for ROI analysis, we will account for the cost of learning for all 20 participants. So, the key is to develop a strategy to obtain responses from as many potential respondents as possible.

Table 3-9 lists a variety of action items to take to ensure an appropriate response rate. Start by providing advanced communication about the evaluation. Clearly communicating the reason for the evaluation ensures that participants understand that the evaluation is not about them, it is about improving the program. Identify those people who will see the results of the evaluation and assure them that they will receive a summary of it. If you are using a questionnaire as a data collection instrument, keep it as brief as possible by asking only those questions that are important to the evaluation. If possible, have a third party collect and analyze the data so participants feel comfortable that their responses will be held in confidence and anonymity will remain.

IDENTIFYING THE SOURCE

Selecting the source of the data is critical in ensuring accurate data are collected. Sometimes it is necessary to obtain data from multiple sources. A fundamental question should be answered when deciding on the source of the data: Who (or what system) knows best about the measures being taken?

The primary source of data for Levels 1, 2, and 3 is the participants. Who knows best about their perception of the program, what they learned, and how they are applying what they learned? Although at Level 3, it may also be important to collect data from other sources, such as the manager, to validate or complement the findings.

TABLE 3-9. Increasing Response Rates

1.	Provide advance communication.	☐
2.	Communicate the purpose.	☐
3.	Identify who will see the results.	☐
4.	Describe the data integration process.	☐
5.	Let the target audience know that they are part of the sample.	☐
6.	Add emotional appeal.	☐
7.	Design for simplicity.	☐
8.	Make it look professional and attractive.	☐
9.	Use the local manager support.	☐
10.	Build on earlier data.	☐
11.	Pilot test the questionnaire.	☐
12.	Recognize the expertise of participants.	☐
13.	Consider the use of incentives.	☐
14.	Have an executive sign the introductory letter.	☐
15.	Send a copy of the results to the participants.	☐
16.	Report the use of results.	☐
17.	Provide an update to create pressure to respond.	☐
18.	Present previous responses.	☐
19.	Introduce the questionnaire during the program.	☐
20.	Use follow-up reminders.	☐
21.	Consider a captive audience.	☐
22.	Consider the appropriate medium for easy response.	☐
23.	Estimate the necessary time to complete the questionnaire.	☐
24.	Show the timing of the planned steps.	☐
25.	Personalize the process.	☐
26.	Collect data anonymously of confidentially.	☐

Source: Phillips, P.P., J.J. Phillips, and B. Aaron. (2013). *Survey Basics*. Alexandria, VA: ASTD Press.

Performance Records

Given the variety of sources for the data, the most credible source is the organization or internal performance records. These records reflect performance in a work unit, department, division, region, or organization. Performance records can include all types of measures that are usually readily available throughout the organization. This is the preferred method of data collection for Level 4 evaluation, since it usually reflects business impact data.

Participants

Participants are the most widely used source of data for ROI analysis. They are always asked about their reaction to the program and the extent to which learning has occurred. Participants are often the primary source of data for Levels 3 and 4 evaluation. They are the ones who know what they do with what they learned and what happened that may have prevented them from applying what they learned. In addition, they are the ones who have insight to what impact their actions have on the business.

While some perceive participants as a biased option, if they understand the purpose of the evaluation and that the evaluation is not about them—it is about the program—participants can remove their personal feelings from their answers and provide objective data.

Participants' Managers

Managers of the participants are another important source. In many cases, they have observed the participants as they attempt to use the knowledge and skills. Those managers, who are actively engaged in a learning process, will often serve as support to the participant to ensure that application does occur. Data from managers often balance the participants' perspectives. In collecting data from the managers, keep in mind any potential bias that may occur from this source of information.

Participants' Peers and Direct Reports

When evaluating at Level 3, participants' peers and direct reports are a good source of data. The 360-feedback evaluation provides one of the most balanced views of performance because it considers the perspective of the participants, their managers, their peers, and their direct reports. While gathering input from peers and direct reports can increase the cost of the evaluation, their perspective may add a level of objectivity to the process.

Senior Managers and Executives

Senior managers and executives may also provide valuable data, especially when collecting Level 4 data. Their input, however, may be somewhat limited if they are removed from the actual application of the knowledge and skills applied. However, senior managers and executives may play a key role in the data collection process when implementing a high-profile program where they have a significant investment.

Other Sources

Internal and external experts and databases provide a good source of data when converting business impact measures to monetary value. The ideal situation is to collect monetary value for the business impact measures from the internal experts or databases outside the organization's records.

DETERMINING THE TIMING OF DATA COLLECTION

The last consideration in the data collection process is timing. Typically, Level 1 data are collected at the completion of the program, and Level 2 data are collected during or at the completion of the program.

Level 3 and 4 data collection occurs after the application is routine—the time in which new behaviors are internalized or the actions are completed. The goal is to collect data as soon as possible, so participants can connect the application to the program. Typically, Level 3 data collection occurs three weeks to two months after the program is complete. Some programs, where skills or actions are applied immediately upon conclusion of the program, should be measured in a matter of days. With Level 4 data, timing may be different than from for Level 3 evaluation, depending on data availability, the stakeholder requirements, and opportunity for the measure to improve. The issue is this: What is the delay or lag time between application and the corresponding impact? Sometimes there is no delay; at other times it may be several months. Usually Level 4 data is collected from three weeks to four months.

While the ROI calculation is an annual benefit, it is unlikely that you will wait a full year to capture Level 4 data. Senior executives usually want to see results sooner rather than later. If the program was introduced to solve a problem (such as unsatisfactory sales revenue), executives and senior managers want the data soon. Otherwise, the decision will be made without the data. It's ideal to collect the Level 4 measures either at the time of Level 3 data collection or soon after, when impact has occurred. Then, those measures should be converted to monetary benefits and included in the ROI calculation.

Sound data collection strategy is imperative for achieving credible results. Ensuring that the most appropriate methods, sources, and timing are employed in the data collection process will yield results that are reliable and useful to stakeholders.

However, it is through the analysis that the real story of learning success is told. Analysis begins with isolating the effects of the program on improvement in business measures.

FINAL THOUGHTS

This chapter introduced the concept of achieving business alignment, which is important for any program, particularly those with significant business impact. It also discussed the importance of evaluation planning (to maintain alignment throughout the evaluation) and data collection. The various methods of data collection were outlined. Using these methods of data collection, you will be able to collect the most credible and timely data and can begin with the data analysis, which is discussed in the next chapter.

4

Data Analysis

T he data collected during the data collection phase must be analyzed. When using the ROI Methodology, data analysis should include the isolation of program effects on the data, calculation of fully loaded program costs, conversion of data to monetary values when appropriate, and the ROI calculation, if needed. This chapter provides a brief overview of each of these issues.

ISOLATING THE EFFECTS OF LEARNING

Isolating the effects of a program on business impact data is one of the most challenging, yet necessary, steps in the ROI Methodology. When addressed credibly, this step links learning through technology directly to business impact.

Other Factors Are Always Present

In almost every situation, multiple factors affect business results. During the time that programs are implemented, many other functions within the organization may be attempting to improve the same metrics addressed by the program. For example, marketing projects are designed to improve sales; and while a technology-based learning program should help a sales professional positively affect sales, the marketing project should also be positively affecting sales. In addition to internal factors, external factors may be affecting business results during the time that the program is occurring.

Without Isolation, There Is Only Evidence, Not Proof

Without taking steps to show the contribution of learning, there is no clear business linkage; instead, there is only evidence that learning may have made a difference. When business results improve during the learning program, it is possible that other factors may have contributed to that improvement. The proof that the program has made a difference on the business comes from isolating the effects of the program or initiative.

For more detail on this methodology, see *The Value of Learning: How Organizations Capture Value and ROI and Translate Them Into Support, Improvement, Funds* (Phillips and Phillips, 2007, Pfeiffer).

Other Factors Have Protective Owners

The owners of the other functions that influence business results are convinced that their processes or programs make the difference. Other processes or programs, such as advertisements, events, reward systems, and job design all have protective owners, and their arguments are plausible. Therefore, program owners are under pressure to build a credible argument for their case to claim value-add to the organization.

To Do It Right Is Not Always Easy

The challenge of isolating the effects of the learning program on the business is critical and can be done; but it is not easy for complex programs, especially when strong-willed owners of other processes are involved. It takes a determination to address this situation every time an ROI study is conducted. Fortunately, a variety of approaches are available.

TECHNIQUES TO ISOLATE THE EFFECTS OF LEARNING

Before reviewing the specific methods, it is helpful to highlight two important issues. First, although it is possible to isolate for the effect of the program at Level 3 application, isolation is usually applied to Level 4 impact. The business impact connected to the program is the key issue; when calculating ROI, the improvement in business measures is reported in monetary terms, and more than any other level, it must be credible. After the business impact data have been collected, the next step is to isolate the effects of the program. This step demonstrates the proof that the program made a difference, whereas reporting results along the chain of impact only presents evidence of the connection between the program and business results.

Another important issue is to attempt to identify the other factors that have contributed to the improvement in the business results measures. This step recognizes that other factors are almost always present and that the credit for improvement is shared with other functions in the organization. Just taking this step is likely to gain respect from the management team.

Several potential sources can help identify these influencing factors. The sponsors of the project may be able to identify the factors. Subject matter experts, process owners, and those who are most familiar with the situation may be able to indicate what has changed to influence the results. In many situations, participants know what other factors have actually influenced their performance. After all, it is their direct performance that is being measured and monitored.

By taking stock in this issue, all factors that contributed to improvement are revealed, indicating the seriousness of the issue and underscoring how difficult it is going to be to isolate the effects of the programs. A variety of techniques can help address the isolation issue, which are discussed next.

Comparison Group Analysis

The most accurate and credible approach to isolate the effects of a learning program is a comparison group analysis, known as the control group arrangement. This approach involves the use of an experimental group that participates in the learning program and a control group that does not. The composition of both groups should be as similar as possible, and, if feasible, the selection of participants for each group should be on a random basis. When this is possible and both groups are subjected to the same environmental influences (for example, market growth, and systems), the differences in the performance of the two groups can be attributed to the program. As illustrated in Figure 4-1, the control group and experimental group do not necessarily have preprogram measurements. Measurements are often taken after the program is implemented only, rather than prior to the program and then again after the program. The difference in the performance of the two groups shows the amount of improvement that is directly related to the program. Chapter 11 provides an example of a comparison group analysis.

FIGURE 4-1. Control Group Design (Post-Test Only)

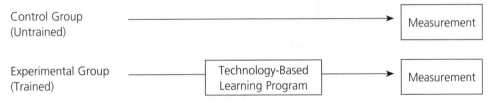

Assumptions

For the comparison group analysis to be used, five conditions must exist.

1. One or two outcome measures represent the consequence of the program. This is the business measure in question.
2. In addition to the program, the factors that influence the outcome measures can be identified.
3. There are enough participants available from which to select the two groups.
4. The program can be withheld from the control group without any operational problems.
5. The same environmental influences affect both groups during the experiment (except that one group participates in the program).

If these assumptions can be met, then there is a possibility for a control group arrangement.

Issues and Opportunities With Comparison Groups

Some issues surface with control group arrangement, which may make it difficult to apply in practice. When addressed properly the issues become opportunities. The first major issue is that the process is inappropriate for some situations. For some programs, it may not be proper to withhold the program from one particular group while it is conducted in another. This particular barrier may prevent many control groups from being used. However, in practice, there are many opportunities for a control group arrangement when a pilot program is implemented.

The second issue is that the control groups must be addressed early enough so that similar groups can be used in the comparison. Dozens of factors can affect employee performance, some of them individual and others contextual. To tackle the issue on a practical basis, it is best to select three to five variables that will have the greatest influence on performance.

A third issue with the control group arrangement is contamination, which can occur when program participants influence others in the control group. Sometimes the reverse situation occurs, when members of the control group model the behavior from the experimental group. In either case, the experiment becomes contaminated because the influence of the program filters to the control group.

Another issue is timing. The longer a control group and experimental group comparison operates, the greater the likelihood that other influences will affect the results. More variables will enter into the situation, contaminating the results. On the other end of the scale, there must be enough time so that a clear pattern can emerge between the two groups. Thus, the timing for control group comparisons must strike a delicate balance of waiting long enough for their performance differences to show, but not so long that the results become seriously contaminated.

A fifth issue occurs when the different groups function under different environmental influences. Because they may be in different locations, the groups may have different environmental influences. Sometimes the selection of the groups can help prevent this issue from occurring.

A sixth issue with using control groups is that it may appear to be too research-oriented for many business organizations. For example, management may not want to take the time to experiment before proceeding with a program, or they may not want to withhold a program from a group just to measure the impact of an experimental program. Because of this concern, some practitioners do not entertain the idea of using comparison groups.

When using a control group to study the effect of a technology-based program, it is important for the program impact to be isolated to a high level of accuracy; the primary advantage of the control group process is accuracy.

Trend-Line Analysis

Another technique used to isolate the impact of programs is trend-line analysis. This approach has credibility when it is feasible. It is also a simpler alternative to the control group arrangement.

A trend line is drawn using preprogram performance as a base and extending the trend into the future. After the program is implemented, actual performance is compared to the projected value, the trend line. Any improvement of performance over what the trend line predicted can then be reasonably attributed to the program. For this to work, the following assumptions must be verified:

- Preprogram data are available. Data represent the impact data—the proposed outcome of the program.
- Preprogram data should be stable, not erratic.
- The trend that has developed prior to the program is expected to continue if the technology-based program is not implemented to alter it.
- No other new variables entered the process after the program was conducted. The key word is "new," realizing that the trend has been established because of the variables already in place, and no additional variables enter the process beyond the implementation of the program.

When the variance of the data is high, the stability of the trend line becomes an issue. If this is an extremely critical issue and the stability cannot be assessed from a direct plot of the data, more detailed statistical analyses can be used to determine if the data is stable enough to make the projection. The trend line can be projected with a simple formula available in software packages or office tools such as Microsoft Excel.

The key element in this approach is to track the trend using historical data; project where the trend would be without help from a program; then after the program occurs, track the actual data over the same period of time as the preprogram data. Then the comparison can be made between what the forecast data show and what the actual data show.

Example

Figure 4-2 shows an example of a trend-line analysis taken from a sales department of a book distribution company. The percentage reflects the level of actual sales compared to sales goals. Data are presented before and after program implementation in July. As shown in the figure, an upward trend on the data began prior to program implementation. Although the program apparently had an effect on sales, the trend line shows that some improvement would have occurred anyway, based on the trend that had previously been established. Program leaders may have been tempted to measure the improvement by comparing the average six months' sales prior to the program (87.3 percent) to the average six months after the program (94.4 percent), yielding a 7.1 percent difference. However, a more accurate comparison is the six-month average after the program compared to the trend line (92.3 percent). In this analysis, the difference is 2.1 percent. Using this more conservative measure increases the accuracy and credibility of the process to isolate the impact of the program.

FIGURE 4-2. Sample Trend-Line Analysis

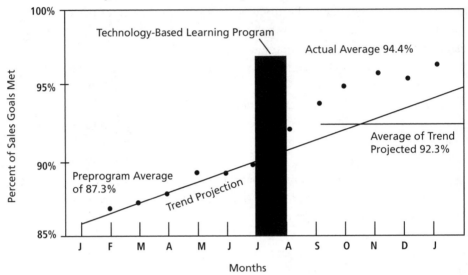

Advantages and Disadvantages of Trend-Line Analysis

The primary advantage of this approach is that it is simple and inexpensive. If historical data are available, a trend line can quickly be drawn and differences estimated. While the approach is not exact, it does provide a quick assessment of a program's potential results.

A disadvantage of the trend-line approach is that it is not always accurate. The use of this approach assumes that the events that influenced the performance variable prior to the learning program are still in place after program implementation, except for implementation of the program. Also, it assumes that no new influences entered the situation at the time the learning program was implemented. Unfortunately, this is not the case most of the time.

Forecasting Methods

A more analytical approach to trend-line analysis is the use of forecasting methods that predict a change in performance variables based on the correlation of other variables. This approach represents a mathematical interpretation of the trend-line analysis when other variables enter the situation at the time the learning program is implemented.

The primary advantage of forecasting is that it can predict performance in business measures with some level of accuracy, if appropriate data and models are available. While there are no absolutes with any technique, using an appropriate level of statistical analysis can provide credible, reliable results.

A major disadvantage with forecasting occurs when several variables enter the process. The complexity multiplies, and the use of sophisticated statistical packages for multiple-variable analyses is necessary. Even then, a good fit of the data to the model may not be possible. Many organizations have not developed mathematical relationships for output variables as a function of one or more inputs. Without them, the forecasting method is difficult to use.

Expert Estimation

An easily implemented method to isolate the effect of a learning program is to obtain information directly from experts who understand the business performance measures. The experts could be any number of individuals. For most learning programs, the participants are the experts. After all, their performance is in question and the measure is reflecting their individual performance. They may know more about the relationships between the different factors, including the impact of the learning, than any other individual.

Because of the importance of estimations from participants, much of the discussion in this section relates to how to collect this information directly from them. The same methods would be used to collect data from others. The effectiveness of the approach rests on the assumption that participants are capable of determining how much of a performance improvement is related to the learning program. Because their actions have produced the improvement, participants may have an accurate perception of the issue. Although an estimate, this value will typically have credibility with management because participants are at the center of the change or improvement.

When using this technique, several assumptions are made:

- A learning program has been conducted with a variety of different activities, exercises, and learning opportunities all focused on improving performance.
- Business measures have been identified prior to the program and have been monitored following the program. Data monitoring has revealed an improvement in the business measure.
- There is a need to link the learning program to the specific amount of performance improvement and develop the monetary effect of the improvement. This information forms the basis for calculating the actual ROI.
- The participants are capable of providing knowledgeable input on the cause-and-effect relationship between the different factors, including learning and the output measure.

With these assumptions, the participants can pinpoint the actual results linked to the program and provide the data necessary to develop the ROI. This can be accomplished by using a focus group or a questionnaire.

Focus Group Approach

The focus group works extremely well for this challenge if the group size is relatively small—in the eight to 12 person range. If much larger, the group should be divided into multiple groups. Focus groups provide the opportunity for members to share information equally, avoiding domination by any one individual. The process taps the input, creativity, and reactions of the entire group.

When conducting a focus group, the following steps are recommended to arrive at the most credible value for learning program impact:

1. Explain the task.
2. Discuss the rules.
3. Explain the importance of the process.
4. Select the first measure and show the improvement.
5. Identify the different factors that have contributed to the performance.
6. Identify other factors that have contributed to the performance.
7. Discuss the linkage.
8. Repeat the process for each factor
9. Allocate the improvement.
10. Provide a confidence estimate.
11. Ask the participants to multiply the two percentages.

Example

Participants who do not provide information are excluded from the analysis. Table 4-1 illustrates this approach with an example of one participant's estimations. The participant allocates 50 percent of the improvement to the learning program. The confidence percentage is a reflection of the error in the estimate. A 70 percent confidence level reduces the estimate to an adjusted percentage of 35 percent (50% x 70% = 35%). In essence, this error adjustment assumes the lowest percentage in an error range. If a person is 70 percent confident in their estimate, that means they are 30 percent uncertain (a 30% error). Given this level of uncertainty, the margin of error is 50% x 30% = 15%. With a margin of error of +/– 15 percent, the range of improvement is 35 to 65 percent. To be conservative, the lowest end of the range, 35 percent, is reported as improvement. Participants who do not provide information are excluded from the analysis.

TABLE 4-1. Example of a Participant's Estimation

Factor That Influenced Improvement	Percentage of Improvement	Percentage of Confidence Expressed	Adjusted Percentage of Improvement
Technology-Based Program	50%	70%	35%
Advertisements	10%	80%	8%
Market Growth	10%	50%	5%
Revision to Incentive Plan	30%	90%	18%
Total	100%		

The use of expert estimations provides a credible way to isolate the effects of technology-based learning when other methods will not work. It is often regarded as the low-cost solution to the problem because it takes only a few focus groups and a small amount of time to arrive at this conclusion.

Questionnaire Approach

Sometimes focus groups are not available or are considered unacceptable for the purposes of isolating the effects of a learning program. The participants may not be available for a group meeting, or the focus groups may become too expensive. In these situations, it may be helpful to collect similar information via a questionnaire. With this approach, participants address the same issues as those addressed in the focus group, but now on a series of impact questions imbedded into a follow-up questionnaire.

The questionnaire may focus solely on isolating the effects of the learning program, as detailed in the previous example, or it may focus on the monetary value derived from the program, with the isolation issue being only a part of the data collected. Using questionnaires is a more versatile approach when it is not certain exactly how participants will provide business impact data. In some programs, the precise measures that will be influenced by the learning program may not be accessible to the evaluation. This may be the case when participants are from many different organizations. In these situations, it is helpful to obtain information from participants on a series of impact questions, showing how they have used what they have learned and how the work unit has been affected. The recommended series of questions is shown in Table 4-2. It is important for participants to know about these questions before they receive the questionnaire. The surprise element can be disastrous in this type of data collection. The specific actions to improve response rates were presented in chapter 3.

TABLE 4-2. Recommended Series of Questions for Isolating Program Results

1. How has your job changed as a result of participating in this program (skills and knowledge application)?
2. What effects do these changes bring to your work or work unit?
3. How is this effect measured (specific measure)?
4. How much did this measure change after you participated in the learning program (monthly, weekly, or daily amount)?
5. What is the unit value of the measure?
6. What is the basis for this unit value? Please indicate the assumption made and the specific calculations you performed to arrive at the value.
7. What is the annual value of this change or improvement in the work unit (for the first year)?
8. Recognizing that many other factors influence output results in addition to the learning gained in the program, please identify the other factors that could have contributed to this performance.
9. What percentage of this improvement can be attributed directly to the application of skills and knowledge gained in the program? (0%–100%)
10. What confidence do you have in the above estimate and data, expressed as a percent? (0% = no confidence; 100% = certainty)
11. What other individuals or groups could estimate this percentage or determine the amount?

Although this is an estimate, the approach has considerable accuracy and credibility. Four adjustments are effectively used with this method to reflect a conservative approach:

- According to Guiding Principle 6, the individuals who do not respond to the questionnaire or provide usable data on the questionnaire are assumed to have no improvements.
- Extreme data and incomplete, unrealistic, and unsupported claims are omitted from the analysis, although they may be included in the intangible benefits.
- Since only annualized values are used, it is assumed that there are no benefits from the program after the first year of implementation.
- The confidence level, expressed as a percentage, is multiplied by the improvement value to reduce the amount of the improvement by the potential error. This is Guiding Principle 7.

Collecting an adequate amount of quality data from the series of impact questions is the critical challenge with this process. Participants must be primed to provide data, and this can be accomplished in several ways, which were explored in the previous chapter. Here are five important ones:

- Participants should know in advance that they are expected to provide this type of data along with an explanation of why the information is needed and how it will be used.
- Ideally, participants should see a copy of this questionnaire and discuss it while they are involved in the program.
- Participants should be reminded of the requirement prior to the time to collect data.
- Participants should be provided with examples of how the questionnaire can be completed, using likely scenarios and types of data.
- The immediate manager should guide participants through the process and review and approve the data, if necessary.

These steps help keep the data collection process with its chain of impact questions from being a surprise. It will also accomplish three critical tasks.

- The response rate will increase. Because participants commit to provide data during the session, a greater percentage will respond.
- The quantity of data will improve. Participants will understand the chain of impact and understand how data will be used. They will complete more questions.
- The quality of the data is enhanced. With up-front expectations, there is greater understanding of the type of data needed and improved confidence in the data provided.

The estimation process is an important technique to isolate the effect of technology-based programs. However, the process has some disadvantages. It is an estimate and, consequently, does not have the accuracy desired by some managers. Also, the input data may be unreliable since some participants are incapable of providing these types of estimates. They might not be aware of exactly which factors contributed to the results or they may be reluctant to provide data. If the questions come as a surprise, the data will be scarce.

Several advantages make this strategy attractive. It is a simple process, easily understood by most participants and by others who review evaluation data. It is inexpensive, takes very little time and analysis, and thus, results in an efficient addition to the evaluation process. Estimates originate from a credible source—the individuals who actually produced the improvement.

The advantages seem to offset the disadvantages. Isolating the effects of learning programs will never be exact, but this estimation process may result in data that are accurate enough for most stakeholders.

SELECTING ISOLATION TECHNIQUES

With several techniques available to isolate the impact of learning programs, selecting the most appropriate techniques for the specific program can be difficult. Estimates are simple and inexpensive, while others are more time consuming and costly. When attempting to make the selection decision, several factors should be considered:
- feasibility of the technique
- accuracy provided with the technique, when compared to the accuracy needed
- credibility of the technique with the target audience
- specific cost to implement the technique
- the amount of disruption in normal work activities as the technique is implemented
- participant, staff, and management time needed with the particular technique.

Multiple techniques should be considered if the reliability of one technique is in question. When multiple sources are used, the most conservative method is recommended. If two methods are credible, the lowest value is used (Guiding Principle 4). The target audience should always be provided with explanations of the process and the various subjective factors involved. Multiple sources allow an organization to experiment with different techniques and build confidence with a particular technique.

Because it is not unusual for the ROI in learning programs to be high, the audience should understand that, although every effort was made to isolate the impact, it is still a figure that is not exact and may contain error. It represents the best estimate of the impact given the constraints, conditions, and resources available.

By isolating the effects of learning, the outcomes are clearly connected to the program, accounting for other factors. By ignoring this step, the reported results lack credibility. To calculate the ROI for the learning program, the next step is to convert business impact data to money.

TYPES OF DATA

ROI is developed through the comparison of the monetary benefits of a program and the cost (or investment) in that program. It is an economic indicator, meaning that the metric indicates the financial return on the investment. To develop this measure, impact data (Level 4 results) are converted to monetary value then compared to the cost of the program. Before we describe the development of the ROI calculation, it is important to review the ways in which impacts are often described.

Hard Data vs. Soft Data

Data fall into one of two categories. They are either referred to as hard data or soft data. Hard data are easy to measure, quantifiable, objectively based, and immediately credible with management. They represent rational, undisputed facts and are usually easy to capture. Hard data can be broadly categorized as output, quality, cost, and time. Examples include sales, new accounts, time to revenue, sales cycle time, downtime, customer complaints, product returns, rework, waste, errors, operating costs, incidents, accidents, absenteeism, turnover, compliance discrepancies, and cycle time.

Soft data represent measures that are difficult to measure and quantify; they are subjectively based and behaviorally oriented. Compared to hard data, these measures, while important, are often perceived as less reliable or less credible when converted to monetary value, due to the inherent level of subjectivity. Examples of soft data are customer satisfaction, customer loyalty, brand awareness, and reputation.

Tangible vs. Intangible Data

Two other categories by which data are often referred are tangible and intangible data. On the surface, measures such as customer satisfaction, teamwork, job engagement, and creativity may seem like difficult soft data items to measure and value, but consider the following:

- Though customer satisfaction seems like a soft measure, quantitative values are assigned to customer satisfaction to create an index. These numbers quantify customer satisfaction.
- When participants apply their newly acquired leadership skills, it may result in improved teamwork. Take that a step further to realize that improved teamwork likely yields greater productivity, leading to increased output and reduced costs—both measures considered as hard data.
- When participants are more creative, this new creative thinking may lead to more efficient business meetings, which results in time savings that can be quantified.
- Employee engagement may seem like a soft measure, but when engagement results in more productivity (revenue per employee), it can be quantified.

Ultimately, soft data lead to hard measures. Some suggest that hard data represent tangible measures; others suggest that soft data represent intangibles. But this is not the case. Both tangible and intangible measures may evolve from either hard data or soft data. This is why to categorize a measure as hard or soft is ambiguous. An alternative categorization scheme is tangible versus intangible.

Tangible benefits of a program are those benefits that have been converted to money. Intangible benefits of a program are those benefits that have not been converted to money. Hard and soft data can be converted to monetary value. Hard data have a direct link to their monetary value, while soft data are converted by tying soft measures to hard measures. Then the measures are converted to money either by associating the measure with cost savings, cost avoidance, or revenue, which is then converted to profit, as shown in Figure 4-3.

FIGURE 4-3. Data Conversion

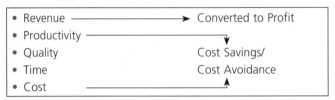

While all measures can be converted to money, several factors should be considered:

- **Cost to convert the measure:** The cost to convert data should not cost more than the evaluation itself.
- **Importance of the measure:** Some measures, such as customer satisfaction and employee satisfaction, stand alone quite well. When that is the case, you might think twice before attempting to convert the measure to money.
- **Credibility:** While most business decisions are made on somewhat subjective data, the source of the data, the perceived bias behind the data, and the motive in presenting the results are all concerns when data is somewhat questionable. Don't risk credibility just to calculate an ROI. For those times when it is difficult to decide whether or not to convert a measure to monetary value, complete the four-part test shown in Figure 4-4.

DATA CONVERSION METHODS

There are a variety of techniques available to convert a measure to monetary value. These are listed in Table 4-3 in order of credibility. The success in converting data to monetary value is knowing which values are currently available. If values are not available, it is possible to develop them. The use of standard values is by far the most credible approach, because standard values have been accepted by the organization. Following those, however, are the operational techniques to convert a measure to money.

Standard Values

Many organizations have standard values for measures of turnover, productivity, and quality. Those organizations that are involved in Six Sigma or other quality initiatives have many measures and the monetary values of those measures. Look around the organization and talk with people to discover what is being measured in various functional areas of the organization. It may be possible to find a monetary value developed and accepted by the organization for a measure you are working with.

Figure 4-4. When to Convert a Measure to Monetary Value

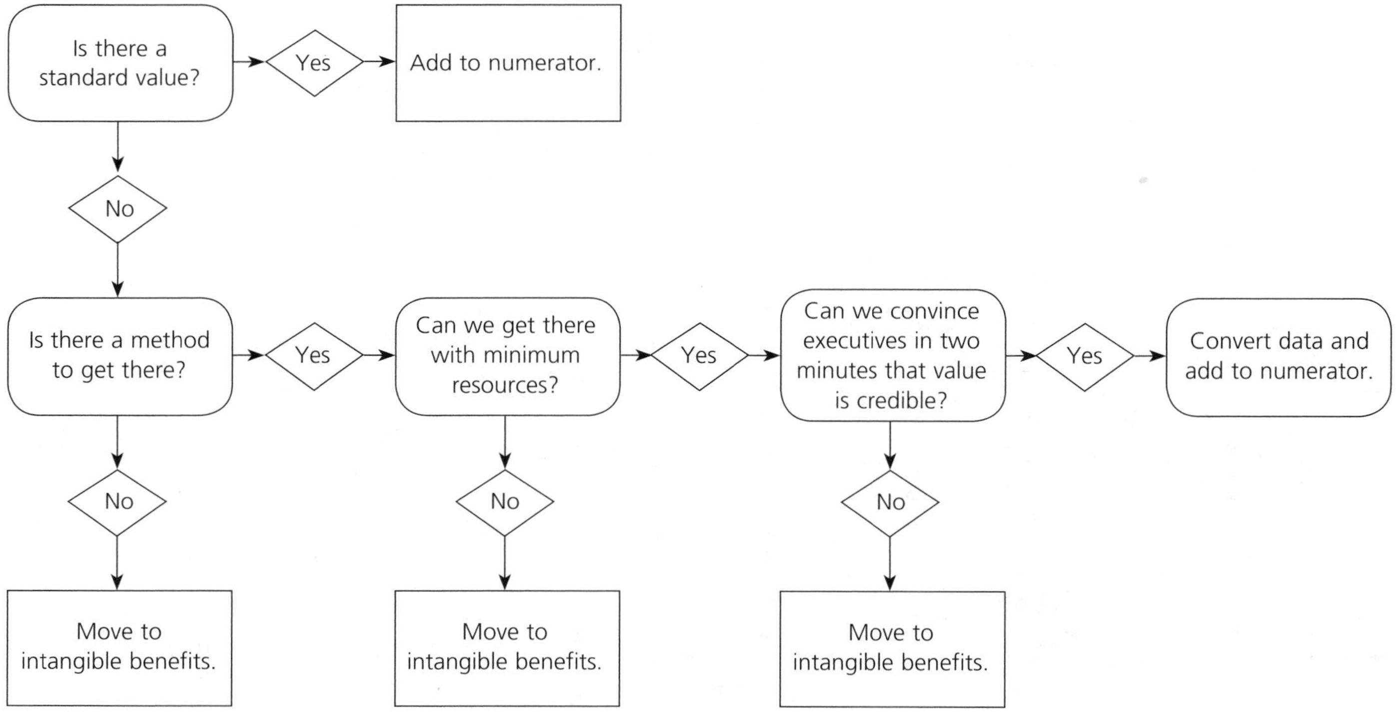

Flowchart:

- **Is there a standard value?**
  - Yes → **Add to numerator.**
  - No → **Is there a method to get there?**
    - Yes → **Can we get there with minimum resources?**
      - Yes → **Can we convince executives in two minutes that value is credible?**
        - Yes → **Convert data and add to numerator.**
        - No → **Move to intangible benefits.**
      - No → **Move to intangible benefits.**
    - No → **Move to intangible benefits.**

TABLE 4-3. Techniques for Data Conversion

Credibility (Higher → Lower)	
Higher	• Standard values:
	○ Output to contribution
	○ Cost of quality
	○ Employee's time
	• Historical cost calculations
	• Internal and external experts
	• External databases
	• Linking with other measures
	• Estimations:
	○ Participants' estimates
	○ Supervisors' and managers' estimates
Lower	○ Learning and development staff estimates

Standard values are defined as output to contribution, quality, and time. When considering output to contribution, the value is based on an additional output. For example, organizations that work on a for-profit basis consider the profit contribution, the profit from the sale, in monetizing an additional sale. Most organizations have a profit margin readily available.

The cost of quality is another standard value in organizations. Quality is a critical issue and its cost is an important measure in most manufacturing and service firms. Placing the monetary value on some measures of quality is quite easy. For example, waste, product returns, and complaints are often monitored in organizations and already have a monetary value placed on them. Other measures, such as errors, can be converted to monetary value by looking at the cost of the work. For example, when employees make mistakes and errors in the reporting, the cost of those mistakes—the value of those mistakes—is the cost incurred in reworking the report.

The third category of standard value is employees' time, probably the simplest and most basic approach to data conversion. If time is saved due to a program, the first question to consider is, "Whose time is it?" Then, to convert time to monetary value, take time saved multiplied by labor cost and add the percentage of additional value for employee benefits. This benefits factor can easily be obtained from the human resources department. A word of caution: When considering employee time as a benefit, the time savings is only realized when the amount of time saved is actually used for productive work. So, if a manager saves time by reducing the number of ineffective meetings the manager attends, the time saved should be applied to more work that is productive.

Historical Costs Calculation

When no standard values exist, historical costs can be utilized by considering what the incident has cost in the past. Using this technique often requires more time and effort than desired. In the end, however, it is possible to develop a credible value for a given measure. This monetary value can eventually become a standard value.

Internal and External Experts

When standard values are unavailable and developing the monetary values through historical costs is not feasible, the next option is to use internal or external experts. When using this approach, ask the expert to provide the cost for the value of one unit of improvement for the measure under investigation. Internal experts have knowledge of the situation and the respect of management. External experts are well published and have the respect of the larger community. In either case, these experts have their own methodologies to develop the values. Therefore, it is important for the experts to understand the intent and the measure with which to develop the monetary value.

External Databases

Sometimes there are no standard values or resources available to develop a monetary value using historical costs. Additionally, there are times when there is no internal expert and it is not possible to locate an external expert who can provide the necessary information. When this is the case, go to external databases. The Internet can provide a wealth of information through online databases and research. External databases provide a variety of information, including the monetary value of many different business impact measures.

Linking With Other Measures

Another technique to convert a measure to monetary value is linking the value of that measure with other measures that have already been converted to monetary values. This approach involves identifying existing relationships showing a correlation between the measure under investigation and another measure to which a standard value has been applied. In some situations, the relationship between more than two measures is connected. Ultimately, this chain of measures is traced to a monetary value. For example, job engagement is linked to sales, productivity, safety, and employee retention. Credibility of data becomes an issue when the assumptions increase as the chain of measures develops further from the actual monetary value. Using this methodology based on the monetary value of other measures is often sufficient for converting measures when calculating the ROI of programs.

Estimations

When the previous methods are unavailable or inappropriate, an estimation process is used that has been proven conservative and credible with executives in a variety of organizations. The estimates of monetary value can come from participants, supervisors, managers, and even the program staff. The process of using estimation to convert a measure to monetary value is quite simple. The data can be collected through focus groups, interviews, or questionnaires. The key is clearly defining the measure so that those who are asked to provide the estimate have a clear understanding of that measure.

FIVE STEPS TO DATA CONVERSION

When it has been decided to convert a measure to monetary value and you've chosen the technique that you are going to use to calculate the monetary value, follow the five steps to complete the data conversion process.

1. **Focus on the unit of measure.** The first step is to review one unit of the measure under investigation. For example, if evaluating a measure of productivity, and the output is one more credit card account, then one credit card account is the unit of measure.

2. **Determine the value of each unit.** In determining the value of each unit, use standard values or one of the other operational techniques. For example, if one new account is worth $500 and that figure is based on standard values using profit contribution, the value is $500 in profit.

3. **Calculate the change in the performance of the measure.** Step three is actually taken during the evaluation process. For example, change in performance or the improvement in the number of credit card accounts is determined during the Level 4 evaluation. How many new credit card accounts were due to the program? For this example, assume that an average two new credit card accounts were sold per month (after isolating all other factors).

4. **Determine the annual improvement in the measure.** Annualize the improvement in the measure. Remember that Guiding Principle 9 says that for short-term programs, report only first-year benefits. You do not necessarily need to wait one year to see exactly how many new credit card accounts are achieved due to the program. Rather, pick a point in time to obtain the average improvement to that date and, then, annualize that figure. In the credit card account example, the unit of measure is one account and the value of the unit is $500. After establishing that the change in performance of the measure due to the program (after isolating the effects) is averaging two new accounts per month, determine the annual

improvement in the measure by simply multiplying the change in performance by 12 months. So, two new accounts per month multiplied by 12 months equals 24 new accounts due to the program.

5. **Calculate the total monetary value of the improvement.** Take the number from step four, annual improvement in the measure (24 in the example), and multiply it by the value of each unit using the standard profit margin ($500 per credit card account in the example). This provides a total monetary value of improvement of $12,000. This annual monetary benefit of the technology-based learning is the value that goes in the numerator of the equation.

FULLY LOADED COSTS

The next step in the move from Level 4 to Level 5 is tabulating the fully loaded cost of the program, which will go in the denominator of the ROI equation. When taking an evaluation to Level 4 only, this step is not necessary; although, regardless of how the learning programs are evaluated, it should be common practice to know the full costs of them. Fully loaded costs mean *everything*. Table 4-4 shows the recommended cost categories for a fully loaded conservative approach to tabulating and estimating costs.

TABLE 4-4. Project Cost Categories

	Cost Item	Prorated	Expensed
1	**Initial analysis and assessment**	✓	
2	**Development of solutions**	✓	
3	**Acquisition of solutions**	✓	
4	**Implementation and application**		
	Salaries/benefits for L&D team time		✓
	Salaries/benefits for coordination time		✓
	Salaries/benefits for participant time		✓
	Program materials, if applicable		✓
	Hardware/software	✓	
	Travel/lodging/meals, if blended		✓
	Use of facilities, if blended		✓
	Capital expenditures, if appropriate	✓	
5	**Maintenance and monitoring**		✓
6	**Administrative support and overhead**	✓	
7	**Evaluation and reporting**		✓

Initial Analysis and Assessment

One of the most underestimated items is the cost of conducting the initial analysis and assessment. In a comprehensive program, this involves data collection, problem solving, assessment, and analysis. In some programs, this cost is near zero because the program is conducted without an appropriate assessment. However, as more program sponsors place increased attention on needs assessment and analysis, this item will become a significant cost in the future. All costs associated with the analysis and assessment should be captured to the fullest extent possible. These costs include time, direct expenses, and internal services and supplies used in the analysis. The total costs are usually allocated over the life of the program.

Development of Solutions

One of the more significant items is the cost of designing and developing the learning program. These costs include time in both the design and development and the purchase of supplies, technology, and other materials directly related to the solution. As with needs assessment costs, design and development costs are usually fully charged to the program. However, in some situations, the major expenditures may be prorated over several programs, if the solution can be used in other programs.

Acquisition Costs

In lieu of development costs, some executives purchase solutions from other sources to use directly or in a modified format. The acquisition costs for these solutions include the purchase price, support materials, and licensing agreements. Some programs have both acquisition costs and solution-development costs. Acquisition costs can be prorated if the acquired solutions can be used in other programs.

Application and Implementation Costs

Usually, the largest cost segment in a program is associated with implementation and delivery. Eight major categories are reviewed below:
- salaries and benefits for learning team time
- salaries and benefits for coordinators and organizers
- participants' salaries and benefits
- program materials, if applicable
- hardware/software
- travel, lodging, and meals, if blended
- facilities (even in-house meetings), if blended
- capital expenditures, if appropriate.

Maintenance and Monitoring

Maintenance and monitoring involves routine expenses to maintain and operate the program. These represent ongoing expenses that allow the new program solution to continue. These may involve staff members and additional expenses, and could be significant for some programs.

Support and Overhead

Another charge is the cost of support and overhead, the additional costs of the program not directly related to a particular program. The overhead category represents any program cost not considered in the above calculations. Typical items include the cost of administrative/clerical support, telecommunication expenses, office expenses, salaries of client managers, and other fixed costs. This is usually an estimate allocated in some convenient way based on the number of learning hours, then estimating the overhead and support needed each hour. This becomes a standard value to use in calculations.

Evaluation and Reporting

The total evaluation cost should be included in the program costs to complete the fully loaded cost. Evaluation costs include the cost of developing the evaluation strategy, designing instruments, collecting data, analyzing data, preparing a report, and communicating the results. Cost categories include time, materials, purchased instruments, surveys, and any consulting fees.

ROI CALCULATION

As explained in chapter 2, ROI is reported in one of two ways: the benefit-cost ratio (BCR) and the ROI percentage. In simple terms, the BCR compares the economic benefits of the program with the cost of the program. A BCR of 2 to 1 says that for every $1 invested, $2 are provided in benefits.

The ROI formula, however, is reported as a percentage. The ROI is developed by calculating the net program benefits divided by program costs times 100. For example, a BCR of 2 to 1 translates into the ROI of 100 percent. This says that for every $1 spent on the learning program $1 is returned, after costs are captured. The formula used here is essentially the same as ROI in other types of investments, where the standard equation is annual earnings divided by investment.

For example, if after you convert Level 4 measures to money and you follow the five steps described previously, you find that the monetary benefits of a learning program result in a sales increase of $350,000, and the learning program cost $200,000, the BCR and ROI are:

$$\text{BCR} = \frac{\$350,000}{\$200,000} = 1.75 \text{ or } 1.75{:}1$$

$$\text{ROI} = \frac{\$350,000 - \$200,000}{\$200,000} \times 100 = 75\%$$

The BCR explains that for every $1 invested in the learning program, the total financial benefit returned is $1.75. The ROI explains that for every $1 invested in learning, that $1 is recovered plus a net return of $0.75. ROI is the "return" on the investment, where the BCR is the total benefit including the investment itself.

So when do you use which? Many times both metrics are reported to give both perspectives. Because the BCR comes from the public sector, it is more often used in public sector reporting. However, the ROI is also gaining traction in those settings. For private sector organizations, the ROI is the primary metric.

Occasionally, a stakeholder will ask to see the time at which an investment will "pay off." This payoff period is the estimated time at which a program will break even. It is then assumed that any time after that period will result in added benefit. The payback period equation is simply the BCR equation turned upside down. Take the total investment of the learning program, divide it by the benefits, and multiply by 12 to get the number of months. Using the previous numbers as the basis for the example, the payback period for the initiative would be:

$$\text{Payback Period} = \frac{\$200,000}{\$350,000} = .57 \times 12 \text{ months} = 6.85 \text{ months to payback}$$

This indicates that in approximately seven months, you can expect to break even on the investment.

INTANGIBLE BENEFITS

As described earlier, intangible benefits are those benefits that are not converted to monetary value; but they are important and sometimes just as important as the actual ROI calculation. When reporting as a result, there must be a connection to these intangibles. Typical intangible benefits not usually converted to monetary value are job satisfaction, organizational commitment, teamwork, and customer satisfaction. These could be converted to monetary value; however, when job satisfaction, organizational commitment, teamwork, and customer satisfaction are improved, the organization is usually satisfied with the improvement in these measures and the dollar value with that improvement is not necessary. The good news is that more of these measures are now being converted to money.

When you report ROI, always balance it with the intangible benefits. This balance places the ultimate benefits of the learning program into perspective.

FINAL THOUGHTS

This chapter discussed the various important aspects of ROI analysis. After following the steps in chapter 3 to collect data, it is important to analyze the data in a credible way. Perhaps the most important aspect of analysis is the isolation of the effects of the learning program on the data. It is crucial to know how this particular program affected the data, outside other influences. Another important part of data analysis is the conversion data to monetary value, various methods were discussed. Finally, the chapter discussed intangible benefits, or those not converted to monetary values. All of these items are critical in the ROI analysis. The next chapter focuses on communicating and using the results of the analysis.

5

Reporting and Using the Results

After the analysis has been completed, perhaps the most important step in the ROI process model is communicating the results of the evaluation to stakeholders. The results from the study will provide insight into the effectiveness of the technology-based learning program, help secure funding for future programs, build credibility for the ROI Methodology, and increase support for learning through technology. However, this will not occur unless the results are properly communicated to the appropriate stakeholders and actions are taken to use the results appropriately. This chapter provides a brief overview to these issues.

THE IMPORTANCE OF REPORTING RESULTS

This final step in the ROI Methodology is critical. Evaluations of technology-based learning programs are essentially useless if the results are never communicated. Communicating the evaluation results of the program allows for improvement and provides the necessary feedback to those interested in the outcomes of the learning. In this way, others in the organization can understand the value the programs bring to the organization. Communication can be a sensitive issue—there are those who will support the technology-based learning program regardless of the results. There are others, however, who are skeptical regardless of what the data show. Some will form their opinions about the program based on how the results are communicated. Different audiences need different information, and the information needs to be presented in a variety of ways to ensure that the message comes across appropriately. There are five steps to take into account when planning your communication strategy:

1. Define the need for the communication.
2. Identify all the audiences for the communication.
3. Select the media for the audiences.
4. Develop the information to be communicated.
5. Communicate the results and evaluate the results of communication.

For more detail on this methodology, see *The Value of Learning: How Organizations Capture Value and ROI and Translate Them Into Support, Improvement, Funds* (Phillips and Phillips, 2007, Pfeiffer).

IDENTIFY THE NEEDS

There are a variety of needs that can be addressed through the communication process. Those needs range from getting approval for programs, to satisfying curiosity about what the program is all about. Sometimes it is necessary to gain additional support and affirmation for programs, or to gain agreement that a change or improvement in a program needs to occur. Often, the purpose of communicating the results of the program is to build credibility for the programs. Many times, the report reinforces the need to make changes to the system to further support the transfer of learning to implementation and business impact. Communicating the results can also serve to prepare the learning team for changes in the organization or, better yet, to give the staff the opportunity to increase their influence.

Communication is often conducted to enhance the entire process as well as to emphasize a specific program's importance to the organization. The communication process is used to explain what is going on, why something might or might not have occurred, and the goals to improve a program when it results in a negative ROI.

When a pilot learning program shows impressive results, use this opportunity to stimulate interest in continuing the program as well as for potential future program participants. The communication process can also be used to demonstrate how tools, skills, or new knowledge can be applied to the organization. Table 5.1 provides a list of possible needs that can be addressed through the communication process. The next step is to identify the audience who can best help address that need.

TABLE 5-1. Reasons for Communicating Results

1. Reasons related to the technology-based learning:
    ❑ Demonstrate accountability for expenditures.
    ❑ Secure approval for a learning program.
    ❑ Gain support for all learning programs.
    ❑ Enhance reinforcement of the learning program.
    ❑ Enhance the results of future learning programs.
    ❑ Show complete results of the learning program.
    ❑ Explain a learning program's negative ROI.
    ❑ Seek agreement for changes to a learning program.
    ❑ Stimulate interest in learning through technology.
    ❑ Encourage participation in learning programs.
    ❑ Market future learning programs.
2. Reasons related to management:
    ❑ Build credibility for the learning team.
    ❑ Prepare the learning team for changes.
    ❑ Provide opportunities for the learning team to increase influence.
3. Reasons related to the organization:
    ❑ Reinforce the need for system changes to support learning transfer.
    ❑ Demonstrate how tools, skills, and knowledge add value to the organization.
    ❑ Explain current processes.

IDENTIFY THE AUDIENCE

When the purpose for communicating results is clear, the next step is to determine who needs to hear the results in order to satisfy the communication need. If the need for communicating results is to secure approval for a new program, consider the client or the top executive as the target audience. If the purpose of communication is to gain support for a program, consider the immediate managers or team leaders of the targeted participant group. If the purpose of communication is to improve the program, target the designers and developers. If it is important to demonstrate accountability for technology-based learning programs, then the target audience would be most—if not all—employees in the organization. It is important to consider the purpose of the communication to determine the appropriate audience. Listed below are the key questions to ask to make this determination:

- Is the potential audience interested in the program?
- Does the potential audience really want to or need to receive this information?
- Has someone already made a commitment to this audience regarding communication?
- Is the timing right for this message to be presented to this audience?
- Is the potential audience familiar with the program?
- How does this audience prefer to have results communicated to them?
- Is the audience likely to find the results threatening?
- Which medium will be most convenient to the audience?

There are four primary audiences who will always need the results of the ROI studies communicated to them:

- **The learning and development team** should receive constant communication of the results of all levels of evaluation. Level 1 and 2 data should be reported to the learning and development team immediately after the program is implemented. This provides them the opportunity to make adjustments to the program prior to the next offering.
- **Participants** are a critical source of data. Without participants, there are no data. Level 1 and 2 data should always be reported back to participants immediately after being analyzed. A summary copy of the final ROI study should also be provided to participants. In doing so, they see that the data they are providing for the evaluation is actually being used to make improvements to the program. This enhances the potential for additional and even better data in future evaluations.
- **Participants' managers** are critical to the success of learning programs. Without managers' support, it will be difficult to get participants engaged in the program, and the successful transfer of learning will be jeopardized. Reporting the ROI study results to immediate managers demonstrates to them that employees'

participation in the program yields business improvement. Managers will see the importance of their own roles in supporting the learning process from program participation to application.

- **The client** (the person or persons who fund the program), should always receive the results of the ROI study. It is important to report the full scope of success, and clients want to see the learning program's impact on the business, as well as the actual ROI. While Level 1 and 2 data are important to the client to some extent, it is unnecessary to report this data to the client immediately after the program is implemented. The client's greatest interest is in Level 4 and 5 data. Providing the client with a summary report for the comprehensive evaluation will ensure that the information clearly shows that the program is successful and, in the event of an unsuccessful program, a plan is in place to take corrective action.

SELECT THE MEDIA

Consider the best means for asking what is needed. As in other steps in the ROI Methodology, there are many options—meetings, internal publications, electronic media, program brochures, case studies, and formal reports. The choice of media is important, especially in the early stages of implementing the ROI Methodology. Make sure to select the appropriate medium for the particular communication need and target audience.

Meetings

When considering meetings as the medium for communication, look at staff meetings and management meetings. If possible, plan for communication during normal meeting hours so as to avoid disrupting the audiences' regular schedules. However, this approach does present the risk of having to wait to present the report until some future meeting when it can be added to the agenda. But, key players will be so interested in the ROI study that getting a slot on the earliest possible meeting agenda should not be a problem. Another meeting might consist of a discussion that includes a participant, and maybe a participant's manager to sit on a panel to discuss the program. Panel discussions can also occur at regularly scheduled meetings or at a special meeting focused on the program. Best practice meetings are another opportunity to present the results of the learning program. These meetings highlight the best practices in each function within the organization. This might mean presenting the ROI study at a large conference in a panel discussion, which includes managers who oversee learning programs and managers from a variety of organizations. Business update meetings also present opportunities to provide information about the program.

Internal Publications

Internal publications are another way to communicate to employees. Use these internal publications—newsletters, memos, postings on bulletin boards—to report program progress and results, as well as to generate interest in current and future programs. Internal hard copy communications are the perfect opportunity to recognize participants who have provided data or responded promptly to questionnaires. If incentives were offered for participation or for prompt responses to questionnaires, mention this in these publications. Be sure to accentuate the positive and announce compliments and congratulations generously.

Electronic Media

Electronic media, such as websites, intranets, and group emailing, are important communication tools. Take advantage of these opportunities to spread the word about the activities and successes related to programs. When using group email, whether organization-wide or targeting certain audiences, make sure that message content is solid and engagingly crafted.

Brochures

Program brochures are another way to promote learning offerings. Reporting results in a brochure that describes a program's process and highlights successes can generate interest in a current program, stimulate interest in coming programs, and enhance respect and regard for the team who owns the programs.

Case Studies

Case studies are an ideal way to communicate the results of an ROI evaluation. Case studies demonstrate the value that learning brings to the organization or to provide others an opportunity to learn from your experience. There are multiple outlets for case studies, including books (such as this one) and learning courses offered within an organization. The ROI Institute uses case studies as a key component in training others in evaluation. Through case studies, others can learn what worked and what didn't.

Formal Reports

A final medium through which to report results is the formal report. There are two types of reports—micro-level reports and macro-level scorecards—that are used to tell the success of programs. Micro-level reports present the results of a specific program and include detailed reports, executive summaries, general audience reports, and single-page reports. Macro-level scorecards are an important tool in reporting the overall success of technology-based learning programs.

DEVELOP THE REPORT

There are five types of reports to develop to communicate the results of the ROI studies. These include the detailed report (which is developed for every evaluation project), executive summary, general audience reports, single-page reports, and macro-level scorecard.

Detailed Reports

The detailed report is the comprehensive report that details the specifics of the program and the ROI study. This report is developed for every comprehensive evaluation conducted. It becomes the record and provides the opportunity to replicate the study without having to repeat the entire planning process. It is possible to save time, money, effort, and a great deal of frustration by building on an existing study. The detailed report contains six major headings:

- need for the program
- need for the evaluation
- evaluation methodology
- results
- conclusions and next steps
- appendices.

Need for the Program

Define and clarify the objectives for the program, making sure that the objectives reflect the five levels of evaluation. Objectives should relate to the participants' perspective, describe what participants are intended to learn, reflect how they are intended to apply what they have learned, and reflect the outcomes that the knowledge and skills gained in the program will have on the organization. Objectives also present the target ROI and how that particular target was determined.

Need for the Evaluation

Typically, if the program is intended to influence Level 4 measures, this presents a need. In some cases, it may be that the Level 4 measures were never developed so the intent of the evaluation is to understand the influence the program has had or is having on the organization. The intent of the evaluation may be to understand the extent to which the program successfully achieved the objectives. The need for the evaluation may depend on the request of an executive. Clearly state the reasons in the report. Although this report will be distributed to key audiences, it will also serve as the tool to refer to in future evaluations and to describe what happened during this particular evaluation.

Evaluation Methodology

This clear and complete description of the evaluation process builds credibility for the results. First provide an overview of the methodology. Then, describe each element of the process, including all options available at each step, which option(s) were chosen, the reasons for those choices, all actions and activities related to each element of the process, and each step taken. For the data collection section of the report, detail how the data were collected, why those data were collected, from whom the data were collected, why the data were collected from that particular source(s), when the data were collected, and why those data collection procedures were selected. Also, display a completed detailed copy of your data collection plan. After the data collection plan has been described, explain the ROI analysis procedures and why the isolation method was selected. Clearly state the various ways the effects of the program could be isolated and explain why the method was chosen. In essence, answer the question, "Why did you do what you did?" When explaining data conversion, describe how the monetary values for the Level 4 impact measures linked to the program were developed, again explaining the range of possibilities for data conversion. After describing the possible data conversion methods, clearly explain why the techniques selected were chosen. Address the cost issue and provide the cost categories included in the ROI analysis. At this point, do not include the actual cost of the program. If the cost of the program is introduced too early, the audience will focus solely on the cost and their attention will be lost. As with data collection, provide a detailed copy of the ROI analysis plan so that the audience can see a summary of exactly what happened.

Results

In this section, the program that has undergone a rigorous evaluation will shine! Provide the results for all levels of evaluation, beginning with Level 1, reaction and planned action. Explain the intent for gathering reaction data, providing the specific questions the reaction data answers, and report the results. Then move on to Level 2, learning. Explain why it's important to evaluate learning and the key questions that learning data answers and report the results. Next, move on to Level 3, application and implementation. This is one of the greatest parts of the story. Provide evidence that what was taught was used. Discuss how frequently and effectively knowledge and skills gained in the program have been applied by the participants. Discuss how the support system enabled participants to apply what they learned. Discuss the barriers to the transfer of learning gained, to behavior change, or implementation and application. It is important to explain what happened. For example, if the work environment did not support learning transfer, report that here. Also explain that when it was recognized (through the evaluation process) that a problem was occurring (the support system was not helping), that action was taken by talking with those who might know or who might provide information about how things could be changed to support the program next time.

Next, discuss Level 4, business impact, including how the program positively influenced specific business outcomes. Reinforce the fact that the effects of the program were isolated; it must be clear to the audience that other influences that might have contributed to these outcomes were taken into account. Describe the options for isolation and explain why those options were chosen.

Then, report on Level 5, ROI. First, explain what is meant by ROI, clearly defining the ROI equation. Address the benefits of the program, the Level 4 measures, and how they were achieved. Explain how the data were converted to monetary value and detail the monetary benefits of the program. Then, report the fully loaded costs. Recall that earlier in the evaluation methodology section of the report, the cost items were detailed, but a dollar value was not identified. It is here, after monetary benefits are reported, where the dollar values of the costs are outlined. The readers have already seen the benefits in dollar amounts; now provide the costs. The pain of a very expensive program is relieved because the audience can clearly see that the benefits outweigh the costs. Finally, provide the ROI calculation.

The last section in the detailed report concerns intangible benefits, which are those items that are not converted to monetary value. Highlight those intangible benefits and the unplanned benefits that came about through the program. Reinforce their importance and the value they represent.

Conclusions and Next Steps
Develop and report the program conclusions based on the evaluation, answering these questions:
- Was the program successful?
- What needs to be improved?

Explain the next steps, clearly pointing out the next actions to be taken with regard to the program. Those actions could include continuing the program, adding a different focus, removing elements of the program, changing the format, or developing a blended learning approach to reduce the costs while maintaining the benefits achieved. Clearly identify the next steps and set out the dates by which these steps will be completed.

Appendices
The appendices include exhibits, detailed tables that could not feasibly be included in the text, and raw data (keeping the data items confidential). The final report is a reference for readers as well as a story of success for others.

Throughout the report, incorporate quotes—positive and negative—from respondents. While it is tempting to leave out negative comments, ethically, they should not be omitted and including them enhances the credibility and respect for the report. By developing a detailed comprehensive report, there will be a backup for anything communicated during a presentation. When conducting a future ROI study on a similar program, the road map is now clear. Table 5-2 presents a sample outline of a detailed report.

TABLE 5-2. Impact Study Outline for Detailed Report

- General Information
  - Objectives of Study
  - Background

- Methodology for Impact Study
  - Levels of Evaluation
  - ROI Process
  - Data Collection
  - Isolation of Program Effects
  - Data Conversion to Money
  - Fully Loaded Costs
  - Assumptions (Guiding Principles)

  } Builds credibility for the process.

- Results
  - General Information
    - Response Profile
    - Relevance of Materials
  - Reaction and Planned Action
  - Learning
  - Application
    - Barriers to Application
    - Enablers to Application
  - Business Impact
    - General Comments
    - Linkage With Business Measures
  - Return on Investment
  - Intangible Benefits

  } The results with six measures: Levels 1, 2, 3, 4, 5, and Intangibles.

- Conclusions and Recommendations
  - Conclusions
  - Recommendations

- Appendices

Executive Summary

Another important report is the executive summary. The executive summary follows the same outline as the detailed report (although it omits the appendices), and each section and subsection is not developed in such great detail. Clearly and concisely explain the need for the program, the need for the evaluation, and the evaluation methodology. Always include the ROI Methodology prior to the results so that the reader understands and appreciates it. The understanding and appreciation build credibility and respect for the results. Report the data from Level 1 through Level 5 and include the sixth measure of success—the intangible benefits. The executive summary is usually 10 to 15 pages long.

General Audience Reports

General audience reports are a great way to describe the success of programs to employees. General audience reports may be published in organization publications, like newsletters or in-house magazines; reported in management and team meetings, where a brief review of the report can be communicated in a meeting setting; and, finally, published as case studies. Case studies can be published internally and externally. There are many opportunities to publish the case study outside the organization, including trade or association publications or academic research publications. The key is to tell the story to show that the programs are working, and that when they don't work, steps are taken to improve them.

Single-Page Reports

A final micro-level report is a single-page report. Success of a program should not be communicated using the single-page report until after the audience understands the methodology. If an audience sees the ROI of a program without having an appreciation for the methodology used to arrive at the number, the audience will fixate on the ROI and never notice, much less form a regard for, information developed in the other levels of evaluation. Therefore, single-page reports are used with great care, but they are an easy way to communicate results to the appropriate audiences on a routine basis.

Macro-Level Scorecards

Macro-level scorecards can provide the results of the overall impact of learning and development programs, such as technology-based learning programs. These scorecards provide a macro-level perspective of success and serve as a brief description of a program evaluation in contrast to the detailed report. They show the connection between the program's contribution and the business objectives. The method of isolation is always included on the report to reinforce that credit is given where credit is due. The scorecard integrates a variety of types of data and demonstrates alignment between programs, strategic objectives, and operational goals.

COMMUNICATE RESULTS AND EVALUATE THE RESULTS OF COMMUNICATION

A final step in the communication process is the communication of results, using the selected media and information, and evaluating the results of the communication. While it is important to evaluate results of the program itself, knowing how successful you are with the communication of those is just as important. Your program may have been flawless, resulting in well over 100 percent ROI. But if the communication was poorly done, then your success may never be known.

So, how do you evaluate the success of your communication? Just like you evaluate your learning program. You observe reaction to the information and the communication process, ask participants if they know what the data mean and understand your evaluation process, follow up on actions taken as a result of the communication, observe subsequent impact (such as funding for a new program), and, if you choose, calculate the ROI on your communication process. How you communicate, to whom you communicate, and when you communicate are critical elements to your overall evaluation strategy.

Remember, there are no perfect ROI studies—someone will find an improvement opportunity in everything you do. As long as you follow the process and the standards, keep your application of the ROI Methodology consistent, and clearly communicate your approach, your results are put into the context of methodology—credible and reliable. With that in mind, good decisions can be made about programs. The case studies in the following chapters provide examples of how the ROI Methodology has been used to evaluate technology-based learning programs in various organizations.

DELIVERING BAD NEWS

One of the obstacles perhaps most difficult to overcome is receiving inadequate, insufficient, or disappointing news. Addressing a bad-news situation is an issue for most project leaders and other stakeholders involved in a project. Table 5-3 presents the guidelines to follow when addressing bad news. As the table makes clear, the time to think about bad news is early in the process, but without ever losing sight of the value of the bad news. In essence, bad news means that things can change—and need to change—and that the situation can improve. The team and others need to be convinced that good news can be found in a bad-news situation.

TABLE 5-3. Delivering Bad News

- Never fail to recognize the power to learn from and improve on a negative study.
- Look for red flags along the way.
- Lower outcome expectations with key stakeholders along the way.
- Look for data everywhere.
- Never alter the standards.
- Remain objective throughout the process.
- Prepare the team for the bad news.
- Consider different scenarios.
- Find out what went wrong.
- Adjust the story line to: "Now we have data that show how to make this program more successful." In an odd way, this puts a positive spin on data that are less than positive.
- Drive improvement.

USING THE DATA

Too often, projects are evaluated and significant data are collected, but nothing is done with the data. Failure to use data is a tremendous obstacle, because once the project has concluded, the team has a tendency to move on to the next project or issue and get on with other priorities. Table 5-4 shows how the different levels of data can be used to improve projects. It is critical that the data be used—they were essentially the justification for undertaking the project evaluation in the first place. Failure to use the data may mean that the entire evaluation was a waste. As the table illustrates, many reasons exist for collecting the data and using them after collection. These can become action items for the team to ensure that changes and adjustments are made. Also, the client or sponsor must act to ensure that the uses of data are appropriately addressed.

TABLE 5-4. How Data Should Be Used

Use of Evaluation Data	Appropriate Level of Data				
	1	2	3	4	5
Adjust program design.	✓	✓			
Improve implementation.			✓	✓	
Influence application and impact.			✓	✓	
Improve management support for the program.			✓	✓	✓
Improve stakeholder satisfaction.			✓	✓	✓
Recognize and reward participants.		✓	✓	✓	
Justify or enhance budget.				✓	✓
Reduce costs.		✓	✓	✓	✓
Market program in the future.	✓		✓	✓	✓

FINAL THOUGHTS

This chapter discussed a crucial area of the ROI Methodology, reporting results. When an ROI analysis has been completed successfully, the results must be communicated to various individuals with interest in the project. Proper communication of results is imperative for successful implementation of the ROI Methodology. The final chapter in part I discusses what is necessary to achieve business results from a design perspective.

6

Designing for Results

This chapter focuses on designing the technology-based learning program to deliver results. Program design has an important connection to the results achieved. This concept involves designing the appropriate communication about the program, changing the role of participants, creating expectations, and designing specific tools and content to make the project results based. This final chapter of the ROI Methodology focuses on these tools for the designer.

COMMUNICATING WITH RESULTS IN MIND

When a learning program is implemented, a chain of communications begins. These communications describe what is expected from the program, for all who are involved. The principal audience for communication is the individuals who will make the program successful; they are often labeled as the participants. The managers of these participants, who are expecting results in return for the participants' involvement in the program, are also a target for information. At least four areas of communication are important.

Announcements

Any announcement for the program—whether a verbal announcement, online blurb, ad, email, or blog—should include expectations of results. In the past, the focus of the announcement may have been on the program's content or learning objectives; this is no longer the case. The focus now is on what individuals will accomplish with a project and the business impact that it will deliver. The measure should be clearly articulated so it will answer the participant's first question, "What's in it for me?" This clearly captures the results-based philosophy of a particular program.

For more detail on this methodology, see *The Value of Learning: How Organizations Capture Value and ROI and Translate Them Into Support, Improvement, Funds* (Phillips and Phillips, 2007, Pfeiffer).

Brochures

If the project is ongoing or involves a significant number of participants, a brochure (digital or paper) may be developed. A brochure is typical for programs that are very important, strategic, and expensive. These brochures are often cleverly written from a marketing perspective and are engaging and attractive. An added feature should be a description of the results that will be or have been achieved from the program, detailing specific outcomes at the application level (what individuals will accomplish) and the impact level, as well as the consequences of the application. These additions can be powerful and make a tremendous difference on the outcome of the program.

Memos

Correspondence to participants before they become fully engaged with their program is critical. These memos and instructions should outline the results described in the announcements and brochures, and focus on what individuals should expect when they become involved in the project. When prework is necessary for participants to connect with the program, the focus should be on the results expected. Sometimes participants are asked to bring specific examples, case studies, problems, measures, or business challenges. Communications should be consistent with the results-based philosophy, underscore the expectations and requirements, and explain what must be achieved and accomplished. Also, the request to provide feedback and document results is explained to participants, emphasizing how they will benefit from responding.

Workbooks

Workbooks are designed with higher-level objectives in mind. Application and impact objectives influence the design of exercises and activities as they emphasize results. Application tools are spaced throughout the workbook to encourage and facilitate action. Impact measures, and the context around them, appear in problems, case studies, learning checks, and skill practices.

CHANGING THE ROLE OF PARTICIPANTS

Perhaps there is no more important individual who can achieve business success than the participant involved in the program. The participant is the person who is learning the skill and knowledge needed for a job setting that will subsequently drive business performance. The participant is the person who is involved in the implementation to achieve the results all the way through business impact. It is often the mindset of this person (in other words, the readiness and motivation of this individual to achieve success) that will make a difference. Sometimes this starts with changing the role of this person, defining more clearly what is expected and perhaps expanding expectations beyond what is traditionally required.

Why This Is Necessary

Many programs and projects fail because the individuals involved didn't do what they were supposed to do. While there are many barriers to achieving success, including those in the workplace, perhaps the most critical one is that the person involved did not want to, did not have time to, or did not see any reason to do what is necessary to achieve success. While they normally blame others (and not themselves), the participant may actually be the problem. The efforts of the participant must change, and this involves two issues, which are described next.

Defining the Role

The first issue is to define the role of the participant, clearly outlining what is expected. For technology-based learning, participants should always understand their specific roles. Table 6-1 describes the new and updated role of a participant. This role clearly defines what is expected throughout the process and engages the participants in expectations beyond the learning sessions. It suggests that the success is not achieved until the consequence of application is obtained, identified as specific business improvements. Most importantly, the role requires participants to provide data. It is only through their efforts and subsequent information that others will understand their successes. At the same time, the participant will clearly see the success of the program.

TABLE 6-1. The Role of the Participant

1. Be prepared to take advantage of the opportunity to learn, seeking value in any type of project or program.
2. Enroll, be on time, stay fully engaged, and become a productive participant.
3. Look for the positives in the program and focus on how the impediments can be removed.
4. Meet or exceed the learning objectives, fully understanding what is expected.
5. Share experiences and expectations using virtual tools, if available, recognizing that others are learning from you.
6. Plan to apply what is learned in a workplace setting.
7. Remove, minimize, or work around barriers to application and success.
8. Apply the learning in a workplace setting, making adjustments and changes as necessary to be successful.
9. Follow through with the consequences of application, achieving the business results from the program.
10. When requested, provide data that show your success as well as the barriers and enablers to success.

Documenting the Roles

The role of the participants should be clearly documented in several places. For formal learning sessions in a blended format, the role is sometimes placed on the name tents so that it is clearly visible at all times during the workshop. In other cases, the role is presented as a handout or downloadable document in the beginning of the program, outlining what is expected of the participant all the way through to impact and results. Sometimes it is included in the workbook material, usually on the first page. It is also placed in catalogs of programs where program descriptions are listed. The role can be included as an attachment to the registration documents as participants are enrolled in a program. It is often included in application documents, reminding the participant of his or her role. Finally, some learning centers place the roles in each conference room so they are clearly visible. The key issue in documenting roles is to place them permanently and prominently so that they are easily understood.

CREATING EXPECTATIONS

With the roles of participants clearly defined, expectations are created. The challenge is to let participants know what is expected and to avoid any surprises throughout the process. Participants resist surprises involving assignments, application tools, or action plans. Also, when a questionnaire, interview, or focus group is scheduled on a post-program basis, participants often resent these add-on activities. The approach is to position any necessary actions or data collection as a built-in process and not an add-on activity.

Identifying Measures Before the Program

For some projects, the participants define the specific business measures that need to improve. For example, in a supervisor safety program implemented in all plants, participants are asked to identify the safety measures that need to improve, but only if those measures can be changed by working with their team using the content of the program. Although this approach may seem dysfunctional, it represents the ultimate customization for the participant, and it applies to many programs. The implementation of lean Six Sigma, for example, requires participants to identify specific business measures that they want to improve by making a process more efficient or effective. Impact measures are identified and become part of the project undertaken by the participant. In the classic GE workout program, pioneered by GE's former chairman, Jack Welch, the participants identified specific projects that needed to improve. All types of process improvement and performance enhancement efforts have this opportunity, ranging from negotiations, creativity, innovation, problem solving, communication, team building, coaching, leadership development, supervisor development, management development, and executive education, among others. This creates the expectation and often comes with a pleasant reaction, because the participant focuses on the measure that matters to them.

Involving the Managers

In addition to creating expectations directed to participants, the participants' managers may be involved. Participants may be asked to meet with their manager to ensure that the manager has input into the involvement in the program. Sometimes this includes an agreement about what must improve or change as a result of the program. One of the most powerful actions that can be taken is having the managers set goals with participants prior to the programs. Another opportunity for manager involvement is to develop a module just for the manager. This is usually a shortened version of the participant module.

Messages From Executives

In addition to immediate manager involvement, having others in executive roles to create expectations can be powerful. In most organizations, the top leaders are often highly respected, and their requirements or expectations are not only noticed, but are often influential. Figure 6-1 shows an opening announcement from a CEO about a safety project. The opening speech was recorded and presented virtually, clearly positions the expectations for business connections, removing any doubt of what was expected. The message is clear: Participants must learn new approaches and tools that they will use or implement; but ultimately, success must be achieved at the business level.

FIGURE 6-1. CEO Message and Expectations

Thank you for taking the time to become involved in this important e-learning project. I am confident that this is the right time and the right place to achieve some major safety improvements. Although we have a safety record that is among the best in the industry, there is still room for much improvement, and it is unacceptable in our minds and in your minds. There is no way we can be pleased with any lost time injuries, let alone a fatality in our workplace.

We have a dozen business measures that you are reviewing in this particular project. The focus of this project is to improve as many of these as possible. The measures will be ranked in the order of the seriousness in terms of pain and suffering for employees and also cost and disruption at the workplace. We expect you to make significant improvements in these measures.

During this project, you will be exposed to a variety of techniques and processes to achieve success. You have our support to make it a reality. Here are our SMART goals for the next two years.

Continued on next page.

Measure	Reduction
Fatalities	50%
Lost time injuries	12%
Accident severity rate	12%
OSHA reportable injuries	13%
OSHA fines	18%
First aid treatments	23%
Near misses	16%
Property damage	29%
Down time because of accidents	18%

I have confidence in you to accomplish these goals with this program. You have my full support. You have the full support of our safety and health team. And you have the full support of your operating executives. There is nothing that we won't do to assist you in this effort. If you have a problem or issue that you need to get resolved and you are having difficulty, contact my office and I will take care of it.

The improvement in these measures is on your shoulders. Only you can do this. We cannot do it at a distance and our safety and health team cannot do it alone. It is your actions with your employees that can really make a difference.

Good luck. We look forward to celebrating these successes with you.

DESIGN FOR RELEVANCE

Blended learning, e-learning, and mobile learning will usually include the acquisition of important knowledge and skills. A prerequisite to achieving results is to make sure that the program is designed for proper relevance.

Sequencing the materials from easy to hard, or for the natural flow of the learning, is helpful. Advanced material is placed near the end. Small quantities of information should be presented sequentially, keeping a balance so not too much content is offered, but enough to keep the individuals challenged.

The content should come at the right time for participants, ideally, just before they need to use it. If it is presented too early, it will be forgotten; and if it is too late, they will have already learned another way to do it. The content must relate to the participants. It must have relevance to the job. Essentially, the challenge is to focus on achieving customized learning to the individual, following the J4 approach:

1. Just for me.
2. Just in time.
3. Just enough.
4. Just right for the task.

DESIGN FOR RESULTS

After designing for learning comes the focus on results. The two issues are connected. As the program is designed for participants to learn the content, the focus shifts ultimately on the business results. At least five areas require attention.

Activities

All activities should focus on situations that define the application of what participants are learning, the consequences of their learning, or both. Activities, exercises, individual projects, and any other assignments should focus on the actions that participants will be taking on the job to achieve business success.

Skill Practices

Sometimes participants will practice skills where the focus is on the use of those skills and the subsequent outcomes. The situational context for the practice is critical for achieving business results. For example, if a learning session is focused on improving employee work habits, a distinct set of skill sets are developed for changing these habits. To provide the focus, an impact objective is needed to define the original problem that must be changed. In one setting, it was absenteeism and tardiness. With that objective known, the skill practices are designed to improve an existing measure of unplanned absenteeism and persistent tardiness, both captured in the system. Without the impact objectives, the skill practice could be focusing on situations where other unrelated work habits and outcomes could be the problem, such as excessive talking, excessive texting, improper dress code, and other distracting habits. The impact objectives clearly defined the problem and signaled for the designer to include absenteeism and tardiness in the skill practices.

Simulations

When simulations are developed to measure learning, they should describe and connect with the ultimate outcomes. This extra effort makes the simulation as real as possible for application and keeps an eye on the consequences (business impact). For example, simulations with the use of software are not only replicating what the participant is doing, but reporting time taken to accomplish steps (time), errors that are made along the way (quality), and the level of accomplishment achieved (productivity). These simulations remind the individuals about the ultimate outcome, business results.

Problems

Some programs involve solving problems, particularly if the program is process oriented. The problems provided should reflect a realistic connection to application and impact. The related activities should focus on a problem that participants will be solving and the measures that they will be improving as the problem is solved, such as output, quality, cost, and time. For example, in an advanced negotiation program, participants were asked to solve a negotiation problem. Given the ultimate outcome needed for the negations (budget, delivery, and quality), the participants used the appropriate skill sets to ultimately achieve their negotiations in a planned process. In solving the problem, participants had to identify the specific skill sets that would be used (application), and arrive at the correct amount for each outcome (business impact).

Case Studies

Case studies are often a part of a learning program. They bring to light real situations. Case studies should be selected that focus on the content, application, and impact for the program. Application items and impact measures should be scattered throughout the case study. The case study includes them, focuses on them, and often results in recommendations or changes to them. This reminds the audience of the ultimate impact that should be an important part of the process.

BUILT-IN APPLICATION TOOLS

Building data collection tools into technology-based learning is perhaps one of the most important areas where designing for results works extremely well. This is particularly helpful for blended learning and e-learning programs where data collection can easily be a part of the program. Ranging from simple action plans to significant job aids, the tools come in a variety of types and designs. They serve as application and data collection tools.

Action Plans

A simple process, the action plan is a tool that is completed during the program, outlining specifically what the participant will accomplish after the program is completed and during its implementation. The action plan always represents application data and can easily include business impact data where a business measure will be improved. Figure 6-2 shows an action plan where the focus is directly on improving a business measure. In this example, unplanned absenteeism in a call center is being improved from a high of 9 percent to a planned level of 5 percent. The actions listed in the plan on the left side of the document are the steps that will be taken to improve the business measure. The information on the right focuses more detail on the data, including the value it delivers. While this tool serves as a data collection process, it also keeps the focus on business impact. As the data are collected, it can even be used to isolate the effects of the program on the impact data, validating that the business alignment did occur. For this to work extremely well, several steps must be taken before, during, and after the action plan to keep the focus on business impact. Figure 6-3 shows the steps that are followed to ensure that the action plan is built into the process and becomes an integral part of achieving the business success.

Figure 6-2. Example of Action Plan

Action Plan

Participant: _____ Program Manager: _____ Follow-Up: <u>Sept. 1</u>

Objective: <u>Decrease unplanned absenteeism.</u> Evaluation Period: <u>March – September</u>

Improvement Measure: <u>Absenteeism rate</u> Current Performance: <u>9%</u> Target Performance: <u>5%</u>

Action Steps		Analysis
Meet team to discuss reasons for absenteeism.	March 10	A. What is the unit of measure? <u>One absence</u>
Review absenteeism records for each employee, looking for trends and patterns.	March 20	B. What is the value (cost) of one unit? <u>$54.00</u>
Counsel with problem employees to correct habits and explore opportunities for improvement.	March 20	C. How did you arrive at this value? <u>Standard value</u>
Conduct a brief performance discussion with each employee returning to work after an unplanned absence.	March 20	D. How much did the measure change during the evaluation period (monthly value)? <u>3.5%</u>
Provide recognition to employees with perfect attendance.	March 20	E. What other factors could have contributed to this improvement? <u>Changes in job market and disciplinary policy</u>
Follow up with each discussion—discuss improvement and plan other action.	March 31	F. What percent of this change was actually caused by this program? <u>40%</u>
Monitor improvement and provide recognition when appropriate.	March 31	G. What level of confidence do you place on the above information? (100% = Certainty and 0% = No confidence) <u>80%</u>

Intangible benefits: <u>Less stress, greater job satisfaction</u> Comments: <u>Great program. It kept me on track with this problem.</u>

FIGURE 6-3. Sequence of Activities for Action

Before	• Communicate the action plan requirement early. • Require business measures to be identified by participants.
During	• Describe the action planning process. • Allow time to develop the plan. • Teach the action planning process. • Have the program manager approve the action plan, if possible. • Require participants to assign a monetary value for each proposed improvement (optional). • If possible, require action plans to be presented virtually to the group. • Explain the follow-up mechanism.
After	• Require participants to provide improvement data. • Ask participants to isolate the effects of the program. • Ask participants to provide a level of confidence for estimates. • Collect action plans at the predetermined follow-up time. • Summarize the data and calculate the ROI (optional).

Improvement Plans and Guides

Sometimes, the phrase "action plan" is not appropriate, if organizations have used it to refer to many other projects and programs, possibly leaving an unsavory image. When this is the case, other terms can be used. Some prefer the concept of improvement plans, recognizing that a business measure has been identified and improvement is needed. The improvement may represent the entire team or an individual. There are many types of simple and effective designs for the process to work well. In addition to improvement plan, the term "application guide" can be used and can include a completed example as well as what is expected from the participant, including tips and techniques along the way to make it work.

Application Tools/Templates

Moving beyond action and improvement plans brings a variety of application tools, such as simple forms to use, technology support to enhance an application, and guides to track and monitor business improvement. All types of templates and tools can keep the process on track, provide data for those who need it, and remind a participant where he is going.

Performance Contract

Perhaps the most powerful built-in tool is the performance contract. This is essentially a contract for performance improvement between the participant in the project or program and her immediate manager. Before a program is conducted, the participant meets with the manager and they agree on the specific measures that should be improved and the amount of improvement. Essentially, they agree on an improvement that will result in the use of the content, information, and materials of the program. This contract can be enhanced if a third party enters the contractual arrangement (this would normally be the program manager for the technology-based learning program).

Performance contracts are powerful, as these individuals are now committing to performance change that will be achieved through the use of content and materials from the program, and has the added bonus of support from the immediate manager and from the facilitator or project manager. When programs are implemented using a performance contract, they are powerful in delivering very significant changes in the business measure.

The design of the performance contract is similar to the action plan. Figure 6-4 shows a performance contract for a sales representative involved in a blended learning program, including a combination of formal learning sessions, online tools, and coaching from the sales manager. The goal is to increase sales with existing clients. The sales manager approves the contract along with the participant and the program manager.

Job Aids

Job aids represent a variety of designs that help an individual achieve success with application and impact. The job aid illustrates the proper way of sequencing tasks and processes and reminds the individual of what must be achieved, all with the ultimate aim of improving a business measure. Perhaps the simplest example is the job aid used at a major restaurant chain, which shows what must go into a particular dish ordered by a customer. The individuals preparing the food use the job aid, which was part of a learning program. The job aid shows how the process flows, using various photographs, arrows, charts, and diagrams. It is easily positioned at the station where the food is prepared and serves as a quick reference guide. When used properly, the job aid is driving important business measures: keeping the time to fill the order at a minimum (time savings), allowing the restaurant to serve more customers (productivity), and ensuring consistency with the meal and reducing the likelihood of a mistake being made on the order (quality).

USE TRANSFER TOOLS

A variety of tools are available to keep the participant engaged and focused on the transfer of learning to the job (application and impact). Figure 6-5 provides a list of techniques to enhance results from learning.

FIGURE 6-4. Example of Performance Contract

Performance Contract

Participant: _____ Manager: _____ Program Manager: _____

Objective: Increase sales with existing clients by 20% Evaluation Period: Jan – March

Improvement Measure: Monthly Sales Current Performance: $56,000/mo. Target Performance: $67,000

Action Steps		Analysis
Meet with key clients to discuss issues, concerns, opportunities.	Jan. 31	A. What is the unit of measure? Monthly sales, existing clients
Review customer feedback data—look for trends and patterns.	Feb. 1	B. What is the value (cost) of one unit? 25% profit margin
Counsel with "at risk" clients to correct problems and explore opportunities for improvement.	Feb. 2	C. How did you arrive at this value? Standard value
Develop business plan for high-potential clients.	Feb. 5	D. How much did the measure change during the evaluation period (monthly value)? $13,000
Provide recognition to clients with long tenure.	Routinely	E. What other factors could have contributed to this improvement? Changes in market, new promotion
Schedule appreciation dinner for key clients.	Feb.15	F. What percent of this change was actually caused by this program? 40%
Encourage marketing to delegate more responsibilities.	Feb.20	G. What level of confidence do you place on the above information? (100% = Certainty and 0% = No confidence) 30%
Follow up with each discussion—discuss improvement and plan other action.	Routinely	
Intangible benefits: Client satisfaction, loyalty	Comments: Excellent, hard-hitting program	

FIGURE 6-5. Examples of Application Techniques

Making Learning Stick	
Action Learning	Sticky Blog
Action Plans	Sticky Heat Map
Application Checks	Sticky Kit for Managers
Do Not Disturb	Sticky Learning Community
Do Now	Sticky Microblog
Feel-Felt-Found	Sticky Objectives
KISS: Keep It Simple or Supervised	Sticky Wiki
A Little Help From Friends	Strategy Link
Live Pilot	Thank-You Note
Manager Module	Threaded Discussion
Note to Self	Transfer Certificate
Picture This	Virtual Tutor
Pop-Up Reflections	What's Wrong With This Picture?
QR Codes	Wrap It Up

Source: Carnes, B. (2012). *Making Learning Stick: Techniques for Easy and Effective Transfer of Technology-Supported Training.* Alexandria, VA: ASTD Press.

INVOLVING THE PARTICIPANT'S MANAGER

A final area of design involves creating a role for the managers of the participants. As mentioned earlier, this is a very powerful group and having specific items, activities, tools, and templates for them can make a tremendous difference in business results.

The Most Influential Group

Research has consistently shown that the managers of a group of participants are the most influential group in helping participants achieve application and impact objectives, apart from their own motivation, desire, and determination. No other group can influence participants as much as their immediate managers. Figure 6-6 shows how learning is transferred to the job, using three important groups of stakeholders involved in this success: participants, their immediate managers, and the program manager. Three timeframes are possible: prior to the program, during the program, and after the program.

This matrix creates nine possible blocks of activities to transfer what is learned from a particular program to the job. The transfer not only includes the behaviors and actions that must be taken (application), but also the impact that must be obtained (impact measures). For example, the participant can be involved in preprogram activities to set specific goals to achieve before the program is implemented (block number

4). During the program, the participant will plan specific actions to improve a business measure (block number 5). After the program is conducted, the participant will apply the material, achieve the business impact improvement, and report it to interested stakeholders (block number 6).

FIGURE 6-6. The Transfer of Success to the Job

| | | Timeframe | | |
		Before	During	After
Roles	Manager	1	2	3
	Participant	4	5	6
	Program/ Manager	7	8	9

In another example, the manager can meet with the participant and set a goal before attending the program (block number 1). During implementation, the manager completes a manager's module or provides coaching as part of it (block number 2). After the program, the manager follows up to make sure the material is used appropriately and the business impact has been achieved (block number 3). The process continues until activities are identified for every block.

Research on this matrix shows that the most powerful blocks for achieving learning transfer to the job are blocks 1 and 3. Unfortunately, managers do not always see it that way. They underestimate their influence. They must be reminded of their influence and provided tools that take very little time to apply to ensure the result of the project is used and drives the business results. This is one of the most powerful areas to explore for improving business results.

Preprogram Activities

At the very least, managers should set expectations for participants involved in any type of activity, program, project, event, or initiative. It only takes a matter of minutes to set that expectation, and the results can be powerful. Preprogram activities can range from a formal performance contract, described earlier, to an informal, two-minute discussion prior to being involved in the program. A full array of activities should be provided that take very little time. Even a script could be helpful. The important point is that managers must be reminded, encouraged, or even required to do this.

During-the-Program Activities

Sometimes, it is important for the manager to have input into the design and development of the program. Possible activities include having managers (or at least someone representing the manager group) help design program content. Also, managers could review the content and serve as subject experts to approve it. Managers could be involved in a manager's module, learning parts of the process, providing one-on-one coaching for participants needing help with specific parts, or just observing the program (or a portion of it). Managers could serve on an advisory committee for the program or review the success of others in the program. The key is to connect the manager to the design and content of the program. Manager involvement will help focus the program on business results, which they will find extremely important.

Post-Program Activities

The most basic action a manager can take is to follow up to ensure the content of the project is being used properly. Suggesting, encouraging, or even requiring application and impact can be very powerful. Managers should be available to provide assistance and support as needed to make the program successful. Just being available as a sounding board or to run interference to ease the application may be enough. Although not necessary, post-program activities can be more involved on a formal basis, where managers actively participate in follow-up evaluations. Managers may sign off on results, review a questionnaire, follow up on action plans, collect data, or present results. In any case, they make a difference.

Reinforcement Tools

In some situations, a management reinforcement workshop is offered to teach managers how to reinforce and guide the behaviors and actions needed to achieve a desired level of performance in business measures. Reinforcement workshops are very brief, usually ranging from two to four hours, but can be extremely valuable. In addition to the workshops, a variety of tools can be created and sent to managers. The tools include checklists, scripts, key questions, resources, and contacts needed to keep the focus on results.

Sometimes managers volunteer for a coaching role where they are asked to be available to assist the participants with a formal coaching process. In this scenario, managers are provided details about coaching, how to make it work, and what is required of them. This is extremely powerful when a participant's immediate manager serves as a coach to accomplish business results.

FINAL THOUGHTS

This chapter focused on what is necessary to achieve business results from a design perspective—designing the communications, expectations, roles, content, and tools that are necessary for a participant to be fully involved. A program with the proper design, combined with a participant who is motivated to learn, will make achieving success a reality. Participants will explore connections to use the acquired knowledge and increase the tenacity to implement the tools and techniques. This approach provides the readiness, motivation, commitment, and tools needed to help achieve business alignment. The remainder of the book presents case studies.

Part II

Evaluation in Action

Case Studies Describing the Evaluation of
Learning Through Technology Programs

Measuring ROI in Work Engagement:
A Blended Learning Solution
PolyWrighton

John Kmiec, Sandra Dugas, Cyndi Gaudet,
Heather Annulis, Mary Nell McNeese, and Susan Bush

Abstract

This case study describes the evaluation of a blended learning program designed to enhance the capabilities of immediate managers to positively influence line employees' work engagement. The study used quasi-experimental research design to analyze changes in work engagement for line employees assigned to two of 14 business units at PolyWrighton, a manufacturer of high-quality, lightweight plastics. The test group of immediate managers in the production business unit received the learning initiative. The maintenance business unit managers did not receive the initiative. Also evaluated were the production unit's participant reaction, learning, application, and business impact data. Production's adjusted return on investment estimate was 598 percent, or $1,265,565.

BACKGROUND

PolyWrighton makes high-quality, lightweight plastics used to package a wide variety of food, beverage, and personal care products. Meeting rigorous hygienic, chemical, and environmental safety standards and specifications for these products requires constant monitoring and testing, state of the art technology and an extensively trained, highly skilled workforce. The chemicals used in the manufacturing process are both toxic and flammable. The plant machinery is very complex, massive in size, and hazardous in its own right. The product itself is processed under high heat and pressure. These conditions combine to demand heightened operational and safety awareness by all employees.

Adding to the complexity of the operation are the costs associated with product waste and rework. In a highly competitive market where raw materials are expensive and frequently in short supply, it is imperative that PolyWrighton generate as little waste and rework as possible. Rework is defined as product that fails to meet customer expectations for quality, and therefore must be reprocessed. Product waste is unusable, because it cannot be reprocessed and must be discarded. The costs associated with rework and waste result in an additional $35,000 for every 1 percent of product rework and $245,000 for every 1 percent of waste per total product produced. The larger of the two expenses, product waste, costs PolyWrighton about $600 per minute for every minute waste is generated.

As with many manufacturing processes, most waste and rework can be prevented, although a smaller amount cannot be prevented and may be considered normal. Controllable waste and rework, for instance, are the result of assignable causes. That is, their causes are identifiable, can be eliminated, and prevented from reoccurring. For example, some controllable waste in the production business unit may represent the cost of a single human error in judgment or decision making that occurred during the manufacturing process. The waste in this example can be traced to the specific cause, and the cause can be diagnosed and eliminated by appropriate intervention. The same holds true for an unexpected equipment failure that must be diagnosed and repaired by the maintenance unit. If the breakdown is preventable, it is controllable. Depending on the nature of the problem, the cause of the mechanical breakdown may be assignable to the maintenance unit (such as improperly performed or neglected servicing procedure), the production unit (for example, operating the equipment improperly), or both. On the other hand, common waste and rework are random and their causes are unknown. Common waste and rework are considered normal byproducts of production, as long as they remain within normal limits of the manufacturing process.

THE NEED

The blended learning program was designed to prepare the production business unit's immediate managers to more effectively create and sustain a motivational work environment to increase the level of engagement in direct reports. The program supposed that, by providing a more motivational work environment, the production business unit managers would have a positive impact on the work engagement of their 32 line employees. The program would evaluate the extent to which any improvements in work engagement led production to higher performance, productivity, business results, and/or profitability.

Work engagement is a positive psychological state of mind that researchers have linked to employee satisfaction and superior job performance. Research suggests that higher levels of work engagement are associated with positive feelings of individual well-being (vigor); a strong sense of commitment to the organization and its mission, goals, and objectives (dedication); and the employees' full concentration and involvement with the work itself, where time passes quickly (absorption). Work engagement is measured by the frequency an employee experiences the three psychological substates of vigor, dedication, and absorption at work. The self-coaching skills taught during the learning program were intended to help the participating managers create and sustain a more favorable environment for work engagement to positively affect employee motivation and performance.

PROGRAM OBJECTIVES

Five self-coaching skills were taught to production business unit managers during a rigorous 90-day blended classroom and online learning program that included on-the-job skills practice, journaling, and peer interaction. The objectives of the program were for each participant to 1) describe, relate, and apply the concepts of motivational work environments, work engagement, and organizational performance; 2) effectively employ the five skills to create and sustain a motivational environment that positively impacts work engagement and organizational performance; and 3) develop a habit of continuous self-coaching for the personal development in, and the practice of, the five skills.

A Summary of the Five Skills

Rooted in self-coaching, or the personal practice of monitoring and assessing one's own job performance, the five skills are self-managing, reflecting, acting consciously, collaborating, and evolving. *Self-managing* refers to clearly knowing one's self and practicing self-discipline and control in one's actions, communications, and interpersonal relations. Self-managing requires managers to understand how they are perceived by others, and how these perceptions can affect the business unit's overall performance. *Reflecting* is the practice of silent observation, or detaching one's self from emotionally charged situations to view these situations with much greater clarity. Helping the manager avoid ineffective or harmful courses of action, reflecting suspends judgment to consider the environment, situation, and possible decision outcomes. When *acting consciously*, managers are more deliberate in their decision making. Because they take the time to understand the facts and nuances of a situation, these managers have a heightened awareness of the consequences and desired outcomes of alternative courses of action. By engaging in informed, conscious decision making, these managers deliberately and decisively act to achieve optimal performance and results. *Collaborating* managers invite team contributions, not just the opinions of a chosen few. Promoting a spirit of inclusion and abundance, these managers fully use the talents of their employees so they can more effectively achieve organizational goals and objectives. *Evolving* managers continue to purposefully grow and develop themselves, both personally and professionally. These managers are open and eager to learn, and they are quick to see work challenges as opportunities for improving their own capabilities and performance.

Basis for Linking Skills to Performance

Research suggests that immediate managers who consistently and effectively practice the self-coaching skills of self-managing, reflecting, acting consciously, collaborating, and evolving play a significant role in shaping motivational work environments that positively affect individual and group performance. Motivational work environments more effectively engage the talents and abilities of employees in ways that positively influence their behavior on the job. Specifically, because motivational work environments lead to greater levels of employee satisfaction, work engagement, and productivity, the more highly engaged employees outperform their lesser-engaged peers. Effective managers afford their people the opportunity to perform well by providing them with critical resources and information needed to do an excellent job. These managers also provide meaningful professional development and growth opportunities, recognition and rewards, and other support valued by their employees. Superior managers build trust, treat people fairly, genuinely appreciate the contributions of their employees, and respect each person as a highly valued member of the team. By clearly communicating organizational plans, goals, and objectives, and by setting and enforcing high standards of performance, these managers successfully align the personal aspirations and efforts of their people with the mission, goals, and objectives of the organization.

PURPOSE OF EVALUATION

This study focused primarily on the production business unit's performance, as measured by the four participating immediate managers' reaction, learning, and application of the five skills taught during the program. Also evaluated were the work engagement levels of the production managers' 32 line employees compared to the control group's 31 line employees assigned to the maintenance business unit. Moreover, the study evaluated the impact and return on investment (ROI) of the initiative in terms of the production unit's controllable waste and rework. The program was evaluated to provide information for PolyWrighton decision makers considering whether to extend the blended learning program to the remaining 13 business units, to make improvements to the program, or to abandon the program altogether.

EVALUATION METHODOLOGY

The ROI Methodology was used to determine five levels of value, including participant reaction, learning, and on-the-job skills application. Also measured were business impact, intangible benefits, and return on investment in the production unit. That is, the evaluation focused primarily on the unit's performance, as measured by the four immediate managers' reaction, learning, and application of the five skills taught during the program. Using the extensively studied and validated Utrecht Work Engagement Scale (UWES), the evaluation also compared the work engagement of the production managers' 32 direct reports to the 31 direct reports assigned to the maintenance unit. The impact and ROI of the program were evaluated in terms of the production unit's controllable waste and rework.

Planning the initiative and its evaluation required a thorough needs assessment to ensure it aligned with organizational priorities. The results of the needs assessment are shown in Figure 7-1.

For the production unit, aligning the initiative with organizational needs meant increasing employee work engagement and reducing controllable product waste and rework. The production unit's work engagement was compared to the maintenance unit's work engagement using the UWES. In a quasi-experimental research design format, work engagement comparisons were generated by taking repeated UWES measurements of both production and maintenance units. Product quality was measured in terms of costs associated with the production unit's monthly percentages of controllable product waste and rework. Trend analysis and participant and management estimates were used to isolate the effects of the initiative. The fully loaded costs of the program were included in the ROI calculation to ensure the monetary benefits were not overstated. PolyWrighton provided standard values for converting controllable waste and rework data into monetary values. At PolyWrighton, rework and waste result in an additional $35,000 for every 1 percent of product rework and $245,000 for every 1 percent of waste per product produced. Data not converted to monetary values, including work engagement, were listed as intangible benefits.

The participating managers' on-the-job application, learning, and reaction data were also collected. The on-the-job application of participant skills was measured using immediate manager self-assessment surveys and UWES data collected from their direct reports after the program. During six of the seven sessions, learning was measured by the participants' summarizing how they practiced the previous session's content on-the-job, and by their completed assignments and skill development journal entries. Learning was also measured using a pre- and post-program skill assessment inventory, and by UWES data collected from the direct reports during the course of the program. Participant reaction data pertaining to program content relevance and importance, as well as the participants' planned implementation actions, were collected at the end of each of the seven learning sessions.

FIGURE 7-1. Business Alignment and Forecasting

Level	Needs Assessment	Program Objective	Measurement and Evaluation
5	**Payoff Needs** ⇨ Avoid costs associated with controllable waste and rework ⇩	**ROI Objectives** ⇨ Target return on investment of 15% ⇧	**ROI** Calculate ROI ⇧
4	**Business Needs** ⇨ Reduce controllable waste and rework Increase work engagement ⇩	**Impact Objectives** ⇨ Monthly percentages of controllable product waste and rework decline Increase work engagement ⇧	**Impact** Percentages of controllable product Waste and rework at 8 months after completion of the program compared to the same measurements taken before the program UWES of direct reports at 6 months ⇧
3	**Job Performance Needs** ⇨ Immediate manager effectiveness in the areas of leadership, setting and maintaining standards, and developing and motivating employees ⇩	**Application Objectives** ⇨ Effectively and continuously apply the five self-coaching skills at work Effectively create and sustain motivational work environments that increase engagement ⇧	**Application** Participant self-assessment at 3 months after completion of the program UWES of direct reports at 3 months ⇧
2	**Learning Needs** ⇨ Increase success skills of immediate managers in the areas of leadership, setting and maintaining standards, and developing and motivating employees ⇩	**Learning Objectives** ⇨ Immediate managers learn to effectively apply the five self-coaching skills of self-managing, reflecting, acting consciously, collaborating, and evolving Learn how to foster motivational work environments that increase engagement ⇧	**Learning** Session content summaries, participant assignments, and skill development journal entries during the program Pre-/post-self-assessment profile Utrecht Work Engagement Scale (UWES) of direct reports during the program ⇧
1	**Preference Needs** ⇨ Learning that is relevant and important to successful job performance	**Reaction Objectives** ⇨ Program content receives favorable rating of 4 out of 5 in relevance and importance 80% of participants identify planned actions	**Reaction** Reaction and planned action questionnaires at the end of each session of the program

Categories/Levels of Data

Corresponding to the ROI Methodology, the categories, or levels, of data included those listed in Figure 7-1. Level 1 reaction data measured participant satisfaction and planned actions for implementing the learning. The organizational need was for the participants to perceive that the learning was relevant and important to successful job performance, and plan to use the learning on the job. The program objectives, in this case, included a mean rating of 4 out of 5 points for content relevance and importance, based on participant reaction surveys, and 80 percent of participants' identifying planned actions.

Level 2 learning measures participant acquisition of knowledge and skills, as well as changes in attitude. The need was for the immediate managers to learn how to effectively apply the five skills on the job, as determined by facilitator assessments of participant discussions, responses to questions, and completed assignments. Also, the facilitator administered pre- and post-program self-assessment profiles to gauge the participants' perceptions of changes in key behaviors related to the five skills. UWES surveys of the production unit direct reports were taken before and at day 45 and 90 of the initiative and compared to those of maintenance unit workers.

Level 3 application measured on-the-job use of the skills taught in the program. The organizational need was for the immediate managers to consistently and effectively apply the five skills, measured through participant self-assessments taken three months after the program. UWES data of production and maintenance direct reports also was taken at three months to assess changes in work engagement.

Level 4 impact measures changes in business impact. The organizational need was to reduce the percentage of controllable waste and rework generated by the production unit. Monthly percentages of controllable rework and waste were used to determine whether program objectives had been met. Also, one last UWES comparison of direct reports was taken six months after the program.

The Level 5 ROI calculation compared the program's benefits to its costs. In this case, a conservative 15 percent target ROI for the reduction of the production units' controllable rework and waste was established.

Data Collection Strategy

The data collection plan in Figure 7-2 shows the level of evaluation, broad program objectives, measures/data collected, collection methods, data sources, timing, and responsibility. Level 1 reaction data collected at the end of each session gauged the participants' perceptions of the program and their intent to apply what they had learned. In addition to Level 2 participant pre- and post-self-assessment profiles and facilitator appraisals of learning, the evaluation used work engagement data collected from the production business unit during the program, and compared it to the work engagement of the maintenance unit. Participant self-assessment profiles and work engagement data taken three months after the program gauged the Level 3 on-the-job application of participant skills. Level 4 data included work engagement measurements taken six months after the initiative and the percentage of controllable waste and rework generated by production at eight months. Level 5 ROI was a calculation of net program benefits over costs.

ROI Analysis Strategy

The ROI analysis for this project, shown in Figure 7-3, depended on tracking the percent of controllable waste and rework for the production business unit before, during, and after the learning initiative. Monetary values were calculated directly, based on the percentage of total product waste and rework generated each month. The researcher used two methods to isolate the effects of the program on controllable waste and rework. The strategy called for trend analysis of the monthly percent of controllable waste and rework per total product, less those outliers identified by PolyWrighton management as nonattributable to the production business unit. Management and participant estimates of the impact of the program and the level of confidence in those estimates were also taken and adjusted. Work engagement was not converted to a monetary value, but was listed as an intangible benefit. Fully loaded costs were calculated and verified by management to ensure the most conservative ROI possible.

Isolation Techniques

Participant and management estimates of the impact of the initiative on business results, corrected for estimate error, were used in conjunction with trend analyses of controllable waste and rework. Outliers identified by PolyWrighton management as nonattributable to the production business unit were removed from the trend analyses.

Data Conversion Techniques

The conversion from percent controllable waste and rework to monetary values was direct. As previously noted, it costs PolyWrighton $35,000 for 1 percent of product rework and $245,000 for 1 percent of product waste. Data not converted to monetary values, including work engagement, were listed as intangible benefits.

Cost Summary

The program cost categories shown in Figure 7-3 included the consulting fees for the learning needs assessment, program design and development, learning delivery, and program evaluation. Printing and supplies, participant salaries, facilities, and travel were also planned costs of the program. In actuality, all fees and expenses were waived, leaving only the cost of participant salaries for PolyWrighton to bear. However, in order to provide the most conservative ROI figure for decision makers, all costs were included in the calculation.

FIGURE 7-2. Data Collection Plan

Program: <u>PolyWrighton Work Engagement Program</u>   Responsibility: _____   Date: _____

Level	Broad Program Objectives	Measures/Data	Data Collection Methods	Data Sources	Timing	Responsibility
1 Reaction	• Program content receives favorable ratings from participants • Participants plan to apply the learning on the job	• Program content receives average favorable rating of 4 out of 5 for relevance and importance • 80% of participants identify planned actions	• Questionnaires	• Participants	• End of each session during the program	• Facilitator
2 Learning	• Learn to effectively apply the five self-coaching skills of self-managing, reflecting, acting consciously, collaborating, and evolving • Learn to foster motivational work environments that increase engagement	• Participants demonstrate successful completion of program learning objectives outlined in the Facilitator and Participant Guides • Self-assessment • Work engagement	• Observations of performance, guided discussions, questioning, and assignments • Skill development journals • Pre-/post-self-assessment profile • Utrecht Work Engagement Scale (UWES)	• Facilitator • Participants • Participants • Direct reports of participants	• Throughout the 90-day learning program • Day 1, Day 90 • Day 1, Day 45, Day 90	• Facilitator

Continued on next page.

Level	Broad Program Objectives	Measures/Data	Data Collection Methods	Data Sources	Timing	Responsibility
3 Application	• Apply the five self-coaching skills at work • Foster motivational work environments that increase engagement	• Self-assessment • Work engagement	• Questionnaires • UWES	• Participants • Direct reports	• 3 months after program completion	• Program manager
4 Impact	• Reduce product waste and rework • Increase work engagement	• Percent controllable waste and rework generated by the production business unit • Work engagement	• Organizational records/databases • UWES	• Business unit manager • Direct reports	• 8 months after program compared to pre-program • 6 months	• Program manager
5 ROI	• Target ROI 15%	• Comments: ROI = (Net Program Benefits ÷ Program Costs) x 100				

EVALUATION RESULTS

Level 1, Reaction Results

The four participating immediate managers from the production unit completed reaction questionnaires at the end of each of the seven learning sessions. The areas surveyed were content relevance to the job, content importance to job success, intent to use the material on the job, facilitator effectiveness, material effectiveness, likelihood the participant would recommend the program to others, and overall satisfaction. Participants rated these items on a scale of 1 (strongly disagree) to 5 (strongly agree). They also indicated planned actions. Evaluation targets were set for a mean rating of 4 out of 5 points for content relevance and importance, and at least 80 percent of participants' identifying planned actions. The targets set for content relevance and importance, and for planned actions were met. Content relevance and importance scored mean ratings of 4.16 and 4.07, respectively. Also, all participants developed plans to apply what they learned during the program.

Level 2, Learning Results

Production unit managers were taught the self-coaching skills of self-managing, reflecting, acting consciously, collaborating, and evolving during seven learning sessions over 90 days. Facilitator observations, participant self-assessments, and UWES measurements of the participant's direct reports were used to evaluate learning.

The pre- and post-program self-assessment profile asked participants to rate how consistently they practiced 25 specific work behaviors anchored to the five skills. Each behavior was rated on a scale of 1 (never) to 5 (always). Administered at Day 1 of the learning initiative, the preprogram self-assessment mean score for all 25 behaviors was 105.0 points. The Day 90 self-assessment mean score was 107.6 points. An increase of 2.6 points for the mean, while statistically inconclusive, suggests the possibility that at least a modest amount of learning occurred during the program. The project team deemed this acceptable, since the learning was designed to become participant self-directed and to continue after the formal program ended. This evolution from facilitated instruction to self-coaching required that learning be evaluated as it was practiced on-the-job. With this in mind, work engagement levels would help evaluate participant skill acquisition during the program.

Taken in the context of the organizational setting, work engagement readings of the production test group and maintenance control group line employees provided additional insight into the participants' on-the-job skill development. A highly disruptive plant fire that occurred toward the end of the learning program produced a significant gap between these two groups; a slight drop in production work engagement compared to a much steeper decline in maintenance.

A thorough assessment of the situation found that the fire should have had no more of an adverse impact on maintenance (control group) compared to production (test group). According to the senior human resource manager, the lead training manager, and the business unit and line managers at PolyWrighton, both groups experienced the same extended period of excessive overtime and intense physical labor. While work engagement was more negatively affected in maintenance compared to production, no apparent reason could be identified. This may suggest that the production immediate managers had been better equipped to deal with the plant fire and its consequences than their maintenance business unit counterparts. In other words, it is possible that the five skills helped keep the production unit from being as negatively affected.

Level 3, Application Results

Self-assessments suggested the self-coaching participant managers from production appeared to be applying their newly acquired knowledge and skills more frequently at Day 180, with a mean score of 112.6, than they were at Day 90, with a mean score of 107.6. While work engagement in both business units was on the increase three months after the program, production maintained a higher response from its direct reports than did maintenance. Managers at PolyWrighton have suggested that the gain in the control group, the maintenance unit, probably was the result of supervisory changes made during that period.

Barriers to Application

Engaged leadership by the lead manager in production and closer communication among all managers in that business unit prevented any notable barriers to application.

Enablers to Application

Production unit leadership was a driving force in enabling the transfer of learning by the participating managers to the job. The lead manager participated in the learning program and practiced the five skills alongside her direct reports, the four line managers. In addition, regular meetings of these managers to discuss application of the five skills, and an improved system of tracking unit performance initiated by these managers, supported the continued use and development of the learning.

Level 4, Business Impact Results

The business impact measures included production's controllable rework and waste summarized in Table 7-1. Also measured were production's work engagement levels compared to those of the maintenance unit. Work engagement data were not converted to monetary values but were treated as intangible benefits.

TABLE 7-1. Production Controllable Rework and Waste

	Pre Intervention 8-Month Average[3,6]		Projected Trend[4]		Post Intervention 8-Month Average[5,6]		Percent Change[7]	Average Monthly Cost[8,10]	12-Month Cost Projection[9,10]
	Percent	Value	Percent	Value	Percent	Value			
Controllable Rework[1]	2.69%	$94,000	0.0%	$0	1.87%	$65,450	1.87%	+ $65,450	+ $785,400
Controllable Waste[2]	0.73%	$178,850	1.5%	$367,500	.22%	$53,900	-1.28%	- $313,600	- $3,763,200
Total Program Benefits (Controllable Waste and Rework Combined)[11]								- $248,150	- $2,977,800

	Impact Estimate[12]	Confidence[13]	Adjusted Estimate[14]	Total Benefit Adjusted for Impact[15]
Isolation of Impact on Total Program Benefits	50.0%	85.0%	42.5%	$1,265,565

Notes:

1. $35,000 is the monetary value of 1 percent of controllable rework per total product produced. Monetary values provided by PolyWrighton.
2. $245,000 is the monetary value of 1 percent of controllable waste per total product produced. Monetary values provided by PolyWrighton.
3. Preprogram monthly percentage and cost averages are based on the data collected during the eight-month period preceding the initiative.
4. The projected trends are based on the preprogram percent waste and rework data collected during the eight-month period preceding the initiative. A linear trend line, generated in Microsoft Excel and extended through the end of the post-program period, returned the projected percentages shown. The dollar values referenced in notes 1 and 2 were then multiplied by the trend percentages to return the projected values.
5. Post-program monthly percentage and cost averages are based on the data collected during the eight-month period following the initiative.
6. Data points, whose causes were not assignable to the production business unit, were treated as outliers and removed from the calculation of the pre- and post-program eight-month averages. PolyWrighton management made the final determination of which data points would be treated as outliers. Examples of causes not assignable to production included new product specifications, ongoing technical issues stemming from the plant fire recovery, an unexpected line freeze attributable to severe weather, and worse than usual supplier material shortages.
7. Percent change is the post-program percentage minus the projected trend percentage for both controllable rework and waste.
8. Average monthly cost is the post-program value minus the projected trend value for both controllable rework and waste.
9. Average monthly cost multiplied by 12 months for both controllable rework and waste.
10. Negative values represent PolyWrighton cost avoidances.
11. Total benefit before factoring in participant and management impact estimates corrected for confidence error.
12. Combined manager and participant estimate of the program's impact on improvement.
13. Combined manager and participant confidence of their estimate of the program's impact on improvement.
14. Combined adjusted impact estimate based on combined manager and participant estimate and confidence.
15. (12-month Total Program Benefit expressed as a positive value) x (Adjusted Estimate expressed as a decimal value) = (Total Benefit Adjusted for Impact): $2,977,800 X 0.425 = $1,265,565

117

Preprogram monthly percentage and cost averages, based on data collected during the eight-month period preceding the program, projected trends for controllable waste and rework through the end of the eight-month period following the initiative. A linear trend line returned the projected percentages shown in Table 7-1. The projected trend values through the end of the post-program period were 0 percent for rework and 1.5 percent for waste.

All rework and waste data the cause of which was not assignable to the production business unit were treated as outliers and removed from calculation of the pre- and post-program eight-month averages. PolyWrighton management made the final determination of which data points would be treated as outliers. Examples of causes not assignable to production included new product specifications, ongoing technical issues stemming from the plant fire recovery, an unexpected line freeze attributable to severe weather, and worse-than-usual supplier material shortages. Controllable rework during the preprogram period averaged 2.69 percent. At a cost of $35,000 for every 1 percent, preprogram rework averaged $94,000 per month. The projected trend value through the end of the post-program period was 0 percent for rework. The post-program monthly average for rework, however, was 1.87 percent, for a cost of $65,450.

Controllable waste during the preprogram period averaged 0.73 percent. At a cost of $245,000 for every one percent, preprogram waste averaged $178,850 per month. The projected trend value through the end of the post-program period was 1.5 percent for waste, or $367,500. The post-program monthly average for waste was $53,900, based on 0.22 percent. The difference between the post-program average and the projected trend represented an average monthly cost decrease of $313,600 for product waste.

Combined, the cost of rework and savings on waste totaled an average monthly cost savings of $248,150, before factoring in participant and management impact estimates and correcting for confidence error, for a total projected annual cost savings of $2,977,800.

Isolation

Also shown in Table 7-1, the combined participant and management estimates of the impact of the initiative on business results, corrected for estimate error, were used in conjunction with the trend analyses of controllable waste and rework. In this case, the 12-month total program benefit (expressed as a positive value of $2,977,800), multiplied by the adjusted estimate of the program's impact on program benefits (expressed as a decimal value of 0.425), returned an annual cost avoidance of $1,265,565 before expenses. This is the total benefit, adjusted for impact, before subtracting total program costs.

Data Conversion to Money

PolyWrighton provided standard monetary values for waste and rework. The company estimated the value of 1 percent of rework at $35,000, and 1 percent of controllable waste at $245,000. The average monthly percentages were multiplied by these values to determine monetary value.

Program Costs

The learning program was provided free-of-charge to the company, but the estimated cost for the program was calculated at $253,761. While the firm's actual cost for the initiative was $3,360, this study provided the more conservative return on investment calculation to allow PolyWrighton managers to make a better-informed decision when considering whether to extend the program to the other 13 business units.

Level 5, ROI

The total projected annual benefit adjusted for impact, before subtracting total program costs, was $1,265,565. The $1,265,565 benefit less the program cost of $253,761 was $1,519,512. The net benefit of $1,519,512 divided by the total program cost of $253,761 was 5.98. Multiplied by 100, the Level 5 ROI calculation was 598 percent.

$$ROI = \$1,265,565 - \$253,761 / \$253,761 \times 100 = 598\%$$

Intangible Benefits

Work engagement was studied throughout the program plus six months afterward. Work engagement is a positive psychological state of mind that researchers have linked to employee satisfaction and superior job performance. Higher levels of work engagement are associated with positive feelings of individual well-being (vigor); a strong sense of commitment to the organization and its mission, goals, and objectives (dedication); and the employees' full concentration and involvement with the work itself (absorption). Work engagement is measured by the frequency an employee experiences the three psychological sub-states of vigor, dedication, and absorption at work. The self-coaching skills taught during the learning program were intended to help the participating production managers create and sustain a more favorable environment for work engagement to positively affect employee motivation and performance. A series of statistical tests examined work engagement in the production and maintenance units using the UWES in a quasi-experimental research design.

An independent sample t-test for differences between the production (test group) and maintenance (control group) means was not statistically significant at Day 1 of the program; the difference between the two groups' work engagement was too small to matter. However, the gap between these two business units widened considerably by the end of the program. By Day 90, mixed-design analysis of variance statistical testing indicated that the difference between production and maintenance work engagement was statistically significant and powerful. Further, Cronbach's alpha testing showed the statistical reliability of the UWES was high. Given the organizational context, including a disruptive plant fire during the final 30 days of the study, the program can perhaps be seen as more preventive in nature. That is, it may be the production managers learned to handle the high stress situation more effectively than their maintenance counterparts.

By Day 270, six months after the program, work engagement in both business units was on the rise. Managers at PolyWrighton indicated the gain in the control group, maintenance, was probably the result of key supervisory changes made after the plant fire that occurred in the last 30 days of the program. While the post-program gap continued to narrow, production maintained high enough levels of work engagement to remain statistically significant at Day 180 and Day 270. In essence, production managers held that increased work engagement led to greater employee satisfaction, improved teamwork and communications, and better decision making.

COMMUNICATION STRATEGY
Results Reporting
Face-to-face meetings with members of the PolyWrighton management team, the participants, the training function, and the director of human resources ensured the results were fully understood and reconciled prior to issuing the final written report.

Stakeholder Response
PolyWrighton had a positive reaction to the results and requested the initiative extend to the 13 remaining business units.

Program Improvement
Stakeholders remained engaged throughout the entire data collection, analysis, and reporting process and offered suggestions to improve future iterations of the learning initiative. PolyWrighton agreed to collaborate with the design team to reduce the 90-day learning period, without sacrificing quality and transfer of skills to the job.

LESSONS LEARNED
Process Learning
Researchers should conduct additional research into programs, particularly in the context of organizational settings and individual business units. For instance, exploring a wider variety of applications for the UWES, including longitudinal studies that link work engagement to tangible business results indicators, may prove useful in assigning monetary values to calculate return on investment. Also, using program research

to move toward a more common and practical engagement construct that links the preconditions, psychological factors, behavioral outcomes, and business results may enhance the evaluation of such programs in an organizational setting.

The study confirmed that practitioners should first take the time and effort to assess relevant business and learner needs in the context of organizational objectives and environmental conditions, before selecting a program. In this case, the blended self-coaching learning initiative was designed to meet the needs of PolyWrighton, and to link program objectives and measures to meaningful business outcomes. The integration of measurement and evaluation into the initiative from the start proved invaluable, because it helped shape a more successful implementation. Finally, programs firmly grounded in research are more likely to succeed.

Organizational Response

Organizational response was favorable and positive. The key element in the overall success of the project was the highly engaged leadership by PolyWrighton managers to ensure the program was implemented on-the-job, as intended. Regular team meetings in production enhanced communications among participating managers, and an element of accountability for implementing the self-coaching skills on the job were leadership-driven enablers of success.

QUESTIONS FOR DISCUSSION

1. How critical do you think the business alignment and forecasting plan in Figure 7-1 was to the success of the program? Explain.
2. Given the time invested into the program, would this online and classroom program be practical to try in your organization? Why was it successful at PolyWrighton?
3. How might the close coordination with the PolyWrighton stakeholders serve as a model for implementing similar initiatives in other organizations?
4. Besides the UWES and self-assessment profiles taken three months after the termination of the program, how would you have measured on-the-job implementation of the five skills? Explain.
5. Guiding Principle 8 states, "Extreme data items and unsupported claims should not be used in ROI calculations." How would you relate that principle to the elimination of nonassignable outliers from production's waste and rework calculations? What about the use of the estimated total cost instead of the actual amount paid for the program? Explain.
6. The authors state that a key element in the overall success of the project was the highly engaged leadership by PolyWrighton managers to ensure the program was implemented on the job, as intended. In what ways do

you believe that level of involvement impacted the outcome, and how can it be nurtured in other organizations, where the environment isn't as user-friendly?

ABOUT THE AUTHORS

John Kmiec, PhD, serves as research associate at the Jack and Patti Phillips Workplace Learning and Performance Institute, The University of Southern Mississippi, where he recently graduated from the Human Capital Development program. A 27-year veteran of the United States Air Force, Kmiec has broad experience training, educating, evaluating, and developing human capital resources in order to improve work processes, products, services, productivity, and performance. His recognitions include the United States Air Force Chief of Staff Team Quality Award and Rochester Institute of Technology/USA Today Quality Cup. He was in Who's Who in American Colleges and Universities in 2010. He can be reached at john.kmiec@usm.edu.

Sandra Dugas, PhD, is a highly respected, nationally recognized executive coach, speaker, and author, with extensive professional experience maximizing workplace learning and performance in many diverse industrial settings. Co-author of *The Savvy Manager: Five Skills That Drive Optimal Performance* (ASTD Press, 2009), Dugas has contributed immeasurably to the seminal research of a learning intervention for work engagement and the university's first human capital development PhD graduate. She can be reached at sandra@dugas.biz.

Cyndi Gaudet, PhD, is professor and director of the human capital development doctoral program, and director of the Jack and Patti Phillips Workplace Learning and Performance Institute, The University of Southern Mississippi. Gaudet was principal investigator for the U.S. Department of Labor's Geospatial Technology Apprenticeship Program. Her workforce development research has received awards from the National Aeronautic Space Administration and the Southern Growth Policies Board. Gaudet has made more than 100 regional, national, and international conferences; and her research has been published in *Performance Improvement Quarterly*, *Performance Improvement Journal*, and *HRD Quarterly* among several others. She can be reached at cyndi.gaudet@usm.edu.

Heather Annulis, PhD, is an associate professor of workforce development and assistant director of the Jack and Patti Phillips Workplace Learning and Performance Institute, The University of Southern Mississippi. Annulis blends teaching and training management experience to coordinate the MS program in workforce training and development and the training and development certificate program for training and human resource development professionals. Annulis was Co-PI for the U.S. Department of Labor's Geospatial Technology Apprenticeship Program. Her research has garnered numerous awards, including recognition as one of Mississippi's Top 40 Under 40. She can be reached at heather.annulis@usm.edu.

Mary Nell McNeese, PhD, serves as associate professor in the department of educational studies and research at The University of Southern Mississippi. She has taught doctoral statistics in three of the university's five colleges. She served as co-principal investigator on the Preparing Mississippi's Teachers to Use Technology Grant, and as Co-PI on the AmeriCorps Campus Link Grant to create a corps of college student volunteers at 11 campus and community sites, who will help develop campus volunteer centers focused on hurricane relief, recovery, and preparedness. Publications include the *International Journal of Diversity in Organizations, Communities, and Nations*, *The International Journal on E-Learning,* and *The Journal of At-Risk Issues*. She can be reached at mary.mcneese@usm.edu.

Susan Bush is the student services coordinator at Gulfport High School's Technology Center (GHSTC). She has been with the Gulfport School District (GSD) for 17 years. Bush's current responsibilities include identifying and assisting students who may have barriers to achieving success in their Technology Center program. Bush has served in leadership positions at GHSTC; most recently as co-chair of the SACS/ AdvancEd and Office of Civil Rights committees. She received both her bachelor of science in business administration and master of education degrees from The University of Southern Mississippi and is currently a student in the human capital development PhD program. She can be reached at susan.bush@gulfportschools.org.

Measuring ROI in Sales Training: A Game-Based Program

Future-Tel Company

Claude MacDonald, CRP
and Louis Larochelle, CRP

Abstract

Future-Tel, a national telecom company in Canada, invited TalentPlus, a professional services firm specializing in business development, to develop and deploy
a unique simulation-based learning program. The one-day training activity,
called The Solution Challenge, was aimed at enhancing the way Future-Tel's
560 sales professionals go about selling solutions to their clients. Specifically,
the training program had to enhance three key competencies: 1) the ability to
create value through skilled questioning, 2) the ability to qualify major opportunities and decide if they are worth pursuing, and 3) the ability to build strong
business proposals.

The program was also aimed at testing, honing, and developing people's
knowledge of Future-Tel's solution portfolio, as well as the key vertical markets
of their clients. To evaluate the effect and profitability of the project, Future-Tel
asked TalentPlus to conduct a Level 5 ROI study. Therefore, data on reaction,
learning, application, business impact, and intangible benefits were collected
during and after the program. After isolating of the effects and converting the
data to monetary value, the ROI study showed that each dollar invested in the
program brought back $1.42 in sales revenues for Future-Tel.

BACKGROUND

Future-Tel is a major Canadian telecommunications company offering a wide variety
of IT and telecom solutions to private and public organizations across the country.
Future-Tel has also developed industry-leading telecom consulting expertise and has

adopted industry recognized assessment tools in order to measure, understand, refine, and fully implement best practices.

Thirty years of experience has enabled Future-Tel to build strong alliances with all major hardware and software manufacturers, including IBM, HP, Cisco, and Microsoft. The company has also forged partnerships with smaller, more specialized IT companies. Those partnerships allow Future-Tel to offer a broad solutions portfolio through its sales force.

Program Description

After observing a decline in sales results, Future-Tel initiated a major reorganization that led to the creation of a new entity: The Future-Tel Business Market Group. The strategic objective of this new group was to improve operational efficiency and enhance customer intimacy.

As part of the overall strategy to accomplish this goal, Future-Tel decided to enhance the competencies of its sales professionals. In this context it was decided to provide all sales professionals with a Solution Selling Training Program.

A survey was conducted by the sales effectiveness team to understand what *Solution Selling* meant for Future-Tel's professionals. Most expressed the importance of understanding and meeting the requirements in their specific vertical markets, such as health, government, financial services, retail, and others. The data from this survey allowed the sales effectiveness team to identify the following key learning objectives with regard to the training program:

- Improve teamwork among sales representatives.
- Develop people's business acumen.
- Develop and refine vertical market knowledge.
- Improve knowledge of the Future-Tel solutions portfolio.
- Develop skills to understand the client's business challenges.
- Develop skills regarding the design and delivery of complex solutions.

In light of Future-Tel's requirements and challenges, TalentPlus was chosen to develop a one-day program, called The Solution Challenge Sales Simulator, a game-based approach that allows acceleration of learning and increases the retention rate of participants. Three hundred twenty-one (321) individuals, including 308 sales professionals, took part in the program.

The learning was structured as follows:

Part 1 (2 hours):
- Vertical forum: most important drivers (four or five) of the vertical market clients evolve in the identification of current projects that focus on such drivers presented by each team.

Part 2 (5.5 hours):
- The Solution Challenge sales simulator, as shown in Figure 8-1.

Figure 8-1. The Solution Challenge Sales Simulator

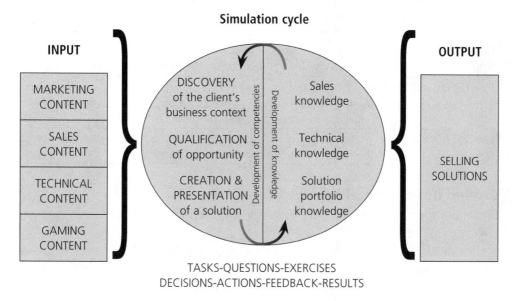

Simulation cycle

TASKS-QUESTIONS-EXERCISES
DECISIONS-ACTIONS-FEEDBACK-RESULTS

EVALUATION METHODOLOGY

In order to validate the relevance and profitability of the training program offered to Future-Tel's sales representatives and solutions specialists, TalentPlus suggested conducting an impact study.

The Phillips ROI Methodology was selected due to its proven and documented use. This approach produces six types of data: reaction, learning, application, business impact, ROI, and intangible benefits. In addition, the methodology uses a systematic logic model to collect, analyze, and report data. Along the way, the process is guided by 12 conservative standards.

The levels of data captured by the ROI Methodology are listed in Table 8-1.

TABLE 8-1. Levels of Data

Level 1: Reaction	• Measures the participants' reactions to training. • Data captured at the end of the session.
Level 2: Learning	• Measures the participants' level of retention. • Data captured at the end of the session and validated in the application survey.
Level 3: Application	• Assesses the frequency of use of what was learned. • Data captured via an online survey, 60 to 90 days after the training.
Level 4: Impact	• Measures variations on KPIs (revenues, margins, etc.). • Data captured via an online survey and through client database, 120 to 180 days after the training.
Level 5: ROI	• Measures the actual ROI by comparing the net monetary contribution of the training program against its fully loaded costs.

General Description of Approach

Figure 8-2 shows that the ROI Methodology was integrated into the entire training project.

Before starting the design of the training content, a meeting took place between TalentPlus CRP's and Future-Tel's stakeholders in order to align (phase 1) the client business objectives and the evaluation objectives. Following the alignment meeting, a data collection plan and an ROI analysis plan were produced and then validated by Future-Tel. Table 8-2 describes the assessment levels.

FIGURE 8-2. Evaluation Methodology

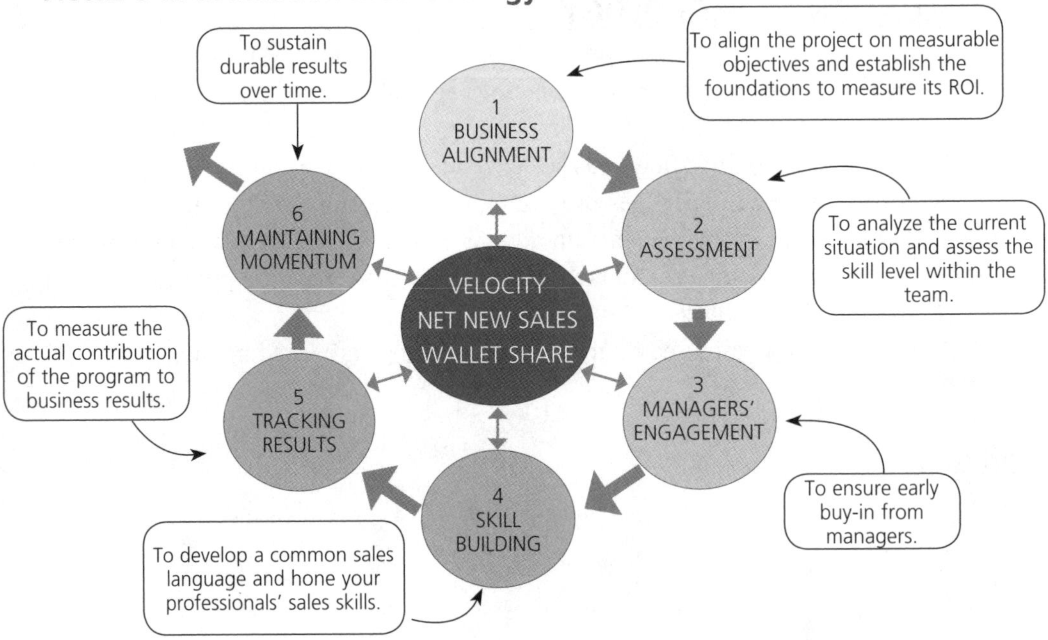

TABLE 8-2. Desired Outcomes

Level 5	Desired ROI	What kind of ROI is required from this project?
Level 4	Desired business impact	To achieve the ROI target, what business impact is required?
Level 3	Behavior outcomes	To get business impact, what kind of behaviors need to change?
Level 2	Learning outcomes	To change those behaviors, what must people learn?
Level 1	Reaction outcomes	To drive learning, what kind of reactions must we provoke?

During the skill-building phase, 24 training sessions (one day) took place. At the end of each training session, the participants, the most credible source of data, had to complete two questionnaires to assess Levels 1 and 2. Sixty days after the completion of data collection at Levels 1 and 2, each sales professional who attended the one-day training session had to complete a Level 3 survey. The collected data allowed assessment of what extent the salespeople were using the knowledge acquired during their one-day training session.

In addition, after 120 days, the sales professionals were given a business impact questionnaire (Level 4) to verify if the changes in terms of attitude and behavior were maintained. This questionnaire also allowed for collection of information on predefined key performance indices (KPI).

At the end of the program, Future-Tel granted TalentPlus access to its business results database. Performance indicators such as average revenue per closed sale, number of opportunities closed with their dollar amount, and sales cycle duration were observed.

To calculate a conservative and precise ROI, one KPI was selected: revenue increase. It was decided to measure the difference between the total sales revenues won by Future-Tel nine months before the training sessions and nine months after the training program.

In order to isolate the effects of the program, the participants were asked to estimate in percentage the actual impact of the training on their sales results as well as their level of confidence in their evaluation. This provides the actual contribution of the program.

The revenue increase measured was then multiplied by the actual contribution to assess the portion of revenue increase that could be associated with the program.

Finally, in order to be as conservative as possible, the ROI was measured by comparing the costs of the program to the net profit generated through the revenue increase. (The net profit considered in this study was chosen based on the lowest net margins observed in Future-Tel's annual reports over the last three years.)

DATA COLLECTION STRATEGY

The data collection plan was developed following the alignment meeting between TalentPlus CRP's and Future-Tel stakeholders. Table 8-3 shows an abstract of the data collection plan.

Level 1 data were captured through a satisfaction questionnaire completed at the end of the training session. Figure 8-3 shows an example of the questionnaire.

FIGURE 8-3. Satisfaction Questionnaire

Trainer:_____   Date:_____

Name (Optional):_____

Title (Optional):_____

Thank you for taking the time to complete this questionnaire. The information we collect will enable us to assess the real impact of this training activity on the business objectives.

Your reactions:
Indicate on a scale of 1 to 4 if you agree with the following statements
(4=Strongly Agree, 3=Agree, 2=Disagree, 1=Strongly Disagree)

Statement		Score			
		4	3	2	1
1	I have acquired new knowledge or additional information in this training activity.				
2	I intend to use what I learned in this training activity.				
3	I would recommend this training activity to my colleagues.				
4	I will be able to apply what I learned in this training activity.				

Enablers
Among the following, identify at least three elements that could facilitate or help you with the implementation of the knowledge and skills acquired during the training activity.
• Support from my supervisor to sustain the implementation of knowledge
• Additional training on the same subjects
• Coaching
• Increased support from the specialist in charge of my vertical
• Better teamwork

• Other: _____

_____

Your comments and suggestions are appreciated: _____

_____

TABLE 8-3. Data Collection Plan

Level	Program Objectives	Measures	Data Collection Method	Data Source	Calendar	Responsibility
1	**Reaction and Perceived Value**					
	• Check whether the participants said they gained additional knowledge and information through the training program (target = 80%).	• Percentage of participants who report having gained new knowledge. Scale of 0 to 100%.	• Satisfaction questionnaire	• Participants	• End of each training session	• TalentPlus
	• Estimate the number of participants intending to use the knowledge gained (target = 80%).	• Percentage of participants who said they plan to use the knowledge gained. Scale of 0 to 100%.	• Satisfaction questionnaire	• Participants	• End of each training session	• TalentPlus
	• Assess how many participants intend to recommend the activity to others.	• Percentage of participants who intend to recommend the activity. Scale of 0 to 100%.	• Satisfaction questionnaire	• Participants	• End of each training session	• TalentPlus
	• Identify elements that could prevent participants from implementing the objectives of the activity.	• Percentage of participants who indicate that the activity is highly relevant. Scale of 0 to 100%.	• Satisfaction questionnaire	• Participants	• End of each training session	• TalentPlus
2	**Learning and Confidence**					
	• Assess whether the participants know how to apply what they learned (target = 80%).	• Percentage of participants who know how to apply what they learned. Scale of 0 to 100%.	• Satisfaction questionnaire	• Participants	• End of each training session	• TalentPlus
	• Evaluate the level of retention of key concepts by participants (target = average results of 80%).	• 5 questions measuring the level of understanding of 5 key concepts.	• Learning questionnaire	• Participants	• End of each training session	• TalentPlus
	• Evaluate the level of retention of key concepts by participants (target = average results of 80%).	• 3 questions measuring the level of retention about 3 key concepts.	• Application questionnaire	• Participants	• 45-60 days after the training session	• TalentPlus

Continued on next page.

131

3	**Application and Implementation**				
	• Check if participants use recently learned techniques such as 6P methodology, the 5 strategies, and the MARS methodology (target = 80%).	• The percentage of participants who use techniques they learned. Likert scale going from strongly agree to strongly disagree.	• Application questionnaire	• Participants	• 45-60 days after the training session	• TalentPlus
	• Evaluate to what extent the training has helped develop the participants' skills to hold professional conversations that enhance their business acumen and their industry knowledge (target = 80% agreeing).	• Percentage of participants who say that the training helped develop this skill. Likert scale going from strongly agree to strongly disagree.	• Application questionnaire	• Participants	• 45-60 days after the training session	• TalentPlus
	• Evaluate to what extent the training has prompted the participants to offer comprehensive solutions (multiple products or services) to their customers (target = 80% agreeing).	• The percentage of participants who say that the training prompted them. Likert scale going from strongly agree to strongly disagree.	• Application questionnaire	• Participants	• 45-60 days after the training session	• TalentPlus
	• Identify which training content has the greatest impact on the respondents' ability to hold quality business conversations, to qualify opportunities, and to prepare high-quality business presentations.	• Multiple choices related to key training concepts.	• Application questionnaire	• Participants	• 45-60 days after the training session	• TalentPlus
	• Identify the factors that could prevent the implementation of knowledge and skills acquired during the training activity.	• Multiple choices, with "other" option.	• Application questionnaire	• Participants	• 45-60 days after the training session	• TalentPlus

#	Objective / Description	Measure	Instrument	Source	Timing	Responsibility
	• Identify the factors that could facilitate the implementation of knowledge and skills acquired during the training activity.	• Multiple choices, with "other" option.	• Application questionnaire	• Participants	• 45-60 days after the training session	• TalentPlus
	• Assess the frequency of use of the newly acquired knowledge (at least a few times a month = 80%).	• The frequency of use of the new knowledge. Likert scale: never, once per month, a few times per month, multiple times per week.	• Impact questionnaire	• Participants	• 90 days after the training session	• TalentPlus
4	**Impacts and Consequences** • Assess the variation of sales revenues before and after the training program.	• $ values	• CRM	• Finance department	• Monthly reports for 2009 and 2010	• Future-Tel: Steve Thomas
5	**ROI** 25% ROI					

ROI Analysis Strategy

Table 8-4 shows the ROI analysis plan for the project.

TABLE 8-4. ROI Analysis Plan

Data Element	Isolation Method	Conversion Method	Costs Categories	Intangible Benefits	Communication Target	Other Influence or Problem
Sales revenues	1. Participants' estimate: • A. How much impact did the Solution Challenge training activity have on your sales funnel since the training activity? (Scale 0 to 100%) • B. How much confidence (in %) do you have in your estimate? Average of A x B = Project's Level of Impact 2. Seasonality: Historic of variation of sales per month in percentage	• Standard Value – profit margin • Internal experts	• External services • Salaries and benefits of the project team, participants, and other employees • Introduction video • Printing and reproduction	• Better preparation for business presentation • Better team work • Greater capability to discover client's concerns	• Project team • Executives	N/A

OBSERVATIONS AND CAPTURED DATA
Reaction (Level 1) Data

Reaction and learning data were captured immediately following each training session. The participants were first given a satisfaction questionnaire. The overall results obtained for all 312 participants (sales representatives) are shown in Table 8-5. The reaction results from the 312 participants surpassed expectations. The objective had been set for each question at 80 percent.

TABLE 8-5. Reaction Data: Percentage of Participants Who Agree or Strongly Agree

Questions	Score
I have acquired new knowledge or additional information in this training activity.	98%
I intend to use what I learned in this training activity.	98%
I would recommend this training activity to my colleagues.	96%
I will be able to apply what I learned in this training activity.	98%

Here are a few examples of comments received during the reaction level evaluation:

- *The course was challenging and exceeded expectations. We were challenged to think on our feet and provide responses to situations in 10 or 15 minutes. That was a great way to make the course relevant to real life.*
- *I believe the 6Ps can be an effective tool for pre-call planning.*
- *Great training session! I really enjoyed the 6P approach—very thorough and applicable.*

Learning (Level 2) Data

As shown in Table 8-6, a knowledge assessment questionnaire was used immediately following the training to measure the participant's level of retention of the key concepts.

TABLE 8-6. Learning Data (Immediately Following the Training)

Number of Questions Answered Correctly	% of Teams That Answered Adequately
5/5	93%
4/5	7%
3/5	0%
2/5	0%
1/5	0%

To verify the participants' retention of the key concepts 60 days after the training, three knowledge assessment questions were included in the application questionnaire. Note that 312 questionnaires were sent and 164 of them were completed. Table 8-7 presents the overall results obtained from the respondents in percentage.

TABLE 8-7. Learning Data (60 Days After the Training)

Questions	Results
Name at least 4 key drivers related to your market that were presented during the Sales Simulator training session.	79% of respondents gave 4 good answers out of 4 for this question.
Name the 5 strategies that can be adopted to push forward an opportunity.	89% of respondents gave 5 good answers out of 5 for this question.
Name the 4 components of the MARS method that allow preparing a strong business presentation.	92% of respondents gave 4 good answers out 4 for this question.

Application (Level 3) Data

As shown in Table 8-8, the application level data were gathered 60 days after each training session. The questions asked were identical for all respondents.

TABLE 8-8. Application Questionnaire

Questions	Results
The Sales Simulator training activity has helped develop my skills to hold professional conversations that show my business acumen and my industry knowledge.	24% Strongly agreed 64% Agreed **Total in agreement 88%**
The Sales Simulator training activity prompted me to offer comprehensive solutions (multiple products or services) to my customers.	17% Strongly agreed 56% Agreed **Total in agreement 73%**
I have used or I intend to use in the near future the 6P Methodology (Perspective and Planning, Projects and Preoccupation, etc.) to improve the way I uncover my clients' business concerns and expectations.	15% Strongly agreed 61% Agreed **Total in agreement 76%**
I have used or I intend to use in the near future one or several of the 5 strategies (frontal, lateral, etc.) to move forward one or many opportunities.	24% Strongly agreed 52% Agreed **Total in agreement 76%**
I have used or I intend to use in the near future the MARS Methodology (Message, Audience, etc.) to prepare one or more business presentations.	29% Strongly agreed 49% Agreed **Total in agreement 78%**

The application questionnaire also identified which key concepts taught to participants had the most impact on their ability to hold quality business conversations, qualify opportunities, and prepare high quality business presentations, as shown in Table 8-9.

TABLE 8-9. Key Concepts With the Most Impact

Rank	Content
1	Increased knowledge of my vertical market's key drivers
2	Opportunity qualification evaluation grid
3 - Tie	5 strategies related to the pursuit of opportunities
3 - Tie	6P Methodology
5	MARS Methodology
6	VCC principle (Value Creation Capability)

Barriers and Enablers

The application questionnaire also captured potential barriers that could hinder the use of the training content. Multiple answers were allowed. Note that 96 people out of 185 respondents to this precise question gave the answer "none" (meaning no barrier).

FIGURE 8-4. Barriers to Implementation

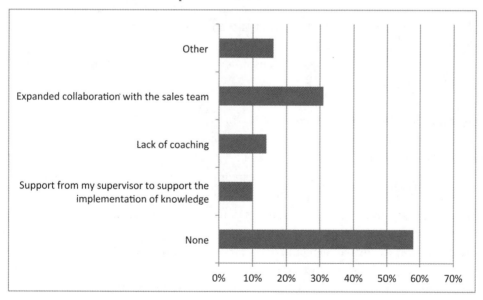

Potential enablers were also captured, such as elements that could facilitate the implementation of knowledge and skills acquired during the training activity. Multiple answers were allowed. Note that 216 people out of 312 participants gave the answer "better team work."

FIGURE 8-5. Enablers to Success

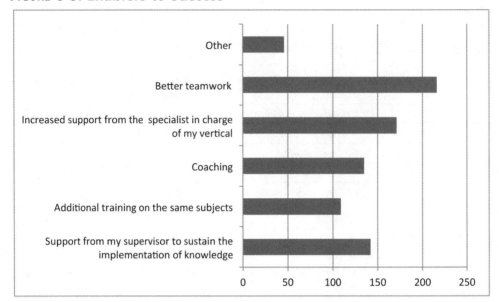

Business Impact (Level 4) Data

The business impact of the project was measured using three methods:
- a questionnaire to isolate the effects of the training solution
- a questionnaire on actual usage of the training content
- an in-depth study of Future-Tel's customer relationship management (CRM) database.

Isolating the Effects of the Program

To assess the contribution the program had on sales revenue, each respondent had to answer two questions:
- How much impact has the Sales Simulator activity had on your sales since the session (for example, 20 percent)?
- How much confidence do you have in your estimate (for example, 60 percent)?

Both answers were multiplied (20% x 60% = 12%) for each participant and then an average was calculated using the results from all participants. This approach is recognized by the ROI Institute as an effective method to isolate the effects of a project or program. Overall, 312 questionnaires were sent and 227 were returned, representing a 65 percent response rate.

The collected data show that participants who confirm the program significantly contributed to their sales are those who most often use the techniques learned. Figure 8-6 shows that the more a sales representative uses the techniques, the higher the contribution percentage was.

FIGURE 8-6. Content Usage Frequency

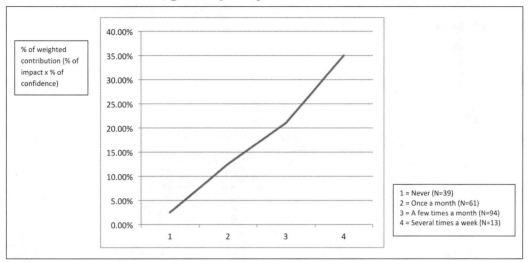

After the calculation of the contribution given by each participant, it appeared that the average contribution was 15.6 percent.

The application/impact questionnaire shown in Table 8-10 was used to obtain each participant's estimate regarding the contribution of the Sales Simulator program to their sales. It also assessed the usage frequency of the specific techniques taught during the training. Please note that 312 questionnaires were sent and 204 of them were completed.

TABLE 8-10. Application/Impact Data Questionnaire (120 Days After the Training)

Questions	Results
How often have you used the 6P Methodology (Power and People, Projects and Preoccupation, etc.) to uncover your clients' concerns and expectations?	80% of respondents use the 6P Methodology at least once a month to discover their customers' requirements and challenges.
How often have you used the MARS Methodology (Message, Audience, etc.) to prepare a business presentation?	79% of respondents use the MARS Methodology at least once a month to prepare a business presentation.
How often have you used the 5 commercial strategies (frontal, lateral, etc.) to move an opportunity forward?	78% of respondents use the 5 commercial strategies at least once a month to move opportunities forward.

Conversion Methodology

The CRM database was analyzed using the following methodology:

- Sales volume (opportunities closed and won revenues) analysis according to Table 8-11.
- Investigation of the seasonality in the sales cycle over the course of a complete year and reduction of the contribution accordingly.

TABLE 8-11. Won Revenues: Before vs. After (from CRM Database)

Director of Sales	CRM Closed Won Revenues Before	CRM Closed Won Revenues After	Variation
Director 1	$26,868,761.85	$15,377,730.51	($11,491,031.34)
Director 2	$13,747,394.63	$28,988,430.62	$15,241,035.99
Director 3	$13,900,757.10	$15,333,933.34	$1,433,176.24
Director 4	$22,071,110.74	$20,908,274.90	($1,162,835.83)
Director 5	$18,118,868.35	$18,497,932.45	$379,064.10
Director 6	$15,172,906.14	$30,115,566.87	$14,942,660.74
Director 7	$6,816,578.26	$10,948,935.45	$4,132,357.19
Director 8	$22,068,795.45	$33,949,732.24	$11,880,936.79
Director 9	$17,142,327.16	$23,464,606.08	$6,322,278.91
Director 10	$9,887,337.21	$7,528,824.48	($2,358,512.73)
Director 11	$19,220,684.40	$31,978,905.88	$12,758,221.48
Director 12	$17,425,731.21	$20,029,077.99	$2,603,346.78
Director 13	$10,938,664.41	$12,620,177.63	$1,681,513.23
Director 14	$40,183,349.32	$22,054,822.13	($18,128,527.19)
Director 15	$10,082,033.32	$11,719,134.64	$1,637,101.33
TOTAL	**$263,645,299.53**	**$303,516,085.21**	**$39,870,785.68**

Since the actual contribution of the Sales Simulator training program on revenue is 15.6 percent, the actual contribution of the Sales Simulator training program is: $39,870,785.68 x 15.6% = $6,299,584 in additional revenue attributed to the program.

Fully Loaded Cost

To calculate a credible ROI, all costs associated to the program were calculated. Table 8-12 provides a detailed description of these costs. The fully loaded cost that will be used to calculate the ROI of the program will therefore be: $392,225.

TABLE 8-12. Fully Loaded Costs of the Sales Simulator Program

Analysis Cost	
Salaries and benefits – Future-Tel team members	$4,125
Total Analysis Cost	$4,125
Development Cost	
Salaries and benefits – Future-Tel team members	$8,000
Salaries and benefits – Other Future-Tel employees	$10,000
Printing and reproduction	$200
Introduction video	$5,300
Total Development Cost	**$23,500**
Delivery Cost	
Salaries and benefits – Future-Tel team members	$30,000
Salaries and benefits – Participants	$150,000
Salaries and benefits – Other Future-Tel employees	$800
Meals, travel, and incidental expenses – Participants	$15,125
External services	$160,000
Facility costs	$4,500
Total Delivery Cost	**$360,425**
Evaluation Cost	
Salaries and benefits – Future-Tel team members	$4,125
Printing and reproduction	$50
Total Evaluation Cost	**$4,175**
Total Program Cost	**$392,225**

ROI CALCULATION

The ROI calculation requires several data points. Here are the different variables calculated up to this point:

- Total variation (before and after) of opportunities closed and won revenues
  = $39,870,785.68
- Estimated contribution by participants = 15.6%
- Additional revenues attributed to the program = $39,870,785.68 x 15.6%
  = $6,299,584
- Fully loaded cost of the Sales Simulator training program = $392,225

However, in order to be as conservative as possible, Future-Tel's CFO decided to use the net contribution of the project as the number to be compared to costs.

Using Future-Tel annual reports from the last three years, the lowest net profit over the three years was 9.8 percent.

- 2009 Operating Revenues: $17.735 million
- 2009 Net Earnings: $1.738 million
- 2009 Net Profit Margin: 9.8 percent

Therefore the real contribution of the Sales Simulator program is: additional revenues attributed to the program x net profit margin:

$$\$6,299,584 \times 9.8\% = \$617,359$$

ROI calculation based on real monetary benefits and fully loaded cost:

$$\text{BCR (Benefit/Cost Ratio)} = \frac{\text{Benefits}}{\text{Costs}} \quad \frac{\$617,359}{\$392,225} = 1.57{:}1$$

$$\text{ROI} (\%) = \frac{\text{Benefits} - \text{Costs}}{\text{Costs}} \quad \frac{\$617,359 - \$392,225}{\$392,225} \times 100\% = 57.4\%$$

Consequently, each $1 invested in the Sales Simulator program created a return on investment (ROI) of $1.57.

To compensate for seasonal variations in sales, we also calculated the ROI based on adjusted revenues. Using financial data (2009–2010) provided by Future-Tel's CFO, a negative variation rate of 9.7 percent was calculated. Consequently, the real contribution of the Sales Simulator program becomes: $617,359 x (1 − 0.097) = $557,475.

ROI calculation with adjusted revenue according to sales seasonality:

$$\text{BCR} = \frac{\text{Benefits}}{\text{Costs}} \quad \frac{\$557,475}{\$392,225} = 1.42{:}1$$

$$\text{ROI} (\%) = \frac{\text{Benefits} - \text{Costs}}{\text{Costs}} \quad \frac{\$557,475 - \$392,225}{\$392,225} \times 100\% = 42.1\%$$

Consequently, each $1 invested in the Sales Simulator program created a return on investment (ROI) of $1.42 (adjusted for seasonal variations).

INTANGIBLE BENEFITS

The intangible benefits were also captured throughout the impact study. Figure 8.7 presents the intangible benefits identified by the participants (multiple answers were allowed).

Note that four of the intangible benefits obtained over 40 percent of support:
- better preparation for business presentation
- better team work
- greater capability to discover client's concerns
- higher capacity to create value for clients.

FIGURE 8-7. Intangible Benefits

LESSONS LEARNED
A High Retention Level Yields a High Impact on Sales

Some learning level questions were included in the application level questionnaire in order to verify the participants' level of retention regarding specific concepts. The results obtained were very revealing. It appears that the questions that received the highest scores overall were about market knowledge and business opportunity development strategies.

In addition, the same application questionnaire revealed that both of these concepts were identified by the respondents as having had the greatest impact on their work. As shown in Table 8-13, it can be concluded that there is a strong correlation between the elements that had the greatest level of retention and those that had the most impact on business development.

This shows the importance of measuring the retention level immediately after the training sessions as well as later on. Both sets of data show a strong correlation with the content elements that have the most impact for the participants.

TABLE 8-13. Retention of Key Concepts

Rank	Key Concepts With Highest Impact	% of Retention About Key Concepts
1	Increased knowledge of my vertical market's key drivers	79% of sales representatives gave 4 out of 4 good answers regarding 4 key drivers related to the vertical market
2	Opportunity qualification evaluation grid	N/A
3 - Tie	5 strategies related to the pursuit of opportunities	89% of sales representatives gave 5 out of 5 good answers regarding 5 strategies to push an opportunity
3 - Tie	6P Methodology	N/A
4	MARS Methodology	92% of sales representatives gave 4 out of 4 good answers regarding 4 MARS communication method components allowing to prepare a business presentation
5	VCC principle (Value Creation Capability)	N/A

A Strong Correlation Exists Between Actual Usage and Contribution to Sales

The application level questions verified to what extent the participants had used or planned to use the key techniques and strategies taught during the training session. It appears that more than 75 percent of the respondents confirm they use or plan to use these techniques.

In addition, the objective of the impact level questionnaire was to assess the usage frequency of the same techniques found in the application questionnaire. The analysis results indicate that more than 50 percent of respondents confirm that they use these techniques at least once a month.

As demonstrated in Figure 8.8, there is a strong correlation between the use of acquired knowledge and usage frequency.

Several Teams Have Taken Ownership of the Content Elements

The results of the Level 4 questionnaire show that the Sales Simulator program contributed a 15.6 percent increase in sales. A more in-depth analysis of the contribution percentage for each director of sales reveals that the contribution percentage varies greatly among them. The assumption can therefore be made that certain senior managers have assumed ownership of key techniques and strategies taught and have integrated them in their business processes more than others.

The assumption can also be made that certain groups felt that the contents of the program were more applicable to their situation (specifically when all the participants were from the same vertical market and worked only in this vertical market).

FIGURE 8-8. Content Usage Frequency

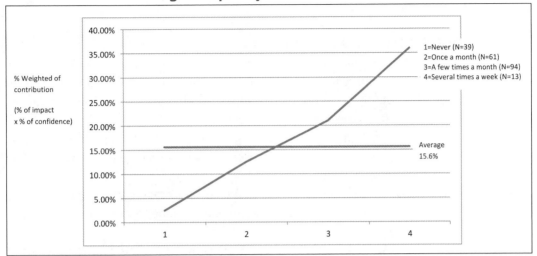

The Data Show a Clear Chain of Impact

The analysis carried out on the Sales Simulator program has a very clear chain of impact between the reaction, application, and impact levels.

- The results from the reaction questionnaire revealed that 98 percent of the participants confirm having the intention of using the knowledge acquired during the training in conjunction with their work.
- The results from the application-level questionnaire indicate that a high proportion (about 78 percent) of the participants use or plan to use three of the most important techniques taught during Sales Simulator.
- The results from the impact level questionnaire reveal that the majority of respondents confirm they use these same techniques at least once per month (79 percent).

In spite of a high usage rate for the concepts taught, the chain of impact shows a gradual decrease in enthusiasm among the people trained regarding the training contents. It would therefore be important to examine the ways of maintaining momentum and encouraging the use of the training's contents.

The Absence of Barriers Correlates With Greater Use

The application level questionnaire reveals that 52 percent of respondents do not see any barriers to the implementation of the knowledge acquired during Sales Simulator. Moreover, the impact level questionnaire shows that more than 79 percent of respondents use the key techniques taught during the training at least once a month. It is therefore very probable that those who do not see any barriers to implementation are those who actually use the knowledge acquired and who grant a higher percentage of contribution.

Teamwork: Mission Accomplished

One of the Sales Simulator program's objectives was to encourage teamwork. Consequently, multidisciplinary teams across specific vertical markets were formed in order to achieve this objective. The importance of teamwork was also questioned in various questionnaires. The results obtained are quite revealing:

- The reaction level questionnaire reveals that 67 percent of the participants say that teamwork is a major facilitating element with respect to the implementation of the knowledge acquired.
- The results from the application questionnaire show that teamwork is the second highest intangible benefit (48 percent) resulting from the Sales Simulator training.

These two observations confirm that the initial strategy regarding the formation of groups was good. Furthermore, should other similar business transformation projects be initiated, Future-Tel would benefit, in our opinion, from repeating this strategy.

The Content Was Not Only Useful but Very Relevant

The analysis of results from the application rates reveals that 78 percent of respondents say they use or plan to use the 6P and MARS techniques. A few eloquent testimonials, among others from a sales professional in the banking sector, prove the usefulness of these techniques. In fact, the use of the MARS technique helped to reactivate and conclude an important multimillion dollar project with a major account. According to the testimonial, the project had been dragging for a while and the MARS technique enabled implementation of the strategy needed to provoke action from the client. This kind of data shows the relevance and effectiveness of the techniques and strategies taught during the Sales Simulator program.

Application of Content Yields Business Results

The majority of participants confirm having acquired useful knowledge. This correlates with the application data, which shows usage rates of up to 78 percent. When asked how much the program contributed to their sales results, overall contribution is 15.6 percent, which is considered very good for a one-day training program. Moreover, the 42 percent ROI shows that the techniques used contributed to improving sales within the Future-Tel business market group.

Finally, 73 percent confirm that it did contribute to increase the number of offers of more complex solutions. Please note that the initial objective was set at 80 percent. It would therefore be important to offer effective means of encouraging the use of the techniques taught and of convincing the participants of their effectiveness.

QUESTIONS FOR DISCUSSION

1. Should all training programs related to business development or sales be submitted to an ROI study?
2. To what extent is it important to adjust revenue variation according to the seasonality of the business?
3. What is the actual impact on the study when scorecards are created and presented to senior management on a regular basis?
4. What is the correlation between the size of a company and the need to measure the outcome of projects?

RESOURCES

Phillips, J.J., and P.P. Phillips. (2007). *The Value of Learning: How Organizations Capture Value and ROI and Translate it into Support, Improvement, and Funds.* San Diego: Pfeiffer.

Phillips, J.J., and P.P. Phillips. (2007). *Show Me the Money: How to Determine ROI in People, Projects, and Programs*, San Francisco: Berrett-Koehler.

ABOUT THE AUTHORS

Claude MacDonald, a graduate from the McGill Executive Institute, is president and founder of Talentuum, a Canadian leader in sales culture enhancement. Over the last 23 years he has trained over 25,000 managers, professionals, and employees from various prominent organizations in Canada. In business since 1996, he has held management positions both in training and business development. Recognized as a true innovator and a business development specialist, MacDonald is also the author of many training programs and conferences offered by Talentuum.

Louis Larochelle. Over the last 20 years, Larochelle has held key business development positions: consultant, sales and marketing executive, project manager, product manager, and sales representative in the software and telecom industry. He has a deep understanding of many business segments, which allows him to offer high-level expertise on the improvement of business processes and the ROI assessment of any project or program. Larochelle is the vice president, professional services of Talentuum.

Measuring ROI in a Sales Program:
A Web-Based Learning Solution
Financial Services Company

Lizette Zuniga

Abstract

This case study focuses on the ROI of an e-learning sales program. Several aspects of this project warrant sharing it with others. It includes competency modeling, competency assessment, and evaluation components for the sales academy at a large midwestern company in the financial services industry, all while undergoing a large merger integration. The learning group enlisted the assistance of an external consultant to provide consultation for the competency development and evaluation aspects. This study outlines the business need for the intervention, e-learning program, and evaluation plan, including how data were collected and analyzed. It concludes with the results from implementing the e-learning program as well as lessons learned.

PERFORMANCE AND BUSINESS NEEDS

A large midwestern company in the financial services industry implemented a revised sales program in its sales academy. There were three drivers for the revised program. First, the learning group identified the knowledge requirements and critical skills for their business and documented key competencies required to move the business forward. Not only did the content of the sales academy need to be revised to match the new competencies, but the time spent in training needed reviewing. Second, the former sales academy consumed three weeks of the new hires' time. A significant impetus for the e-learning version of the sales academy was the need to reduce the amount of time spent in training and get sales associates generating sales earlier in their tenure. Finally, the company was in the process of acquiring a large company and wanted to capitalize on cross-selling its products. This meant that sales associates needed to increase knowledge of all the products and develop new transactions with existing customers.

Two additional considerations were a new product launch and the fact that the call center was undergoing customer service training, which could affect customer satisfaction. An audience analysis confirmed that e-learning was an appropriate medium for the sales associates. The analysis showed that there were 3,000 sales associates scattered throughout the United States and more than 200 other countries. Many of those associates were remote employees. As road warriors, they used laptops with company intranet connections.

THE E-LEARNING SOLUTION

The learning group enlisted an external consultant to assist with competency modeling, competency assessment, and evaluation components of this project. Additional outsourcing assistance was obtained to develop web-based training.

The e-learning program was designed to improve the skills in the following seven competencies: general sales skills, technical knowledge of the products, customer focus skills, prospecting, negotiating, managing resistance, and gaining business results. A basic sales skills segment permitted the associates to test their foundational skill level. Refresher content guided the learners through specific competencies before moving into the remaining sales topics.

The assessment provided immediate input on strengths and areas of improvement for each member of the sales team. This information was tracked in a database and triggered an automatic individual development plan to improve skills in the seven competencies. The skill-gap assessment, coupled with the e-learning design, allowed individual sales associates to customize their learning experience. If the sales associate already had strengths in negotiating skills, then the program allowed the learner to bypass negotiating skills and focus on specific areas needing improvement.

EVALUATION PLAN AND OBJECTIVES

The learning management system (LMS) was the primary vehicle used to launch, score, and track the modules and evaluations. At the close of each module, the learner was triggered to automatically complete a Level 1 evaluation. Figure 9-1 presents the full data collection plan.

FIGURE 9-1. Data Collection Plan

Evaluation Purpose: To demonstrate monetary benefits from impact of sales academy on sales performance

Program: Online Sales Academy   **Responsibility:** Consultant   **Date:** March 3

Level	Broad Program Objective(s)	Measures	Data Collection Method/Instruments	Data Sources	Timing	Responsibilities
1	Reaction, Satisfaction, and Planned Action	Item #6 *I am generally satisfied with this course*	Course evaluation hosted on online assessment Website. Distribution method: email to participant with hyperlink to website with course evaluation.	Online assessment database	Upon completion of course	Facilitator
2	Learning	85% correct on mastery learning check	Mastery learning checks hosted on online assessment website.	LMS tracking system	Before and after course	Facilitator
3	Application/ Implementation	Increased skill assessment ratings on sales competencies	Skill gap assessment launched through LMS; Automated through LMS	LMS competency management system	Before course and 90 days post online training	Monitored by consultant
4	Business Impact	Increased new accounts; Increased $$ made from sales	Database fields for number of new accounts and dollars from sales	Sales workforce database	180 days post-training	Consultant
5	ROI	Baseline Data: 5,000 new accounts opened $15,000,000 sold in those new accounts Comments:				

The goal for satisfaction was set for an average rating of 90 percent. Mastery learning checks (Level 2) were embedded in the design of the e-learning modules. The learner was required to complete the mastery checks before completing the module. A goal of 85 percent correct was set for the mastery checks. Pre- and post-training skill-gap assessments (Level 3) were administered online to measure and track the level of sales competencies among the sales associates. A minimum score for the post-training skill assessment, administered three months after training, was set for 80 percent. Other performance and business impact measures, which were tracked in an online sales workforce database, included the following:

- ability to contact 10 new prospects and conduct needs assessment on those prospects within a week after attending the sales academy
- number of sales proposals that the sales associates generated based on the assessments within 30 days
- number of new accounts opened
- weekly amount of dollars earned from sales in the first four weeks after sales academy
- monthly amount of dollars earned from sales thereafter
- number of customers retained out of total customer load
- dollar amount gained from new accounts
- reduction of time spent in training
- amount gained from cross-selling products (new initiative).

Figure 9-2 presents the ROI analysis plan. To isolate the impact of the e-learning program, participants and their managers were asked to estimate the impact of the e-learning program on the business results. Confidence levels for estimates were used to adjust for any indecision.

Program Cost

The total cost of the former sales academy was $18,890,800. This included analysis, design, marketing, delivery, evaluation, and overhead costs. Each sales associate already had an assigned personal laptop, and the company had already purchased an LMS; nevertheless, a proportionate amount of the hardware and software was allocated to this project. The costs of the program are illustrated in Table 9-1.

FIGURE 9-2. ROI Analysis Plan

Data Items (Usually Level 4)	Methods for Isolating the Effects of the Program/Process	Methods of Converting Data to Monetary Values	Cost Categories	Intangible Benefits	Communication Targets for Final Report	Other Influences/Issues During Application	Comments
Number of new accounts generated	Control group		Net profit from sales Cost of online sales academy	Customer satisfaction	• Senior vice president of sales • Vice president of sales • Vice president of sales academy • Sales academy project work team • Company's online newsletter • LMS (messaging for registrants)	• New product launch • Call center undergoing customer service training, which could affect customer satisfaction	
Dollars made from sales	Control group	Dollars made from sales in both groups pre- and post-training; convert gross sales to net	Cost of lost productivity				

TABLE 9-1. E-Learning Cost Tabulation Worksheet

Item	Itemized Cost	Total Cost
Upfront Costs		
Servers (to accommodate learning technology)	$10,000	$10,000
Software (authoring software, LMS, survey software, virtual classroom setup): depreciation rate per year x number of years	$60,000	$60,000
Hardware (PCs)	$18,000	$18,000
Total Upfront Costs		**$88,000**
Recurring Technology Costs		
Annual software maintenance	$500	$500
Upgrades for software	$300	$300
Total Recurring Technology Costs		**$800**
Analysis Costs		
# of employees x average salary x benefits x # of hours on project	$6,500	$6,500
Meals, travel, and incidental expenses		
Office supplies and expenses		
Outside services	$2,000	$2,000
Equipment expense		
Other miscellaneous expenses		
Total Analysis Costs		**$8,500**
Development Costs		
# of employees x average salary x benefit rate x # of hours on project	$6,500	$6,500
Program materials and supplies		
CDs/diskettes		
Artwork/graphics		
Other		
Outsourced services	$300,000	$300,000
Internal services (for example, information technology staff), including salaries and charge-backs for services: # of employees x average salary x benefit rate x # of hours on project OR amount billed by department	$7,500	$7,500
Registration fees		
Other miscellaneous expenses	$5,500	$5,500
Testing (alpha and beta testing): # of testers x average salary x benefit rate x # of hours on project	$5,500	$5,500
Total Development Costs		**$325,000**

Marketing Costs		
Marketing staff: # of marketing employees x average salary x benefit rate x # of hours on project	$1,000	$1,000
Meals, travel, and expenses		
Office supplies		
Printing and reproduction		
Outsourced services		
Internal services		
Equipment expense	$150	$150
Hardware expense	$175	$175
Software expense	$175	$175
Miscellaneous expenses		
Total Marketing Costs		**$1,500**
Delivery Costs		
Participants' time in training: # of employees x average salary x benefit rate x # of hours of training time (tracked by either timestamp actual or average)	$4,557,000	$4,557,000
Lost production (explain basis)		
Program materials and supplies, if required		
Instructor costs for synchronous learning		
Instructors' salaries and benefits		
Meals and travel expenses for synchronous learning, if applicable		
Outside services		
Facility/rental costs (synchronous, satellite studio, distance learning lab)		
Facilities expense allocation		
Hardware expense		
Software expense		
Miscellaneous expenses		
Total Delivery Costs		**$4,557,000**
Evaluation Costs		
# of employees x average salary x benefit rate x # of hours on project	$6,800	$6,800
Meals, travel, and incidental expenses		
Participants' costs for interviews, focus groups, surveys, and so forth		
Office supplies and expenses		

Continued on next page.

Printing and reproduction		
Internal services		
Outsourced services	$8,000	$8,000
Hardware expense	$100	$100
Software expense	$100	$100
Other miscellaneous expenses		
Total Evaluation Costs for Program/Project		**$15,000**
TOTAL PROGRAM/PROJECT COSTS		**$4,995,800**

Source: Adapted from Phillips, J.J. (1997). *Return on Investment in Training and Performance Improvement Programs.* Boston: Butterworth-Heinemann.

E-LEARNING PROGRAM RESULTS

As a result of the new e-learning program, the number of hours spent in training were cut from 105 hours to 49 hours per sales associate. Annual earnings show a revenue increase of approximately 13 percent. One-year tracking showed the following: Within a week after attending the sales academy, sales associates were contacting 10 new prospects and conducting needs assessment 80 percent of the time; the number of sales proposals that the sales associates generated based on those analyses within 30 days increased 22 percent; the number of new accounts opened increased 32 percent; and the number of customers retained increased 8 percent.

Intangible benefits included improved customer satisfaction and retention. There was also a notable increase of motivation among the sales associates (Table 9-2).

TABLE 9-2. Level 4 Results of the Sales Academy Program

Level 4 Evaluation Item	Results
Hours reduced in training per sales associate	56-hour reduction
Annual revenue	13 percent increase
New prospects contacted	10 per week
Needs assessment conducted	80 percent of the time
Number of sales proposals generated based on those analyses within 30 days	22 percent increase
Number of new accounts opened	32 percent increase
Number of customers retained	8 percent increase
Dollars earned from new accounts	19 percent increase ($20,000,000 to $23,800,000)
Dollars earned from cross-selling	$120,000,000

The amount of dollars earned from new account sales increased 19 percent, from $20,000,000 to $23,800,000. Participants and their managers estimated that the revised sales academy contributed to 70 percent of the new account sales with a confidence level of 65 percent. The amount gained from cross-selling was $120,000,000. The participants and their managers estimated that the revised sales academy contributed to 45 percent of the cross-selling earnings with a confidence level of 25 percent. The two revenue figures were converted to profit margin using a 30 percent margin rate, according to the financial averages of the company (Table 9-3).

TABLE 9-3. Benefits Adjusted for Isolation and Confidence Estimates

Hours Reduced in Training	Amount Saved	Isolation Adjustments	Final Result
56	$3,124,800	70% Estimate 65% Confidence	$1,421,784
Amount of increased dollars generated from new account sales	$3,800,000 ($23,800,000 – $20,000,000)	70% Estimate 65% Confidence 30% Profit margin	$518,700
Amount of increased dollars earned from cross-selling	$120,000,000	45% Estimate 25% Confidence 30% Profit margin	$4,050,000
		TOTAL BENEFITS	**$5,990,484**

$$BCR = \frac{\$5,990,484}{\$4,995,800} = 1.2$$

$$ROI = \frac{\$5,990,484 \text{ (benefits)} - \$4,995,800 \text{ (e-learning program costs)}}{\$4,995,800 \text{ (e-learning program costs)}} \times 100 = 19.9\%$$

An ROI of 19.9 percent means that for every $1 invested in the program, there is a return of $1.20 in net benefits, after costs are covered. These benefits are representative of annual benefit, showing the amount saved or earned for one year following the launch of the e-learning sales academy program. The benefits will continue after the first year and are likely to increase in the case of this program. Although the impact sometimes decreases in traditional learning settings after the first year, this is not always true for e-learning programs. Given the up-front technology and development expenses in e-learning, the benefits may increase significantly after year one.

This case study shows annual benefits, but ROI practitioners should consider the multiyear impact of e-learning programs. Accountants frequently use depreciation and amortization to spread out the costs of assets during the years a company intends to use the assets. Companies often use a conventional straight-line method of depreciation, which depreciates the same amount of cost each year rather than depreciating more during the first few years after the purchase of a major asset. Overall, the straight-line method results in lower expenses, and, consequently, higher profits in the first few years after the purchase. Another method—particularly for technology investments—is the accelerated method. It is strongly recommended to partner with the financial analyst to follow the preferred method of depreciation. When considering long-term impact, the shelf life of the e-learning program in its current format must be determined.

COMMUNICATION OF RESULTS

Communication of the results is a critical step in the ROI process. It is also important to remember to customize communication according to the needs of the recipient. This particular study required three different forms of reporting. Figure 9-3 outlines the medium and the target audience for communicating of the ROI results from this study.

FIGURE 9-3. Communication Plan for Evaluation Reporting

Communication Approach	Recipient of Communication
Detailed report of the ROI study	• Project sponsor • Project team
Executive summary	• Executive team • Program participants
Summary of findings	• Future participants • Future managers

LESSONS LEARNED

The process of designing and evaluating an ROI study is not all smooth sailing. In fact, there are several areas to highlight as lessons learned in the hope that other ROI practitioners can learn and avoid unnecessary work in their projects:

1. **Get early executive support.** The HR or learning group often feels ownership of employee development processes and is hesitant to let them be developed independently. Initial barriers occurred because of putting the project ahead of collaboration. Early partnership and consensus building is critical to the success of the project. Without the early and intermittent involvement of key business executives, the project is doomed to failure.

2. **Partner with the financial analyst within the client organization.** This partnership provides the ROI practitioner with a couple of advantages: First, it helps establish credibility from the CFO organization early in the project,

and second, it helps the ROI practitioner learn about the preferred method of depreciation.

3. **It is helpful if the project team is cross-functional.** Early credibility suffered during this project because it was initially seen as another HR initiative. Create a project team that comprises the right mix of functional representatives and skills to complete the study in a timely and credible manner.

4. **Enlist an expert in the ROI process.** Whether internal or external, these skills are a must for developing a credible ROI study. Without such expertise, confidence levels could weaken.

QUESTIONS FOR DISCUSSION

1. What steps would you take to ensure executive support in your ROI project?
2. What accounting approach does your company take when calculating the costs of assets during the years a company intends to use the assets?
3. Would you have shown the results in terms of annualized benefits from a single year or multiple-year results?
4. How could you ensure that you had the right mix of team members (skills and function) on your project team?
5. Are there other impact measures that you would have included in this study?
6. What would you have done differently in this study?

ABOUT THE AUTHOR

Lizette Zuniga, PhD, presently serves as vice president of ROI implementation for the ROI Institute. With more than 10 years of professional experience, Zuniga has expertise in leadership and organizational development, learning and development, survey design, and ROI. She facilitates certification courses for ASTD in Measuring & Evaluating Learning and ROI Skill Building. She also serves as faculty on the United Nations System Staff College. Zuniga holds an MS degree in psychology from Georgia State University, and a PhD in leadership and HRD from Barry University. She is certified in the ROI Methodology and has authored and co-authored several articles and books about the application of the ROI Methodology. She can be reached at Lizette@roiinstitute.net.

Measuring ROI in an English-as-a-Second-Language Program: An Online Learning Solution

Performance Medica

Edward P. Nathan

Abstract

This case study examines the methodology used to determine the ROI of an online English-as-a-second-language (ESL) program. The program was implemented in more than 20 countries, and the scope of the analysis includes data from all participating countries. A form of ROI analysis had been conducted annually prior to the addition of the ROI Methodology. The latest analysis follows the ROI Methodology approach step-by-step and has provided greater credibility as a result.

BACKGROUND

The organization evaluated is a multinational research-based pharmaceutical company. In order to respect the privacy of the client company and for purposes of this project, the company will be called "Performance Medica." The ROI evaluation described here represents the sixth year of evaluating the online English-as-a-second-language (ESL) course from a company called GlobalEnglish (GE). Due to its previous history as a holding company for many different types of businesses, Performance Medica has an HR function that does not include technical skills training, but focuses more on senior management and leadership development. While the company has shed many of the nonpharmaceutical businesses and now focuses exclusively on healthcare, technical training still resides in the various business units in the organization. As a result, the GE program was originally sponsored and rolled out by the company's learning and performance (L&P) department. This group is responsible for training (directly and indirectly through global affiliates) more than 8,000 employees in the commercial organization (sales and marketing).

THE TRAINING NEED

Due to the size of the organization and the scope of the initiative, good metrics were very important to this project. As the process is described, this study references the 12 guiding principles of the ROI Methodology. For the company to meet its succession planning and career ladder goals, it needed to move a number of high-talent and high-potential people from country to country with an expected rotation in the United States. Succession planning was a stated business objective whereby the company was committed to develop and promote highly talented people. Those people were identified as tomorrow's company leaders. As a U.S.-based multinational corporation, the lingua franca was English. Developing the English language skills for these non-native speakers was a major concern, but one that had been left up to the local affiliates to resolve on their own.

Historically, the affiliates tried to hire high-potential employees who already had suitable English language skills—although no standard for what was "suitable" was ever established. When ESL skills were less than "suitable," it was up to the local affiliates to offer local ESL solutions to their staff. As a result, the outcomes of ESL training have been mixed. A number of affiliates suggested it would have been more effective if the company considered leveraging its global economy of scale to drive a standard ESL learning initiative.

KEY STAKEHOLDERS

A number of stakeholders were involved in this effort. However, it was a complex set of relationships. While the HR group (a key stakeholder) was responsible for the succession planning process, that group offered no ESL training to support the effort. A significant number of succession planning candidates in the affiliates came from their sales and marketing departments, therefore it was felt the global L&P department (another key stakeholder) should be tasked with supporting the ESL training. In addition, the affiliate HR managers were also key stakeholders responsible for implementing the local succession planning process. These managers were also critical decision makers in terms of both funding the ESL solution and enrolling affiliate learners.

ADDRESSING THE NEED: ONE FAILURE

Because succession planning was the driving factor in developing English language skills in high-potential affiliate personnel, the solution had to be cost-effective, minimize time away from work, and accommodate students at various levels of English capability. After repeated requests from overseas affiliates for support of this activity, several global ESL training companies were located and reviewed. Ultimately, a global contract meant to leverage global buying efficiencies was negotiated with Berlitz language services. However, after the first year the approach was abandoned for the following reasons:

- Despite global pricing, many affiliates were able to find local classroom training at lower prices—usually from a local university.
- Classroom training sponsored within the company's local offices presented a challenge in scheduling.
- To keep costs reasonable, classes had a wide range of learners at various skill levels. Beginner, intermediate, and advanced learners sat in the same classroom, which created a lot of challenges.

The affiliates refused to participate in the Berlitz program after the first year, so the Berlitz contract was allowed to expire without renewal. An alternate solution needed to be located—one that addressed the problems experienced with the Berlitz program and one that the markets would embrace. An online ESL training system was found to be the potential solution. At the time, GlobalEnglish (GE) was one year old and had been started by a venture capital company. GE's premise was simple:

- English is the global language of business.
- All resources would be put into developing interactive learning tools to support just one language—English.
- There were 11 levels of business English covered in the GE program.
- There were different course tracks for different English language skills, such as grammar, writing, speaking, and listening.
- The approach would allow a learner with level 10 skills in writing to take the level 10 writing track. However, if the learner had level five English grammar skills, the learner would be placed in the level five grammar track. This allowed for unprecedented customization not possible in a group classroom setting.
- Instructions on using the system in the first five levels are provided in local languages until the learner had sufficient English language skills to follow both lesson instructions and the lesson content completely in English.

A pilot program for GE was commenced for 50 people in several affiliates. The ROI Methodology was not applied to the pilot. What was used was a simple measure of Level 1–3 results. Specifically, learners provided feedback on their experience using the GE system (Level 1). Their improvement (or lack thereof) in English test scores from their original placement to when they completed the pilot were measured through assessment in the GE system (Level 2). Simulated application exercises, also within the GE system, were measured from the benchmark placement process at the beginning of the pilot to the learner's final performance at the end of the pilot (Level 3). Based on the results of the pilot, which were favorable, the GE system was adopted.

MEASURING RESULTS

The L&P department, the program sponsor, was tasked with organizing the global roll-out of the program. Since then, a limited ROI analysis has been added to the original pilot measures and is conducted in the fourth quarter every year. The original ROI method simply asked the learners to provide an estimate of how much time was saved due to their new English language skills. Once an "hour" value was established, conducting a ROI was relatively easy. On average, the company has seen an 800 percent ROI for each of the five years the program has been employed. However, many stakeholders were skeptical about the results of those earlier ROI analyses. Therefore, after five years, elements of the ROI Methodology were also added. For the first time, learners and their managers were asked: In addition to how much time was saved due to improved English language skills, how confident are learners and their managers in that estimate and how certain are they that the GE program was the reason for the results? This approach created a more defensible and credible ROI analysis. The balance of this study focuses on this improved process. The year the ROI Methodology was adopted there were 426 users on the system, an all-time high. Therefore, a more credible and rigorous ROI analysis was critical to measuring the value of the program.

Evaluation Objectives

Level 1, Reaction Objectives

1. Determine learner satisfaction with the GE learning methodologies using a 5-point scale from "dissatisfied" to "extremely satisfied."
2. Determine learner self-satisfaction with progress improving English skills using a 5-point scale from "dissatisfied" to "extremely satisfied." This last point can be correlated to actual Level 2 and 3 assessment results to see if learner perception matches reality.

Level 2, Learning Objectives

1. Objective test scores for knowledge based on placement assessment and progress assessment in order to progress through the 11 levels. An assessment score of 80 percent or higher is required to move to the next level in a particular skill set.
2. Learning objectives will focus on knowledge of vocabulary and rules of grammar.

Level 3, Application Objectives

1. Objective test scores for skill application based on placement assessment and progress assessment in order to progress through the 11 levels. An assessment score of 70 percent or higher is required to move to the next level in a particular skill set.

2. Application objectives, which focus on reading, writing, listening, and speaking skills as applied to specific, real job tasks, as differentiated from simulated tasks or assignments for reading, writing, listening, and speaking skills within GE. It is important to note that, with regard to reading, writing, listening, and speaking skills—whether applied to a simulated task (as within a course lesson) or when applied to a real job task or activity—the methods used for evaluation will be quite similar. The difference in this case is that the simulated Level 3 situations within GE can be automatically assessed by the administration module within the GE system. The real-world job application will need to be evaluated by qualified assessors on the job.

3. Assessment by the learners and their managers (or qualified assessors) using an on-the-job checklist of 12 business situations will be conducted. Ratings will be ranked on a measure of five levels of improvement.

Levels 4 and 5, Business Impact and ROI Objectives

1. Determine level of importance of English skills to the learner's job and career aspirations.
2. Determine learner's estimate of time saved due to improved English language skills.
3. Determine learner's confidence estimate of how much time was saved due to improved English skills.
4. Determine learner's percent estimate of GE's contribution to the improvement in the learner's English language skills.

DATA COLLECTION PLAN

Table 10-1 provides a detailed look at the data collection plan. It is important to note that Level 2 and 3 data are actually collected through placement and progress assessments within the GE program administrative module and are not extraneous data collection tools. As an integral part of the program, these assessments meet the recognized generally accepted standards and criteria of ESL assessment methodology.

TABLE 10-1. Data Collection Plan

Purpose of the Evaluation: Determine the personal and business impact, including ROI of employee use of the online ESL training program known as GlobalEnglish.

Program/Project: GlobalEnglish online ESL program

Level	Broad Program Objective(s)	Measures	Data Collection Method/ Instruments	Data Sources	Timing	Responsibilities
1	REACTION & USAGE Positive reaction to program Usage pattern	Feedback on 1-5 Likert scale Number of hours of use	Annual survey Compare satisfaction levels with previous years. GE User data	Participants Participants' supervisors GE admin. software	October every year	GlobalEnglish support services
2	LEARNING & CONFIDENCE Vocabulary and grammar for placement and progress.	There are 11 levels of vocabulary and grammar in GE. To progress from one level to the next learners will need exam scores of 80% or higher in vocabulary and grammar to move to the next level.	Online assessments (11 levels for vocabulary and grammar)	Participants through GE assessments	For placement to begin using the GE program Also for progress as each course is completed to continue to the next level	GlobalEnglish online program
3	APPLICATION & IMPLEMENTATION (SIMULATED) Listening, reading, writing, and speaking for placement and progress	There are 11 levels of listening, reading, writing, and speaking in GE. To progress from one level to the next learners will need exam scores of 80% or higher in each of these areas	Online assessments (11 levels for listening, reading, writing, and speaking)	Participants through GE assessments	For placement to begin using the GE program Also for progress as each course is completed to continue to the next level	GlobalEnglish online program

CONVERTING DATA TO MONETARY VALUES

Based on the data collected, the Level 1 through 3 objectives contribute to the development of a positive case for the use of GE in delivering ESL learning. Translating that learning into a monetary value comes from the Level 4 and 5 assessments, which ask learners how much time they and their managers believe was saved due to improved English language skills. To add to the credibility of this estimate, the respondents' level of confidence in that estimate was captured and ultimately combined with the respondents' level of confidence in GE's contribution to that result to develop a very conservative and credible estimate of the time saved due to new ESL skills. Once a time saved value is determined (for instance, one hour per week), a financial value will be associated with that time (such as a fully loaded labor cost) and an ROI cost determined by taking into account the annual estimate of the value of the time saved, less the annual value of the time spent studying, divided by the annual cost per learner for the program. This approach will provide a very solid ROI case for the program.

ISOLATING THE IMPACT OF TRAINING

A chain of evidence is an essential component of demonstrating the impact and ROI of a training solution used as a performance improvement intervention. Specifically, conducting Level 1, 2, 3, 4, and 5 evaluations. Level 5 evaluation is critical to developing a supportable and credible foundation for the overall ROI analysis.

It is important to note that the learners and their managers are scattered around the globe. With 426 users (and associated supervisors) around the world, the most efficient method to gather learner reaction (Level 1), business impact (Level 4), and ROI (Level 5) was in a single survey. The critical element is that the survey had to be crafted in such a way that learner (and manager) reactions and expectations are aligned with a perception of the metrics that are relevant to the measure of success used by these learners, supervisors, and their organization. By linking Level 1, 4, and 5 data questions into a single survey, collating the data from potentially more than 850 people (426 learners and the same number of managers) from around the globe, the data collection became a much more manageable task. It is also important to keep in mind that in addition to this annual survey, which captures Levels 1, 4, and 5, the learners are constantly taking Level 2 and 3 assessments as they progress through the program.

Another factor in planning to conduct a global ROI study for an ESL program was the quality of English of both the beginning learners and the supervisors. Just because the learner is *learning* English language skills does not mean all the skills to answer a survey were mastered or that the learner's supervisor(s) have mastered enough English as well (in order to respond to the survey). In addition, there are no resources to translate the survey into all the languages that might be required. As a result, it was important to keep the survey as short as possible, keep the form of English as simple as possible, and leave enough time for respondents to complete the survey. These factors were treated as prerequisite issues and potential constraints that had an impact on the design of the evaluation tools.

Consistent with the ROI Methodology Guiding Principle 5—"At least one method must be used to isolate the effects of the solution"—to isolate the contribution of training to improve job performance as a result of better English language skills, a number of the ROI Methodology techniques were employed. Two of the nine methods of data isolation were used in this ROI analysis.

Guiding Principle 7 states that estimates of improvements should be adjusted for the potential error of the estimate. To accomplish this, a questionnaire to gather data from learners was developed. The three key questions in order to capture data for the ROI analysis were:

1. How much time has been saved due to improved English language skills? _____ hours have been saved each week.
2. On a percentage basis, what is the confidence level concerning the number of hours saved each week? ___ %
3. On a percentage basis, what is the confidence level that GlobalEnglish is the reason this time has been saved? ___ %

Again, consistent with Guiding Principle 7, a second questionnaire was developed to gather data from the learners' supervisors. The key questions for the supervisors were:

1. If one were to assume that improved English language skills allow an employee to work more effectively due to the ability to read and respond to English language emails, telephone calls, teleconferences, and meetings with greater skill and confidence, what would an estimate be of how many minutes or hours per week the learner(s) save(s) due to a perceived improvement in English language skills? ____
2. On a percentage basis, what is the confidence level concerning the number of hours saved each week? ___ %
3. On a percentage basis, what is the confidence level that GlobalEnglish is the reason this time has been saved? ___ %

With the data that resulted from these questions, a unit of measure, that is, time saved, was established, converted into a dollar value, and ultimately used to generate a benefit-cost ratio (BCR) and an ROI. This is an approach that, while not terribly sophisticated, is simple to measure, very defensible to management, and fits within the constraints of conducting a global ROI analysis.

EVALUATION RESULTS

Determining the Benefits

As mentioned earlier, for the company to meet its succession planning and career ladder goals it needs to move a number of high-talent and high-potential people from country to country with an expected rotation in the United States. No financial analysis of the value of such a program has been conducted by the company, and such an analysis is beyond the scope of this study. Succession planning is, however, a stated business objective whereby the company is committed to develop and promote highly talented people. The assumed and accepted benefit of such a program is key to the company's growth, and effective English language skills are required for the succession planning process to be successful. That said, the financial benefit of the GE ESL program can be found in Table 10-2.

TABLE 10-2. Calculation of Dollar Benefits of the Online ESL Program

Item #	Measure	Objective	Source	Value
1	Average number of hours per month each learner spends on the GE system	To determine how much time each learner spends using the GE system	Administrative report from the GE system	3.06 hours online per month per learner in 2008
2	Not all hours spent using GE system are while the learners are at work	To determine how many work hours are lost due to learners using GE while at work	Learners (from survey)	Learners used GE at work only 26% of the time.
3	Time spent using GE system while at work	To determine the average actual monthly study hours used by learners when they are at work	Calculated	3.06 hours online per month per learner x 26% while at work = 0.80 hours per month online at work per learner.
4	Estimated work hours saved per week due to improved English skills	To determine how many work hours are saved each week due to improved English language skills	Learners and supervisors (from survey)	1.68 hours per week

Continued on next page.

5	Total estimated work hours saved per month due to improved English skills	To determine how many work hours are saved each month due to improved English language skills	Calculated	1.68 hours per week x 4.3 weeks per month = 7.2 hours saved per month per learner
6	Net estimated work hours saved per month due to improved English skills (total saved less time consumed online at work)	To determine the amount of hours saved each week due to improved English language skills less time online using GE while at work	Calculate	7.2 hours saved per month – 0.80 hours spent online using GE = 6.4 hours net savings per month per learner.
7	Confidence level of estimated work hours saved	To determine confidence level in the estimate of how many work hours are saved each month due to improved English language skills	Learners and supervisors (from survey)	Respondents indicated only a 37% confidence level in their estimate of the time saved by the learner per week.
8	Confidence level that the GE training contributed to the estimated work hours saved	To determine confidence level in how much the GlobalEnglish training program contributed to the estimated number of work hours saved each month due to improved English language skills	Learners and supervisors (from survey)	Respondents indicated only a 49% confidence level that GE was the reason the learners' English skills improved.
9	Calculation of work hours saved per month per learner.	Take estimate of work hours saved and apply the two confidence level estimates to the value to determine a best estimate of work time saved due to participation in GE	Calculated	Item # 6 x Item # 7 x Item #8 = Item #9 6.4 hrs x 0.37 x 0.49 = 1.17 hrs saved per month per learner

10	Calculation of hours saved per year	Take the monthly hours estimated saved and convert the number to an annual value	Calculated	Item# 9 x 12 months = Annual hours saved per learner 1.17 hrs. saved per month x 12 months per year= 14.04 hours savings per learner per year
11	Calculation of dollar value of work hours saved per year per learner	Take the estimated time saved per year per learner and multiply it by the fully loaded labor cost	Calculated	Item # 10 x $ of fully loaded labor cost 14.04 hours x $50.00 = $702 saved per learner per year
12	Total dollar value of hours saved per year by 426 GE learners	Calculate the annual dollar benefit of the GE program for 426 learners	Calculated	Item # 11 x 426 learners $702 x 426 learners = $299,052

Calculating the Costs

For the five years since the GE program was introduced, an older annual ROI analysis has been conducted. Each previous year in which the older ROI analysis was conducted, the analysis was applied to just that year. This is consistent with Guiding Principle 9: "Only the first year of benefits [annual] should be used in the ROI analysis of short-term solutions." Since most learners are only in the system for 12 to 15 months, each year can be considered the "first year" for that audience. That is why the survey is conducted annually. Its ongoing value to each year's audience needs to be established. By adding the concepts offered by the Phillips Methodology, the quality and credibility of these annual ROI analyses will be enhanced. In fact, the costs that need to be captured for this project are quite easy to calculate. In the previous ROI calculations, a fully loaded labor cost per hour was provided by HR and it includes opportunity cost, that is, what work the employees could be doing if they were not taking the GE program. This aligns with Guiding Principle 10, which states, that the costs for the solution should be fully loaded for the ROI analysis. Additional costs include the per-user license fee for one year of access to GlobalEnglish, as well as the cost of broadband access. Because the cost of broadband access turned out to be miniscule, it was not used in the ROI analysis. This decision is in keeping with Guiding Principle 8, extreme data items and unsupported claims should not be used in the ROI analysis of short-term solutions. That measure, while having been calculated, turned out to be inconsequential in the final analysis. The details of that calculation can be found in Table 10-3.

Table 10-3. Annual Cost of T1 Broadband Access for 450 GE Learners

Item #	Measure	Objective	Source	Value
1	Cost of broadband connectivity	To determine the cost of company T1 broadband per person	SBC communications (a broadband supplier)	$23/month/1,000 users or $0.023 per user per month The cost for the 426 GE learners for an entire month (450 x $0.023) is $9.80
2	% and number of hours per month learners spend online with GE	To determine monthly broadband usage per GE learners	GlobalEnglish	4,821 hours online through April 30, 2008 4,821 hours/4 months = 1205.25 hours for all GE learners per month
3	Cost of broadband usage by GE learners	To determine how much of the overall cost of broadband is utilized by GE learners	Calculated	Hours per month per person = 730 Total hours available for 426 GE learners: 730 x 426 = 310,980 hours available % of monthly hours used by GE learners: 1,205/310,980 = 0.39% Cost of 426 GE learners use of broadband per month = 0.39% x $9.80 = $0.0382 $0.0382 x 12 months = $0.46/year)
4	Total cost per year of T1 broadband access for 450 GE learners	Determine annual cost of T1 broadband access for all GE learners	Calculated	$0.46 per year

The entire calculation of all costs for the GE program implementation can be found in Table 10-4.

TABLE 10-4. Annual Cost of GlobalEnglish Usage for 426 Learners

Item #	Measure	Objective	Source	Value
1	GE cost per Learner	To measure the cost of the actual training program	GlobalEnglish	$350/learner/year
2	# of Learners	To determine how many learners require an annual license	Performance Genetica (Client)	426 learners
3	Administration	To determine the cost of administering the GE program	GlobalEnglish	GE handles its own administration as part of the user fee.

Performance Pharmaceuticals' administration costs come to $4,500 per year ($150/year/ affiliate x 30 affiliates). |
| 4 | Materials | To determine if there are any material costs | GlobalEnglish | $0 since the entire program is online and using computers already assigned to learners there are no material costs.

The $350/learner/year fee covers all materials and support costs. |
| 5 | Cost of broadband connectivity | To determine the cost of company T1 broadband per person | Calculated in Table 10-1 | Less than $1.00 per year |
| 6 | Total annual cost of GE | Total cost of implementing GE for 450 users for 1 year | Calculated (Items #1 x #2) + Items #3, #4, and # 5 | Total cost of GE for 426 learners for one year: $153,601 |

Using the data from Tables 10-2, 10-3, and 10-4, the final ROI cost calculation is provided below:

$$\frac{\$299,052 - \$153,601}{\$153,601} = 0.9469 \times 100\% = 94.7\% \text{ ROI}$$

The benefit-cost ratio (BCR) is calculated as follows:

$$\frac{\$299,052}{\$153,601} = 1.95:1 \text{ or approximately 2:1 BCR}$$

COMMUNICATION PLAN

Guiding Principle 12 states, "The results from the ROI Methodology must be communicated to all the key stakeholders." After determining the ROI and BCR for the GE learning initiative, it was critical to communicate those results to key stakeholders who influence the availability of resources to continue the program. Without communicating the results of the study, there is a very high risk that in a budgetary downturn the program could be cut because key stakeholders were unaware of the impact of the program. Putting together an effective communication plan required the following elements:

- Communication had to be timely.
- Communication was targeted to specific audiences.
- Media used were carefully selected.
- Communication was unbiased and modest.
- Communication was consistent.
- Testimonials were more effective coming from individuals the audience respects.
- The audience's opinion of the learning and development staff and function had influence on the communication strategy.

CONCLUSIONS

This case study has demonstrated that by using a disciplined comprehensive approach to evaluating the GE online ESL program, it is quite possible to make a strong qualitative and quantitative case for investing in this learning intervention. The ROI Methodology approach has provided valid and persuasive tools and methods to tease out the financial impact, specifically the ROI, of implementing the program. The added rigor, discipline, and operating standards brought to the evaluation process helps to insulate the program and the study from critics who use subjective criteria to attack the value of the program. This process moves the entire evaluation methodology for learning programs from a soft, subjective assessment to a concrete, comprehensive, and objective analysis of the impact of the program on learner performance and company business results. These are very powerful tools for learning professionals to support their recommendations for investments in future technology-based learning programs.

DISCUSSION QUESTIONS

1. Are the results of this study credible? Explain.
2. Although participants are guided to think of program evaluation as including five distinct levels, for reasons of practicality, this study clearly combined the qualitative aspects of Levels 1, 3, 4, and 5 into one survey tool. Is this acceptable? If so, why? If not, why not?

3. Why is the chain of impact so important in a study such as this one?
4. An important part of this ROI case study was the ability to determine an increase in workplace application of improved English-as-a-second-language (ESL) skills by using percentages of time and converting those percentages to dollar values. Were there other methods one could use to determine the financial impact of new ESL skills? Please explain.
5. How might the ROI process in this case study be improved?

REFERENCES

Phillips, J.J. (2003). *Return on Investment in Training and Performance Improvement Programs*. Oxford, UK: Butterworth-Heinemann.

Phillips, J.J. (2006). Return on Investment Measures Success [Electronic version]. *Industrial Management*, 48, 2.18–23.

ABOUT THE AUTHOR

Edward (Ed) P. Nathan PhD, CRP, CPT, has over 25 years' experience in global learning and development. Having worked in more than 40 countries with global companies such as Pfizer, Wyeth Pharmaceuticals, Lederle Laboratories, and Walmart, he has conducted research in developing global e-learning programs and measuring the ROI of online ESL learning.

Nathan earned his PhD in education with a specialization in training and performance improvement from Capella University. He holds a CRP (Certified ROI Professional) from the ROI Institute and a CPT (Certified Performance Technologist) from the International Society for Performance Improvement. With numerous papers published, over a dozen conference presentations, and two textbook chapters, he is currently working on a book focusing on the use of organic learning methodologies in the classroom. Properly applied, these methods help facilitate learners' self-mastery of complex business and academic processes. He makes his home in West Chester, Pennsylvania, and can be reached at EPNathan1@gmail.com.

11

Measuring ROI in an Upgrade Selling Program: A Mobile Learning Solution

Transsoft Inc.

Jack J. Phillips and Patti P. Phillips

Abstract

This project involves a mobile learning application for sales associates of a large software firm specializing in software solutions for the trucking industry. Sales associates were provided a mobile learning solution for their iPads, designed to describe and sell an upgrade to its most popular software product. Although the release occurred at the same time for all sales associates, not all of them logged onto the learning portal through their iPads, which allowed an opportunity for a comparison group. This case study highlights the key issues in calculating the impact and ROI of a mobile learning solution on business results. The case is arranged in a multiple part format to allow readers to experience the issues and recommended actions and solutions.

BACKGROUND
Organizational Profile

Transsoft is one of the largest software companies for the trucking industry. With more than 12,000 users, Transsoft dominates the trucking landscape. Transsoft provides software solutions for carriers, brokers, logistics companies, and shippers. A variety of software solutions are available, including products for financial operations, fleet management, document systems, dispatch operations, freight management, and broker management. Its most popular software, ProfitPro, integrates a variety of software solutions, all aimed at improving the efficiency and profitability of the trucking company. The trucking industry is highly competitive, often producing low margins. Having an efficient operation is usually the difference in profit or loss. ProfitPro has a reputation for helping trucking companies meet profit goals.

Situation

Transoft has an extensive network for sales and marketing, with more than 200 sales associates serving all of North America. Sales associates are strategically located across the United States and most work from their homes. Bringing sales teams into three regional offices for training has become a thing of the past, unless extensive formal development of new sales associates is needed.

Transoft has just completed an upgrade on its most popular software, ProfitPro, and has released it to the sales team to begin selling the upgrades. An upgrade costs the client from $1,000 to $3,000, depending on the scope of operations. For the client, the upgrade provides some new features and streamlines some of the previous processes. It should help make clients more profitable by reducing the time to complete certain documents, ensuring on-time filing, reducing invoicing errors, and improving other operating efficiencies.

Solution

The learning and development team agreed on a solution that would involve a mobile learning application directly accessible on an iPad. Previously, sales teams were furnished with iPads for work. With five modules, the program would take about two hours to complete, which would prepare a sales rep to sell the upgrade. The specific modules include:

- rationale for the upgrade
- key features of the upgrade
- how the upgrade will increase profits (time savings, quality improvements, and productivity)
- pricing options
- implementation and support.

Each module contains tools to check learning and to encourage and plan for application. In addition, brief summaries of each module are produced for review just before meeting a client. The program provides an integration with Salesforce.com to set up appointments with customers to discuss the upgrade. This feature identifies the target clients, listed by potential sales volume. It also develops the pricing options based on the client's use of ProfitPro. Modules were designed to develop an understanding of the upgrades and to assist, encourage, and even require a sales associate to sell the upgrade.

A mobile solution was selected because of its flexibility, convenience, and cost. It was not feasible to train the sales force in face-to-face workshops. A half-day workshop would have required sales associates to lose an average of a day at work, and more than 80 percent of them would have incurred travel costs. A mobile solution was not only ideal for this type of program, but it was the only way to go from an economic and convenience perspective.

Rationale for ROI

Although mobile learning appeared to be the only feasible solution in terms of cost, time, and convenience, the management team wanted to know whether it was working, perhaps at the same level as a face-to-face workshop. Executives wanted an evaluation that would show how well the program was working, how quickly it was working, and what issues were inhibiting the success of this type of learning. While executives were convinced that this approach was necessary for a diverse sales force scattered around the country, there was still a nagging concern about the effectiveness of mobile learning programs. Although they would see the sales numbers, they wanted to know more in terms of costs versus benefits. The learning team was challenged not only to secure data but also to evaluate the program up to and including the financial ROI. They insisted that the analysis should be credible, separating the influence of this program from the special promotion for the upgrade.

Exercise

1. Is this level of accountability typical? Please explain.

_____

_____

2. What do you think the broad objectives should be at each level?
Reaction

_____

_____

Learning

_____

_____

Application

_____

_____

Impact

_____

_____

ROI

_____

_____

OBJECTIVES

After the decision was made to go with the program, the next step was to develop the detailed objectives at all five levels. This step was completed with input from a project manager, a sales manager, and subject matter experts. At Level 1, it was decided that participants should see this program as relevant to their work and important to their success. It should have content that they intended to use and that they would recommend to others.

In terms of learning, a self-assessment on the five modules included a simple true/false quiz at the end of each module. Each module had five questions, representing 25 questions total. A participant should score at least 20 out of 25, allowing for one missed question for each module. The score would not be punitive as there would not be any consequences for missing the desired score. This was only a gauge for participant success, as they immediately saw the correct answers with an explanation. Sales associates were encouraged to repeat the exercise if they scored less than four out of five correct answers for each module.

For application, the objectives focused on sales associates using the skills quickly and to make the first scheduled call within a week of completing of the program. By the end of the month, the goal was to see routine use of each of the major tasks, actions, or skills from the five modules.

For business impact, sales should occur within three weeks of program completion, and the associates should reach $10,000 in sales per month within three months. This was suitable to the management team and should result in success for the program.

For the Level 5 objective, a 20 percent ROI was set. This is slightly above what Transoft would use for capital expenditures (for example, the headquarters building), and it would seem reasonable to executives. The objective was the minimum acceptable performance, not only for this level of ROI, but for the other levels as well.

Exercise

Based on these objectives, what is your recommended approach for data collection and analysis? Please complete the data collection plan and the ROI analysis plan for this program. See Figures 11-1 and 11-2.

FIGURE 11-1. Data Collection Plan

Program: _____   Responsibility: _____   Date: _____

Level	Broad Program Objective(s)	Measures	Data Collection Method/Instruments	Data Sources	Timing	Responsibilities
1	REACTION & PLANNED ACTION					
2	LEARNING & CONFIDENCE					
3	APPLICATION & IMPLEMENTATION					
4	BUSINESS IMPACT					
5	ROI					

Baseline Data:

Comments:

Figure 11-2. Action Plan

Name:_____ Facilitator Signature_____ Follow-Up Date_____

Objective:_____ Evaluation Period_____ To___

Improvement Measure:_____ Current Performance_____ Target Performance_____

Action Steps	Analysis
1._____	A. What is the unit of measure?_____
2._____	B. What is the value (cost) of one unit? $_____
3._____	C. How did you arrive at this value?_____
4._____	_____
	_____
5._____	D. How much did the measure change during the evaluation period? (monthly value)_____
6._____	E. List the other factors that have influenced this change._____
7._____	F. What percent of this change was actually caused by this program?_____%
Intangible Benefits:_____	G. What level of confidence do you place on the above information? (100%=Certainty and 0%=No Confidence)_____%
Comments:_____	

PLANNING

Data Collection Plan

The evaluation planning meeting was conducted with the program manager, the designers and developers who were on contract, and the project manager for the program. In addition, the evaluator moderated the meeting. In this case, the evaluator was an external consultant who was conducting the ROI study. Figure 11-3 is the data collection plan, which details the methods, source, and timing for collecting data at four levels. Level 1 and 2 data were captured in the system as the participants completed five modules in the mobile learning program. Level 3 was a web-based questionnaire with simple questions. To achieve a good response rate, 20 techniques were used, which are shown in Table 11-1. Level 4 impact data were retrieved directly from the Salesforce.com system at Transoft.

TABLE 11-1. Techniques to Increase Response Rates

1. Provide advance communication.
2. Communicate the purpose.
3. Identify who will see the results.
4. Describe the data integration process.
5. Let the target audience know that they are part of a sample.
6. Design for simplicity.
7. Make it look professional and attractive.
8. Use the local manager's support.
9. Build on earlier data (Level 1 and 2).
10. Pilot test the questionnaire.
11. Recognize the expertise of participants.
12. Have an executive sign the introductory letter.
13. Send a copy of the results to the participants.
14. Report the use of results.
15. Introduce the questionnaire during the program (first and last module).
16. Use follow-up reminders.
17. Consider the appropriate medium for easy response.
18. Estimate and report the necessary time needed to complete the questionnaire.
19. Show the timing of the planned steps.
20. Collect data anonymously or confidentially.

Figure 11-3. Completed Data Collection Plan

Program: Product Upgrade With Mobile Learning   **Responsibility:** _____   **Date:** _____

Level	Broad Program Objective(s)	Measures of Success	Data Collection Method/ Instruments	Data Sources	Timing	Responsibilities
1	REACTION & PLANNED ACTIONS Achieve positive reaction on: • Relevance to my work • Recommend to others • Important to my success • Intent to use	Rating of 4 out of 5 on a composite of four measures	LMS survey, built into program	Participant	End of program	Program manager
2	LEARNING Learn to use five concepts to sell new upgrade: • Rationale for upgrade • Features of upgrade • How upgrade will increase client profit • Pricing options • Implementation and support	Achieve 4 out of 5 correct answers on each module Achieve 20 of 25 total correct answers	True/False quiz	Participant	End of program	Program manager

3	APPLICATION/ IMPLEMENTATION Use of five skills: • Explain rationale for upgrade • Identify key features of upgrade • Describe how upgrade increases client profit • Identify pricing options • Explain implementation and support • Make the first call in 5 days	Rating (4 of 5) on a 1-5 scale System check	Questionnaire, web-based Performance monitoring	Participant Salesforce. com	1 month after program 1 month after program	Evaluator
4	BUSINESS IMPACT • Increase in sales to $10,000 per month • Sell first upgrade in 3 weeks	Monthly sales per associate Actual sale	Business performance monitoring Business performance monitoring	Salesforce. com Salesforce. com	3 months after program 1 month after program	Evaluator
5	ROI 30%	Comments:				

ROI Analysis Plan

Figure 11-4 shows the ROI analysis plan, which is straightforward for this type of analysis. The two business measures collected were the monthly sales per associate for the upgrade and the time for the first sale. The method of isolation was a comparison group method—a classical experimental versus control group method. As a fallback, participant estimates would be used to sort out the effects of this program. During the evaluation meeting, there was discussion about the possibility of setting up the comparison group. Based on previous experience, some of the sales team might not use the module for several weeks, or at all, depending on their schedules, their interest in the upgrade, and their eagerness to learn through mobile technology. At the same time, some will get involved immediately. Given this situation, there could be an opportunity for a comparison group. Also, it is helpful to know that some, if not all, would sell the upgrade without taking part in the mobile learning program. They would flip through the brochure and attempt to make the sale—and succeed in doing so. The challenge was to match the first 25 users with a corresponding group of nonusers. Because of timing (when they might have started the program) the matching group would be larger so that, as users logged in, they would be dropped out of the control group. This was the best shot at having a comparison group, and the planning team realized at the onset that it might not work. Consequently, participant estimates were used as a backup, adjusted for error.

Converting data to money was very easy. The sales were adjusted with the profit margin for the new product. This was developed by the product launch team and was actually known to the sales force. For this upgrade, the margin was 20 percent. The time for sale was a measure that was monitored but not converted to data. This sales data actually would be included in the overall sales and to include them again would be double counting the sales. The cost categories are routine and listed in the figure, including a small prorated cost for the iPads and the design and development cost prorated for the 25 participants. The expected intangibles included customer satisfaction and engagement, job satisfaction for the sales team, brand awareness, reputation of the company, and stress reduction for sales associates. The individuals who needed to see the results were the complete sales team, sales managers (including the vice president of sales and vice president of marketing), the participants who provided the data, and their immediate managers.

FIGURE 11-4. Completed ROI Analysis Plan

Program: Product Upgrade With Mobile Learning   **Responsibility:** ___   **Date:** ___

Data Items (Usually Level 4)	Methods for Isolating the Effects of the Program/Process	Methods of Converting Data to Monetary Values	Cost Categories	Intangible Benefits	Communication Targets for Final Report	Other Influences/Issues During Application	Comments
• Monthly sales per associate	• Control group analysis • Participant estimates (both measures)	• Direct conversion using standard profit contribution	• Needs assessment • Design • Content development • Mobile device • Participants' salaries plus benefits (time) • Cost of coordination and administration (time) • Project management (time) • Evaluation	• Customer engagement and satisfaction • Job satisfaction of sales associates • Stress reduction • Reputation	• Program participants • Sales managers • Product manager • Senior executives—regional and headquarters • Learning coordinators, designers, and managers • All sales associates	• No communication with control group	
• Time to first sale	• Control group analysis • Participant estimates (both measures)	• N/A					

RESULTS

The first 25 people signed up within three days of the program's announcement. Level 1 reaction data were collected at the end of the fifth module and are presented in Table 11-2. Reactions were as expected, with the exception of intent to use, which was very high.

Level 2 learning seemed appropriate, and quiz scores were above targets, as shown in Table 11-3. Scores were slightly lower than desired for the quiz for implementation and support. This was not a huge concern, as this information is clearly in the documents and the product brochures.

Level 3 application data seemed to be on track as shown in Table 11-4. Identifying pricing options and explaining implementation and support were off a little, but overall the objectives were met. The time for the first call was below the objective, which was very good. As expected, there were some barriers and enablers to success, as shown in Table 11-5. The barriers were minimal. However, there was a concern that 9 percent of sales associates were not encouraged by their managers to use the program. As expected, the number one enabler was management encouragement.

TABLE 11-2. Reaction Results

Rate the Following	Rating
Relevant to my work	4.3
Important to my success	4.1
Intent to use	4.7
Recommend to others	4.2
Target: 4.0	Average: 4.3
(Scale: 1 = not at all; 2 = some; 3 = average; 4 = above average; 5 = very much)	

TABLE 11-3. Learning Results

Module	Quiz Categories	Avg. Number of Correct Responses
1	Rationale for the upgrade	4.3
2	Key features of the upgrade	4.2
3	How upgrade will increase client profit	4.3
4	Pricing options	4.1
5	Implementation and support	3.9
Possible score: 25		Average: 20.8
Target: 20		

TABLE 11-4. Application Results

Extent of Use in One Month	Rating
Make the first call (target: 5 days)	3.5 days
Explaining the rationale for upgrade	4.2
Identifying key features of upgrade	4.3
Describing how the upgrade increases client profit	4.1
Identifying pricing options	3.9
Explaining implementation and support	3.8
Target: 4.0	Average: 4.06

(Scale: 1 = not at all; 2 = some use; 3 = moderate amount of use; 4 = significant amount of use; 5 = very significant amount of use)

TABLE 11-5. Barriers and Enablers

Barriers	% Reporting
Lack of time to be involved	12%
Lack of management encouragement	8%
Took too long to complete	8%
Technology issues	4%
Other	4%
Explaining implementation and support	3.8
Enablers	**% Reporting**
Management encouragement	60%
Easy to use	52%
Timely	48%
Convenient	40%
Relevant	36%
Other	16%

Isolating the Effects of the Program

An important and perhaps the most challenging issue was to determine the effects of this program from other influences. The best way to do this was to use a classic experimental versus control group, although that became tricky with this program and it was questionable whether or not it would work throughout the program. At first, 25 sales associates were selected based on the first 25 to complete the modules. This was accomplished within the first three days. This group of 25 was matched to a group of other sales associates. The first challenge was finding an appropriate match; the second was to have enough remaining in the control group, since they drop out of the experiment when they complete the program. Some people would wait weeks or months to take the program, or they would choose not to take it at all. And some dropouts are a reality when mobile learning is left entirely up to the individual. Instead of forcing participants to use the program, the team wanted the program to be taken voluntarily. The communication for the program, which emphasized that learning is needed in order to sell this upgrade properly, was presented in hopes that this plea would cause them to sign up.

To select the control group, the factors that should affect sales were considered. The four most important considerations were:

1. current sales level, on an annual basis
2. tenure with the company
3. performance rating in human resource system
4. total selling experience.

Although the fourth item was a little more difficult to determine because it counted selling experience in other companies, a quick review of human resource records revealed the total number of years of selling experience. Given these factors, more than 80 associates matched with the 25 in the trial group. Fifty of those were selected randomly as the control group, recognizing that some of them may drop out of the control group when they started this mobile learning program.

Impact Results

Table 11-6 shows the impact data comparing the experimental group of 25 sales associates with the control group of 22. As expected, almost every one of the control group (19 of 22) was actually selling the upgrade though not participating in the program, but the difference of the two groups was very impressive. The difference for that second month is then annualized, producing an annual improvement of $1,140,000. The time of the first sale was impressive for the group involved in the program—11 days compared to 21 days for the control group.

TABLE 11-6. Sales Data in Three Months After Launch

Group	Avg. Sales (Month 3)	Avg. Time to First Sale
Trial (Experimental) Group: 25 sales associates	$7,500	11 days
Comparison (Control) Group: 19 sales associates (out of 22)	$3,700	21 days
Difference =	$3,800	
Annualized = $3,800 x 12 x 25 = $1,140,000		
20% profit = $228,000		

Comparing Data to Money

Converting data to money was easy. As outlined on the ROI analysis plan, the profit margin had to be used. This new upgrade had a predicted profit margin of 20 percent, and this value was used in the analysis. This yields a monetary value of $228,000. The time of the first sale was not converted to money, as that sale was actually already in the total sales number.

Cost

As shown in Table 11-7, the fully loaded costs were included to make the ROI calculation credible. The initial needs assessment represented very little cost, because the need was precipitated by the new product and the solution was dictated by the time and cost constraints. A charge of $3,000 was estimated for the time to pin down needs. The design and development cost was estimated to be $56,000. This amount was prorated over the evaluation for the 25 participants. To be conservative, it was assumed that half the sales team (110) would not use the program. The design and development cost per participant was $509, resulting in $12,725 for 25 participants. The project manager's time was included, as was time for participant involvement. Although many sales associates complete technology-based learning on their own time, this program was planned for use during regular work hours between calls or just before calls. In sales, work hours can be anytime. A conservative estimate was two hours per associate, recognizing that some of them completed the program on their own time. Some cost was prorated for the use of the iPad, albeit minor as the iPad is used for other purposes. An external evaluation was used in order to ensure objectivity, which created a high evaluation cost. Still, this evaluation will suffice for the entire sales force, although it's for the sample. Also, internal evaluation would have cost about $5,000. When costs and monetary benefits are combined, the benefit-cost ratio and ROI can be calculated.

TABLE 11-7. Costs

Needs assessment (est.)	$3,000
Design and development ($56,000/110 x 25)	$12,725
Mobile device (prorated)	$1,700
Sales associate time	$2,524
Administration time (est.)	$6,000
Project management (est.)	$14,500
Evaluation	$15,000
Total	$55,449

Exercise

1. Calculate the BCR and ROI below.

BCR =

ROI =

2. What should the approach be to communicate the results to the appropriate audiences?

Figure 11.5 shows the benefit/cost ratio and the ROI calculation. As anticipated, results exceed the ROI objective.

FIGURE 11-5. BCR and ROI Calculations

$$BCR = \frac{\$228,000}{\$55,449} = 4.11$$

$$ROI\ (\%) = \frac{\$228,000 - \$55,449}{\$55,449} \times 100 = 311\%$$

Intangible Benefits

In addition to the tangible sales increase converted to money, several intangibles were connected to the program, as presented in Table 11-8. Receiving the first sale within the time period is intangible, because it was not converted to money and used in the calculation (this would be double counting). In addition, the other intangibles are connected to the program as indicated on the questionnaire distributed for Level 3 data. This questionnaire contained an extra question about the extent to which this program influenced these measures. At least five participants had to rate 3 or more on a 5-point scale. There is no neutral point on a scale.

TABLE 11-8. Intangible Benefits

- Made the first sale in 11 days, average
- Customer satisfaction
- Brand awareness for ProfitPro
- Job satisfaction of sales associates
- Stress reduction for sales associates
- Reputation of company

COMMUNICATING RESULTS

Because this project was very successful, communicating its results was not difficult. At first there was a briefing with an executive who asked for the ROI study. The 30-minute briefing provided an opportunity to see the power of mobile learning technology and how it could affect business measures.

Data were sent to the 25 participants, along with their immediate managers, within three weeks of data collection. Also, some minor adjustments were made to the program as a result of the evaluation. These were announced in the same communication.

An executive summary of the evaluation was provided to all sales associates to show them the success of the program and to entice others to get involved in this and future programs.

A brief article (about 1,000 words) was placed in the company newsletter for all employees to read. Results were presented at a technology-based learning conference as a case study. All sales and support managers received an executive summary. The learning and development team received a full copy of the study, along with a two-hour workshop.

RECOMMENDATIONS

Some barriers to success were underscored. These barriers led to minor adjustments to the program, including a reduction from four hours to three hours and 15 minutes. Also, support for the program was strengthened.

LESSONS LEARNED

This study results in several important lessons.
1. Early planning was crucial, before any design and development took place. Had the team waited until the program was designed, developed, and implemented before planning the evaluation, it would have been incomplete.
2. The objectives gave the designers, developers, and participants the proper focus. There was no mystery about what was expected of participants.
3. The control group versus experimental group method was the best one for isolating the effects of the program; however, there were some concerns about the matching of the groups. The problem with the approach of matching groups was that the evaluation team was at the mercy of the time when participants signed up for the program. If everyone were required to participate, the matching group technique would not work, and other processes would be involved.

QUESTIONS FOR DISCUSSION

1. Is this study credible? Please explain.
2. What other methods might be used to isolate the effects of the program? Please explain.
3. What other ways could data collection be accomplished? Please explain.
4. Is the three-month follow-up for impact data appropriate? Please explain.
5. Was a year of impact data appropriate? Please explain.
6. How should this data be presented to management in terms of sequencing, emphasis, and approach?
7. Could this study be replicated? Please explain.

ABOUT THE AUTHORS

Jack J. Phillips, Phd, is a world-renowned expert on accountability, measurement, and evaluation. Phillips provides consulting services for Fortune 500 companies and major global organizations. The author or editor of more than 50 books, he conducts workshops and presents at conferences throughout the world.

His expertise in measurement and evaluation is based on more than 27 years of corporate experience in the aerospace, textile, metals, construction materials, and banking industries. This background led Phillips to develop the ROI Methodology—a revolutionary process that provides bottom-line figures and accountability for all types of learning, performance improvement, human resource, technology, and public policy programs.

Phillips has undergraduate degrees in electrical engineering, physics, and mathematics; a master's degree in decision sciences from Georgia State University; and a PhD in human resource management from the University of Alabama. He has served on the boards of several private businesses—including two NASDAQ companies—and several nonprofits and associations, including the American Society for Training & Development and the National Management Association. He is chairman of the ROI Institute, Inc., and can be reached at 205.678.8101, or by email at jack@roiinstitute.net.

Patti Phillips, PhD, is president and CEO of the ROI Institute, Inc., the leading source of ROI competency building, implementation support, networking, and research. A renowned expert in measurement and evaluation, she helps organizations implement the ROI Methodology in 50 countries around the world.

Phillips's academic accomplishments include a PhD in International Development and a master's degree in public and private management. She is a certified in ROI evaluation and has been awarded the designations of Certified Professional in Learning and Performance and Certified Performance Technologist. Patti Phillips can be reached at patti@roiinstitute.net.

12

Measuring ROI in a Sales Program: An E-Learning Solution

United Petroleum International

Patrick Whalen

Abstract

This case addresses measuring the effectiveness and return on investment of an e-learning solution in an international sales environment. This can be especially challenging when management wants the program to pay for itself in the first year. This case demonstrates that, with a proper needs assessment and support from the organization, a well-designed e-learning program can influence business measures significantly. The program contribution to sales and other business measures determined by using one or more methods to isolate the effects of the program. The $500,000 projected price tag of the training was a key factor in management's decision to support an impact study to determine the return on investment.

BACKGROUND

United Petroleum International (UPI) is an international organization headquartered in the southwestern United States. UPI operates several refineries and engages in the sales and service of petroleum products worldwide. UPI has approximately 17,500 employees. International sales of petroleum products have plummeted during the last three quarters, and the outlook shows this trend will continue.

Increased competition abroad and a diminishing quality of sales relationships with customers/prospects were determined to be the major reasons for the lack of performance. The results from quarterly customer satisfaction surveys revealed specific areas of low performance. The executive vice president (EVP) of international sales asked for an assessment of the performance improvement needs of the UPI International Sales Organization (ISO). International Sales has 117 sales engineers and eight sales managers. They are supported by 50 administrative employees who maintain

195

the customer/prospect database, develop sales quotes for the sales engineers, maintain pricing and inventory lists, and provide HR services.

A senior representative from corporate HR and two of UPI's internal consultants teamed with an external consultant to implement the Performance Assessment and Analysis Process to identify problems, opportunities, and solutions in ISO. The report provided to the EVP identified overall findings, performance gaps, and recommended solutions. At the end of the presentation, the EVP agreed to fund an intense improvement effort, including sales training and restructuring of the ISO incentive pay plan, which was no longer competitive in the changing markets. Funding was also made available for the consultant to design and implement a comprehensive evaluation system to determine business impact and return on investment. The EVP was particularly interested in knowing the ROI for the program. A business objective was established to improve three business measures. Measures to be tracked were identified as sales, monthly closing ratios, and customer satisfaction. Because measurement is an inherent component of the process, the methods and timing were designed and put into place. Baseline data were collected from UPI's performance records.

DESIGNING AND IMPLEMENTING THE SOLUTIONS

The HR department worked with the design team to design and implement a more appropriate and competitive incentive plan. This new incentive plan was designed after a review of several models and an analysis of application to UPI's markets. The plan was approved and scheduled for implementation in June.

The second solution, addressing the skill and knowledge needs within the sales force, was more difficult to design and implement. Client workload, time constraints, and the scattered locations of the sales engineers were impediments to implementing traditional instructor-led learning. Electronic learning methods were considered a viable alternative. A plus for this delivery method at ISO was that all sales engineers had online capabilities on their laptop computers. Another plus was that the flexibility of the electronic delivery method allowed it to be available at any time of the day. This flexibility is attractive to participants who are compensated principally through incentive pay and who desire to spend their available time making customer contacts. The decision was made that the 117 sales engineers and eight sales managers would receive an electronically delivered interactive program to improve their skills and effectively achieve the business objectives. During the performance analysis, it was discovered that the corporate HR group had identified sales competencies from a previous project and had already begun developing a curriculum. Much of this in-work product served as an important input for the new initiative and greatly assisted the on-time completion of the project.

The design called for a more focused e-learning effort, paying specific attention to the sales relationships engaged by sales engineers and allowing for significant practice of the required skills. The program had to present numerous job scenarios and challenges currently being encountered in the marketplace. The EVP of International Sales assigned the project to the manager of sales training, who subsequently established a project team to provide the coordination, design, and development of this project.

Several modules were developed with the support of corporate professionals, including technical writers, learning technology specialists, graphic designers, information technology specialists, and consultants. The team consisted of five full-time employees and four external consultants. Given the short timeframe for completion (management allowed a few months to design and implement the program), work began immediately to develop focused e-learning programs based on the desired business impact (the business objectives), job performance competencies, and field sales encounters. Several members of the design team were concerned that traditional face-to-face learning methods could not be replaced by an interactive e-learning program. The learning technology specialists addressed these concerns, and field testing established the design as a success in achieving learning goals. The e-learning program that was developed for the sales engineers became known affectionately as the TLC program, the Technology Learning Competency program. After design completion, it was implemented in June and July, shortly after the new incentive plan was implemented.

The Technology Learning Competency (TLC) Program

The TLC program was an interactive, self-paced learning process designed to assess current skill level and needs of the sales engineer. Each module was designed to build on a specific set of UPI sales skills (that is, client partnerships, product pricing and contracting, selling more profitable products, uncovering objections, handling objections, defining product features as unique benefits for the customer, expanding existing contracts, handling dissatisfied customers, building community awareness of UPI, and UPI product awareness/knowledge).

The TLC program was designed to allow the participant to respond to various sales-relationship scenarios and to determine the appropriate decision to move closer to a sale. Each decision made by the engineer activated another scenario, which allowed additional choices or decisions to be made. The program continued on a predetermined path initiated by the engineer until a string of choices confirmed the responses as appropriate or until the decision was redirected. Video of a subject matter expert provided analysis of decision choices and helpful suggestions. This took maximum advantage of learning opportunities presented when a participant worked through the program. The engineer experienced real-world issues and situations, had the help of an expert, and was able to learn from mistakes in a nonthreatening manner.

A pretest at the beginning of each module was used to determine the skill areas that needed improvement and to load the appropriate learning modules. All the 117 sales engineers were pretested to establish a baseline. The program then linked participants to recommended modules that addressed their skill gaps. Each engineer was allowed a two-month window to complete the required e-learning, either during or after hours as his schedule allowed. So that they could be more effective coaches, the eight managers completed all modules plus a coaching module.

The TLC program contained a programmed mechanism that captured the results from the various decision paths chosen by the participant. After each learning module, an individual report was generated, which highlighted the learning achievement and the decisions made by the engineer. This report was provided to each participant and his manager for discussion in the follow-up coaching session. This provided additional learning opportunities and a means for recognition and feedback. Sales engineers were asked to schedule the follow-up planning and coaching meeting with their managers to occur within two weeks of their TLC program implementation.

MEASUREMENT METHODS AND DATA ANALYSIS

Measures to evaluate the effectiveness of a program can be designed and tracked through five distinct levels, as shown in Table 12-1. In addition to the five levels of data illustrated in this table, intangible benefits are reported for important outcomes that cannot be converted to monetary values.

The executive vice president of international sales requested that the return on investment (Level 5) be calculated for this program because of the high cost and potential business impact of the TLC program. Therefore, it became necessary to analyze data at the five levels, plus any intangible benefits.

TABLE 12-1. Five Levels of Data

Level and Type of Measure	Measurement Focus
Level 1: Reaction/Planned Action	Measures participant satisfaction and captures planned actions
Level 2: Learning	Measures changes in knowledge, skills, and attitudes
Level 3: Application	Measures changes in on-the-job actions and behavior
Level 4: Business Impact	Measures changes in business impact variables
Level 5: Return on Investment	Compares program benefits with the costs

ROI Model and Process

Executive management expressed concern that the process used to evaluate TLC was a credible process. Figure 2-3 in chapter 2 illustrates the ROI Process Model used to address this concern. This process has been applied in virtually every industry and in numerous international settings to evaluate training programs, HR programs, technology initiatives, and performance improvement programs. The process flows sequentially from step to step until the ROI is developed. The impact study captures both Level 3 (application) and Level 4 (business impact) data. The ROI (Level 5) is developed from Level 4 data. Improvements that cannot be converted to monetary values are reported as intangible benefits. A conservative approach is used to ensure that only benefits that can be legitimately attributed to the program are captured.

The Data Collection Plan and ROI Analysis Plan

After the business measures were determined and the framework for the TLC training program was known, the data collection plan focusing on Level 3 (application) and Level 4 (business impact) measures was developed. The Level 3 measures were behavior changes and frequency of application linked to the TLC program objectives. After exploring performance data availability in the ISO unit, the quality of the specific data, and the perceived linkage to the TLC program, the Level 4 measures were targeted and included in the data collection plan, which is presented in Figure 12-1.

The Level 4 data items were then transferred to the ROI analysis plan so that the planning process could be completed. The methods for isolation, data conversion, cost categories, and other items were determined and documented on the ROI analysis plan, which is presented in Figure 12-2.

Level 1 and 2 Data

Level 1 data were captured through an online feedback questionnaire that assessed course content, usefulness of the TLC program, and job applicability. Participants rated questions on a Likert-type scale from 1 to 7. Participant average for the overall course content was 6.6, and overall usefulness of the system was 6.5. Applicability of the course to the job was rated 6.8. Level 1 data are consolidated in the first three columns of Table 12-2.

Level 2 data were assessed using pre- and post-testing. The pre- and post-testing for TLC was designed based on job performance expectations. Subject matter experts (SMEs) determined the testing components, which were then validated by sales managers.

The SMEs, working with the program designers, validated program content based on competency requirements and skill gaps of the sales organization. They also provided input to design pre- and post-tests. Pretests were administered electronically at the beginning of each learning module to determine individual knowledge and skill gaps. The results showed that participants averaged a 50 percent knowledge level on the pretest and averaged a 91 percent knowledge level on the post-test. These Level 2 data are consolidated in the last two columns of Table 12-2.

FIGURE 12-1. Data Collection Plan: United Petroleum International

Program: Technology Learning Competency (TLC) **Responsibility:** _____ **Date:** _____

Level	Objective(s)	Measures/Data	Data Collection Method	Data Sources	Timing	Responsibilities
Level I Reaction and Satisfaction	Employee positive reaction to: • Appropriateness of the technology delivery program • Usefulness of the TLC • TLC application to the job	• Participants' perception and attitude	• Online questionnaire	• Participant	• End of each segment (3-5 modules) • End of program	• Program coordinator
Level II Learning	Module learning assignment based on knowledge/skill gaps: • Client partnerships • Product pricing & contracting • Identification & handling objections	• Skill gaps identified • Learning occurs as gaps are closed through each module implemented	• Online pretest questionnaire on all modules • One post-test by module	• Participant	• Prior to training to establish baseline • Prior to each module as required • At end of each module	• Program coordinator
Level III Application & Implementation	• Review post-course report and participate in follow-up planning meeting with managers • Application of skills to achieve business goals	• Goals set and achieved • Skills applied in sales planning and sales situations	• Follow-up questionnaire	• Participants • Managers	• Coaching and planning session within two weeks of TLC • Follow-up questionnaire four months after TLC	• Program coordinator initiates follow-up • Manger and participants initiate planning and coaching

Level IV Business Impact	• Improve closing ratio • Increased revenue • Customer satisfaction	• Increase in monthly closes • Increase in profit margin • Customer satisfaction index	• Performance monitoring • Performance monitoring • Customer survey (existing)	• Sales record – marketing • Sales record – Marketing • Customer quarterly survey	• Monthly • Monthly • Monthly	• Program coordinator
Level V ROI	Because of strict requirement for development costs (see comments) an ROI at 20% will be acceptable.	Comments: Because training will be completed for all current engineers within the first year of roll-out, management desires to achieve a return on investment during the first year. Therefore, development costs will not be prorated over the life of the program as is customary.				

Level 3 and 4 Data

Level 3 (application) included three components to evaluate results: 1) follow-up planning and coaching sessions between sales engineers and sales managers, (2) self-assessment of skill application using a follow-up questionnaire, and (3) managers' assessment of skill application using a follow-up questionnaire.

Engineers completed follow-up planning and discussion meetings with their respective managers within two weeks of completing the TLC program. A plan including goals and expectations was created as a result of each discussion. To allow appropriate time for evaluation and application of skills, it was imperative for managers to have these planning and coaching sessions as close to the end of the training as possible. The sessions occurred during July and August and averaged two hours in length. Because of the dispersed locations of the engineers and managers, some of these meetings were conducted face-to-face and some by telephone or video conferencing.

TABLE 12-2. Reaction and Learning Results—1 to 7 Scale

Reaction: Overall Course	Reaction: Overall Usefulness of TLC	Reaction: Job Applicability	Learning: Pretest Overall Score	Learning: Post-Test Overall Score
6.6	6.5	6.8	50%	91%

The follow-up questionnaire was developed during the program design phase and field-tested with a random sample of sales engineers and sales managers. By advice of the sales managers, the questionnaire was administered four months after the completion of the TLC program. Four months was deemed an appropriate timeframe to determine the successful application of skills. A series of questions on the follow-up questionnaire also focused on engineers' progress with the improvement goals established in the follow-up discussions between managers and sales engineers. In addition, sales managers each received a follow-up questionnaire focusing on the performance of sales engineers and isolating the effects of the TLC program. These performance data were consolidated and documented in the final evaluation report. Figure 12-3 presents a summary of the follow-up questions from the sales engineers' questionnaire.

Business impact data (Level 4) were monitored by reviewing the quarterly customer satisfaction index scores, the monthly sales closing averages, and the profit margin of monthly sales revenue. These data were readily available within the organization, and all but customer satisfaction were used in the determination of business impact and the return on investment of the TLC program. Customer satisfaction data were reviewed for progress, but a standard monetary value did not exist for improvements; therefore, there was no conversion to a monetary value.

FIGURE 12-3. Summary of Follow-Up Questions

1. Did you have a follow-up coaching session with your sales manager?
2. Did you complete a follow-up plan and set related goals?
3. How do you rate the quality of the planning and discussion session with your manager?
4. Based on the discussion and planning session you had with your manager, what specific improvement goals have you completed? What improvement goals still need to be completed?
5. How have you and your job changed as a result of participating in TLC?
6. How are you specifically applying what you learned as a result of participating in TLC?
7. What is the impact of these changes for the customer and the ISO organization?
8. Rank (estimate the percentage) the effect each of the following had on any improvement in your sales performance. Allocate from 0 to 100% to the appropriate factors (the total percentage of all items selected must equal 100%):

   TLC Training Program Influence ____%   Executive Management ____%

   Market Influences ____%   New Products ____%

   Manager Coaching Influences ____%   Other (specify) ____%
9. What barriers (if any) were a deterrent as you applied what you learned?
10. List any skills you did not have an opportunity to apply during the evaluation timeframe.
11. Estimate the total hours you were involved in accessing/completing TLC training during regular company work hours: _____hours.

Isolating the Effects of the Program

To assess the Level 4 and 5 data accurately, it was imperative that the various influences on any improvement in sales performance be isolated. To isolate the effects of how each factor influenced sales (that is, TLC training, the new incentive plan, market changes, management influence, and so on), each had to be assessed by a credible source. The influence of each factor was determined by using participant and manager estimates regarding each factor. Because the managers work closely with the sales engineers (participants), it was felt that managers could respond credibly to these issues. The data were gathered from the participants in the Level 3 and 4 follow-up questionnaires and from the managers in a separate follow-up questionnaire. Table 12-3 reports the consolidated data.

Design and Implementation Costs

The development costs of $354,500 for this project included the salaries for development time of one project manager, five full-time employees, and four contract consultants. The costs associated with time spent in meetings and interviews with executive management, senior sales staff, and SMEs were also included. This included the time of the interviewer, as well as the people being interviewed. The cost of travel, meals, and lodging during development was also included.

TABLE 12-3. Consolidated Estimates—Isolating the Effects

Influencing Factor	Sales Engineers Average From 104 Respondents	Sales Managers Average From 8 Respondents	Lowest Value
New Incentive Plan	38%	37%	37%
TLC Training Program	38%	37%	37%
Executive Management Influence	7%	6%	6%
Coaching by Sales Manager	17%	18%	17%
Other (market changes, new products, product improvements, etc.)	2%	2%	2%

The material costs of $68,500 included a comprehensive workbook for participants, distribution of tutorial CDs, and some additional networking software.

The equipment cost of $91,000 included upgrades (systems, processors, and video/graphics capability) to the specified hardware setup. This cost category also included the purchase of several new laptops for the sales engineers, digital editing equipment for editing the video and graphics in each module, and two platform servers capable of handling the multi-operational usage.

Eight SMEs were assigned to the project. These eight lead sales engineers were paid their sales average ($150 per day) for the 18 days each spent on the module designs, video shoots, and other project duties.

The analysis and evaluation costs of $71,000 included all costs associated with the initial performance analysis and evaluation process (for example, employee time during interviews and questionnaires). This cost category also included the use of an outside consulting firm to plan and implement the performance analysis and evaluation methodology for this project.

All the 117 sales engineers reported completing all modules during their personal time. Because they were compensated mostly by commissions, they usually spent their work hours conducting sales planning and call activities. Table 12-4 summarizes the fully loaded costs for the TLC program.

Because no sales were occurring for SMEs during the 18 project days, the commission payments may represent a cost to the sales bottom line. The management team felt the lead sales engineers would be able to maintain their average sales throughout the year even with their involvement in this project. Therefore, they did not feel that lost sales should be included as an opportunity cost. Salaries and benefits and opportunity costs for the "actual training time" are not included in the calculations because none of the 104 sales engineers reported implementing the TLC training during normal company work hours.

TABLE 12-4. Fully Loaded Costs

Development costs	$354,500
Materials/software	$68,500
Equipment	$91,000
SME time (commission paid to expert sales engineers for lost opportunity) eight people @ $150/day × 18 days	$21,600
Analysis and evaluation costs	$71,000
TOTAL	$606,600

Level 3 and 4 Results

The results of the initiative were encouraging. Prior year sales records revealed that sales engineers' overall performance showed an average of 14 closes per month at $980 profit margin per close. Six months after the implementation of TLC, the engineers averaged 16.65 closes per month at $1,350 profit margin per close. From the previous year, this was an average increase of 2.65 closes per month and an additional $370 profit margin on revenue.

The design team decided to use the ROI Methodology's conservative process when calculating the ROI based on revenue generated from new or increased closes. This decision helped to enhance the credibility of the data because participant and manager estimates were the only methods used to isolate the impact of training. The profit margin portion of the revenue increase attributable to the training (TLC) was used as a basis for the ROI calculation.

The Level 5 data were calculated by comparing the cost with the net benefits attributable to the TLC implementation. The benefit attributed to the use of TLC for improvement was considered to be 37 percent, based on the lowest value of the two estimates (manager estimates) from Table 12-3.

The benefits, except for improved customer satisfaction, were then converted to a monetary value, and a return on investment was calculated. Customer satisfaction improvements and other data that could not be converted to monetary values were captured as intangible benefits. Level 3 and 4 performance data and intangible benefits were documented in the final evaluation report.

ROI Results

Monitoring the performance records revealed the total increase in sales attributable to all influencing factors was $5,022,810. There was an average of 2.65 additional closes per month (16.65 – 14.0). However, based on the lowest estimates, only 37 percent of this increase in sales was influenced by the TLC program.

The conservative adjustment of benefits resulting from the TLC program was a factor of 0.98 additional closes per month (2.65 × 0.37). This resulted in an average of $1,323 profit margin per close ($1,350 × 0.98). Multiplied by 12 months and 117 engineers to annualize, this produced $1,857,492 in monetary benefits attributable to TLC.

- 2.65 closes × 0.37 = 0.98 factor for additional closes attributable to TLC program
- 0.98 × $1,350 per close = $1,323
- $1,323 × 12 months = $15,876 × 117 sales engineers = $1,857,492

The total cost of the TLC training program was $606,600. After rounding the benefits from the program, the ROI for the TLC program was calculated as follows:

$$\text{ROI (\%)} = \frac{\$1,867,000 - \$606,000}{\$606,600} \times 100 = 206\%$$

In addition to the impact of the TLC training, participants and managers reported the new incentive plan implemented in June had influenced an increase in sales by 36 percent, or $1,808,000.

Intangible Benefits

The results from quarterly customer satisfaction surveys were used to compare the previous year with the current year. Positive improvements and trends were identified. These data were not converted to a monetary value because management had no standard monetary value for an increase in customer satisfaction. It was also difficult to determine how much the skills and behavior from the training actually influenced the improvement in customer satisfaction. Data to isolate and substantiate this would need to come directly from customers because many factors could influence their satisfaction level. When using estimates, only customers are likely to know the extent of such influences. However, executive management felt the customer satisfaction scores were a good indicator of how the organization was responding to the market.

The customer satisfaction scores showed an average improvement of 23 percent since the previous year. Sales engineers and sales managers reported additional intangible benefits, such as increased job satisfaction, better understanding of expectations, reduced turnover, and increased recruiting effectiveness of future sales engineers.

LESSONS LEARNED

This program demonstrated favorable results. The results can be attributed to several things: a comprehensive front-end analysis process that accurately identified the appropriate gaps and solutions, the support of corporate HR, the support of executive management, and the sales organization providing the resources and clarification of expected outcomes prior to designing this initiative.

A major learning issue involved meeting management's requirement for a short lead time to design and implement the program. Executive management expected the program to be implemented within a few months because the competitive environment and need for improved skills were having a negative impact on sales. This created little time to conduct a pilot program. Also, there was not enough time to create all the modules needed for the full range of competency and skill needs of the sales organization. The most salient competencies were targeted and given development priority.

The need to more accurately isolate the effects of this initiative was another learning issue. Several factors influenced the results. Although participant estimates can be effective (participants know what influences their performance), additional methods, like a control group arrangement or trend-line analysis, can often isolate the impact more convincingly.

REPORTING TO STAKEHOLDER GROUPS

The target population for this initiative included four groups: the sales engineers, the leaders of the sales organization, the SMEs, and the executive management team of UPI. All played a critical role in the success of the TLC program. All were provided a final report showing the results from the impact study.

The primary group was the 117 sales engineers who actually participated in the TLC program. They were the most instrumental of the groups in creating the success enjoyed by TLC. They dedicated the time to the system and took full advantage of the opportunity to improve performance based on what they learned from the technology-supported training. They also provided tremendous constructive feedback to enhance the system for future engineers.

The second group consisted of the leaders of the sales organization, who were responsible and accountable for the success of sales at UPI. Ten people—including one executive vice president, one director, and eight sales managers—were key factors in the success. They supported the up-front analysis and the validation of the job skills and gaps that were to be measured. By conducting planning and coaching sessions with sales engineers and by discussing expectations, the leaders of the sales organization were essential factors in the transfer and application of skills on the job.

The third group was the SMEs, who provided timely and accurate feedback about each module being developed, and the corporate professionals and consultants, who demonstrated diligence and expertise. On frequent occasions, they worked beyond normal work hours to keep the project on track.

The fourth group was the members of the executive management team of UPI, who funded the project and showed interest in the entire training process. The executive management team supported the project by allocating the necessary resources and setting the expectations for outcomes.

QUESTIONS FOR DISCUSSION

1. Identify the influencing factors that contributed to the success of the TLC program.
2. How would you convince management that a control group arrangement would be beneficial to the study?
3. What recommendations would you make to management to convert customer satisfaction improvements to a monetary value?
4. How credible are the estimates in this evaluation?
5. How credible is this study?

ABOUT THE AUTHOR

Patrick Whalen, PhD, PHR, is an experienced training, consulting, and human resource professional with expertise in management, performance and succession management, competency modeling, facilitation, employee development, needs analysis, evaluation methods, and program design and development. Whalen is currently the senior director of global consulting for the International Center for Performance Improvement (ICPI). He is also the managing director for TeamEffective. He consults with a broad range of clients and organizations on talent management, performance analysis, organizational development, strategic planning, needs analysis, and measurement and evaluation.

About the ROI Institute

The ROI Institute is the leading resource on research, training, publications, networking, and advice for metrics and analytics. Founded in 1992, the ROI Institute is a service-driven organization that assists professionals in improving their programs through the use of the ROI Methodology and other analytical tools. The ROI Methodology is a critical process for measuring and evaluating programs in 20 different functional applications in more than 70 countries.

The ROI Institute offers a variety of consulting services, learning opportunities, and publications. With over 60 books (translated into 38 languages) supporting metrics, analytics, and ROI—the ROI Institute is the global leader for documentation of successful analytics applications. In addition, the ROI Institute conducts consulting and research activities for organizations in business, public sector, non-government organizations, nonprofits, and universities.

BUILD CAPABILITY IN THE ROI METHODOLOGY

The ROI Institute offers a variety of workshops to help you build capability through the ROI Methodology. Among the many workshops offered through the institute are:

- One-day "Bottomline on ROI" workshop—provides the perfect introduction to all levels of measurement, including the most sophisticated level, ROI. Learn the key principles of the ROI Methodology and determine whether your organization is ready to implement the process.
- Two-day "ROI Competency Building" workshop—the standard ROI workshop on measurement and evaluation, this two-day program involves discussion of the ROI Methodology process, including data collection, isolation methods, data conversion, and more.
- Two-day "Human Capital Analytics" workshop—explores the various approaches to analytics with a focus on case studies and how to make analytics work in an organization.

ROI CERTIFICATION

The ROI Institute is the only organization offering certification in the ROI Methodology. Through the five-day ROI Certification workshop, you can build expertise in implementing ROI evaluation, conducting ROI studies, and sustaining the measurement and evaluation process in your organization. As part of this process you receive personalized assistance while conducting an impact ROI study. When competencies in the ROI Methodology have been demonstrated with your own impact study, certification is awarded. No other process provides access to the same level of expertise as our ROI Certification. To date, more than 8,000 individuals have participated, with more than 4,000 achieving the designation Certified ROI Professional (CRP).

For more information on these and other workshops, learning opportunities, consulting, and research, please visit us on the web at www.roiinsititute.net, or call us at 205.678.8101.

Index

A

Accountability, 8, 16, 27
Accuracy, of data collection methods, 38
Acquisition costs, 68
Acting consciously, 107
Action plans, 43, 94–96, 182
Activities, 93
Activity-based approach, 27
Announcements, 87
Appendices, of detailed report, 80–81
Application and implementation (Level 3)
    case study examples of, 128, 136–138
    data, 17–18, 37
    key questions for, 18
Application guide, 96
Application objectives, of technology-based learning programs, 32–33
Application tools, 94–97

B

Bad news, 83–84
Benefit-cost ratio (BCR), 16, 69, 157, 192
Best practice meetings, 76
Blended learning, 5, 92, 106
Bring your own devices, 6
Brochures, 77, 88
Business alignment
    achieving of, 28–34
    case study of, 110
    process of, 30
    program evaluation, 34
    program objectives, 31–34
    stakeholder needs, 28–29, 31, 162, 207–208
Business impact (Level 4)
    case study examples of, 128, 138–140, 202
    data, 18, 37
    detailed report description of, 80
    importance of, 50
    isolating the effects of learning programs applied to, 50
    key questions for, 19
Business results, 8–9, 49–50
BYOD. *See* Bring your own devices

C

Case studies
    communicating the results through, 77, 94
    description of, 22
    e-learning, 149–159, 195–208
    English-as-a-second language program, 161–175
    financial services company, 149–159
    Future-Tel, 125–147
    mobile learning, 177–194
    Performance Medica, 161–175
    PolyWrighton, 105–123
    publishing of, 82
    Transoft Inc., 177–194
Client, communicating the results to, 76
cMOOCs, 7
Coaching role, 101
Collaborating, 107
Communication of results
    announcements for, 87
    audience considerations, 75–76
    brochures used for, 77, 88
    case studies used for, 77, 94
    case study examples of, 120, 158, 174, 193
    electronic media used for, 77
    evaluation of, 83
    formal reports used for, 77
    importance of, 24, 73
    internal publications used for, 77
    media for, 76–77
    meetings used for, 76
    memos for, 88
    reasons for, 74
    reports used for. *See* Report(s)
    workbooks for, 88
Comparison group analysis, 52
Conclusions section, of detailed report, 80
Contamination, of control groups, 52
Control group design, 51
Cost(s)
    case study examples of, 191–192, 203–204
    of data collection methods, 40
    of e-learning, 154–156
    fully loaded, 67–69, 80, 112, 140–141, 191, 205
    of technology-based learning programs, 67–69
Cost of quality, as standard value, 64
Creative Commons, 7
Customer satisfaction, 61, 206

D

Data
    application and implementation, 17–18
    business impact, 18
    failure to use, 84
    hard, 60–61
    intangible, 61–62
    lack of, 11–12
    learning, 17
    Level 1. *See* Level 1 data
    Level 2. *See* Level 2 data
    Level 3. *See* Level 3 data
    Level 4. *See* Level 4 data
    from participants, 46, 55–59, 75
    from participants' managers, 46, 75–76
    reaction and planned action, 17
    reporting of, 24
    soft, 60–61
    sources of, 44–47
    tangible, 61–62
Data analysis
    conversion of data to monetary value. *See* Data
        conversion
    description of, 23–24
Data collection
    case study examples of, 130–133, 151–152,
        165–166, 181, 183–185, 199–201
    from databases, 47
    description of, 23
    from executives, 47
    importance of, 48
    Level 1, 41, 47, 113–114
    Level 2, 41, 47, 113–114
    Level 3, 41, 47, 113–114
    Level 4, 41, 47, 60, 113–114
    plan for, 35–37
    response rates for, 44–45
    from senior managers, 47
    sources of, 44–47
    timing of, 47–48
Data collection methods
    accuracy of, 38
    action plans, 43, 94–96, 182
    cost considerations, 40
    focus groups, 40, 43
    improvement plans and guides, 96
    interviews, 40, 42–43
    overview of, 41
    performance contracts, 43, 96–98
    performance records, 43–44, 46
    questionnaires, 40–42, 44
    reliability of, 40
    repeatability of, 40
    time requirements, 40
    utility of, 40–41
    validity of, 40

Data conversion
    case study examples of, 119, 167, 191
    description of, 62
    estimations for, 66
    external databases used in, 65
    external experts used in, 65
    historical costs used in, 65
    internal experts used in, 65
    linking of measures for, 65
    standard values used in, 62–64
    steps involved in, 66–67
    success factors, 62
Databases, 47, 65
Detailed reports, 78–81
Development of solutions costs, 68
Digital content, 4
Domain massive open online courses, 8
During-the-program activities, 101

E

E-learning
    case study examples of, 149–159, 195–208
    description of, 4
    factors that affect, 5
Electronic media, for communication of results, 77
Employee engagement, 61
Employees' time, as standard value, 64
English-as-a-second language program case study,
        161–175
Estimations, for data conversion, 66
Evaluation
    costs associated with, 68–69
    planning of, 23, 150–156
Evaluation framework, of ROI Methodology, 17–19
Evaluation methodology section, of detailed
        report, 79
Evolving, 107–108
Executive summary, 82
Executives
    description of, 47
    expectations and, 91–92
    technology-based learning and, 9–10
Expectations, 90–92
Expert estimation, for isolating the effects of
        technology-based learning programs, 55–59
External databases, 65
External experts, 65

F

Facilitator-led learning, 10
Financial services company case study, 149–159
Focus groups, 40, 43, 56
Forecasting
    advantages of, 55
    disadvantages of, 55

isolating the effects of learning programs
    through, 54–55
technology-based learning programs, 25
Formal reports, 77
Fully loaded costs, 67–69, 80, 112, 140–141, 191,
    205
Future-Tel case study, 125–147

G

Game-based learning, 6
General audience reports, 82

H

Hard data, 60–61
Historical costs, in data conversion, 65

I

Impact objectives, of technology-based learning
    programs, 34, 93
Implementation, 22–23, 28, 68
Improvement plans and guides, 96
In-person interviews, 42–43
Initial analysis and assessment costs, 68
Intangible benefits, 24, 70–71, 80, 119–120,
    142–143, 156, 192, 206
Intangible data, 61–62
Internal experts, 65
Internal publications, for communication
    of results, 77
Internet, 4, 65
Interviews, 40, 42–43
Isolating the effects of learning programs
    case study examples of, 118, 189–190, 203–
        204
    comparison group analysis for, 52
    expert estimation for, 55–59
    forecasting methods for, 54–55
    importance of, 49–50
    Level 4 application of, 50
    selecting techniques for, 60
    trend-line analysis for, 53–54

J

J4 approach, 92
Job aids, 97

K

"Knowledge broadcast" model, 4

L

Lean Six Sigma, 90
Learning
    accountability for, 27
    activity-based approach to, 27
    blended, 5, 92, 106

facilitator-led, 10
flow of, 92
game-based, 6
mobile. *See* Mobile learning
results-based approach to, 27
ROI Methodology benefits for, 25
technology-based. *See* Technology-based
    learning
Learning (Level 2)
    case study examples of, 128, 135–136
    data, 17, 36
    key questions for, 18
Learning and development team, 75
*Learning Everywhere: How Mobile Content
    Strategies Are Transforming Training*, 8
Learning management systems, 4–5, 150
Learning needs, 31
Learning objectives, of technology-based learning
    programs, 31–32
Learning program(s)
    acquisition costs, 68
    application costs, 68
    business needs addressed in, 29, 31
    costs of, 67–69
    development of solutions costs, 68
    evaluation costs, 68–69
    forecasting of, 25
    fully loaded costs of, 67–69, 80, 112
    implementation costs, 68
    initial analysis and assessment costs, 68
    input needs addressed in, 31
    intangible benefits of, 61–62, 70–71, 119–120,
        156
    justifying spending on, 24–25
    learning needs addressed in, 31
    maintenance and monitoring costs, 69
    manager support for, 26, 75–76
    objectives of, 28, 31–34
    overhead costs, 69
    payoff needs addressed in, 29
    performance needs addressed in, 31
    preference needs addressed in, 31
    questions to ask before implementation of,
        28–29
    reporting costs, 68–69
    stakeholder needs and, 28–29, 31, 162,
        207–208
    supervisor support for, 25
    support costs, 69
    support for, 25–26
    tangible benefits of, 61–62
    unsuccessful, 25
Learning program evaluation
    business alignment and, 35
    data collection plan for, 35–37

plan for, 34–38
ROI analysis plan, 35, 38
Learning technologies, 4
Learning transfer, 79
Level 1 data. *See also* Reaction and planned action
application of, 85
case study examples of, 110–111, 115, 128–129, 164, 199
collection of, 41, 47, 113–114
Level 2 data. *See also* Learning
application of, 85
case study examples of, 110–111, 115–116, 128–129, 164, 188, 199
collection of, 41, 47, 113–114
Level 3 data. *See also* Application and implementation (Level 3)
application of, 85
case study examples of, 110–111, 114, 116, 128–129, 165, 188, 202
collection of, 41, 47, 113–114
Level 4 data. *See also* Business impact (Level 4)
application of, 85
case study examples of, 110–111, 114, 116, 118–119, 128–129, 165, 202
collection of, 41, 47, 60, 114
Level 5. *See* ROI (Level 5)
Likert scale questions, 42

M
Macro-level reporting, 24
Macro-level scorecards, 82–83
Maintenance and monitoring costs, 69
Managers
coaching role of, 101
communicating the results to, 75–76
expectations and, 91
involvement of, 99–101
learning program support from, 75
participants', data from, 46, 75–76
senior, 47
technology-based learning program support from, 26
Marketing programs, 49
Massive open online course
description of, 7–8
domain, 8
Measurement, 15–16
Measures
case study examples of, 164
conversion of, to monetary value, 62–66
identifying of, 90–91
linking of, 65
Meetings, for communication of results, 76
Memos, 88
Mobile learning

business benefits from, 9
case study of, 177–194
description of, 5–6, 92
Monetary value, converting data to, 62–66, 119, 167
MOOC. *See* Massive open online course

N
Need for the evaluation section, of detailed report, 78
Need for the program section, of detailed report, 78

O
Objectives, of technology-based learning programs, 28, 31–34, 93, 180
OER. *See* Open educational resources
Open Badges framework, 6
Open educational resources, 6–7
Operating standards, 20
Output to contribution, as standard value, 64
Overhead costs, 69

P
Participants
business measures defined by, 90
communicating the results to, 75
data from, 44–47, 55–59
peers of, 46
role of, 88–90
Participants' managers
communicating the results to, 75
data from, 46
involvement of, 99–101
Payback period, 70
Payoff needs, 29
Payoff period, 70
Peers, data from, 46
Performance contracts, 43, 96–98
Performance Medica case study, 161–175
Performance needs, 31
Performance records, 43–44, 46
PolyWrighton case study, 105–123
Post-program activities, 101
Preference needs, 31
Preprogram activities, 100
Preprogram forecasts, 25
Priority setting, 25
Problem solving, 93–94
Process learning, 120–121

Q

Questionnaires
  data collection use of, 40–42, 44
  isolating the effects of learning programs as focus of, 57–59

R

Reaction and planned action (Level 1)
  case study examples of, 128, 135
  data, 17, 36
  key questions for, 18
Reaction objectives, of technology-based learning programs, 31–32
Reflecting, 107
Reinforcement tools, 101
Reinforcement workshops, 101
Relevance-based design, 92
Reliability, 40
Report(s)
  detailed, 78–81
  executive summary, 82
  general audience, 82
  macro-level scorecards, 82–83
  single-page, 82
Reporting of results
  audience considerations, 75–76
  brochures used for, 77, 88
  case studies used for, 77, 94
  costs associated with, 68–69
  electronic media used for, 77
  evaluation of, 83
  importance of, 24, 73
  internal publications used for, 77
  media for, 76–77
  meetings used for, 76
  reasons for, 74
  reports used for. See Report(s)
Response rates, for data collection, 44–45
Results
  case study examples of, 169–176, 188–192, 205–206
  communication of. See Communication of results
  e-learning program, 156–158
  technology-based learning program design for, 87–102
Results-based approach, 27
Results section, of detailed report, 79–80
Return on investment. See ROI
ROI
  benefit-cost ratio versus, 69
  calculation of, 24, 69–70, 141–142, 157, 192, 206
  case study examples of, 179
  definition of, 16–17

  equation for, 16, 70, 141–142
  key questions for, 18–19
  rationale for, 179
  0 percent, 33
ROI (Level 5), 110–111, 114, 119, 128–129, 165, 205
ROI analysis plan
  case study examples of, 112, 134, 153, 186–187, 199
  description of, 35
  key areas of, 38
  sample, 39
ROI Methodology
  benefits of, 24–26
  case applications and practice, 22, 109. See also Case studies
  evaluation framework, 17–19
  in executive summary, 82
  guiding principles of, 20, 22
  implementation of, 22–23
  learning benefits of, 25
  operating standards, 20, 22
  process model of, 19, 21
  reporting. See Reporting of results
  spending on technology-based learning programs justified using, 24–25
  summary of, 26
ROI objective, of technology-based learning programs, 33
ROI process
  case study example of, 198–199
  chain of impact in, 20
  data analysis, 23–24
  data collection, 23, 36–37. See also Data collection
  evaluation planning, 23
  model of, 19, 21
  reporting, 24
ROI studies
  communicating the results of. See Communication of results
  costs of, 40
  Future-Tel case study, 125–147
Role of participants, 88–90

S

Sales training programs, 140–141
Self-coaching skills, 107–108
Self-managing, 107
Senior managers, 47
Sequencing of materials, 92
Simulations, 93
Single-page reports, 82
Six Sigma, 90
Skill practices, 93

Skype, 5
Soft data, 60–61
Spending on technology-based learning, 24–25
Stakeholders, 28–29, 31, 162, 207–208
Standard values, 62–64
Structured interviews, 42
Succession planning, 162
Support costs, 69

T
Talent management, 5
Tangible data, 61–62
Technology, 3
Technology-based learning, 1–13
    barriers to, 11–13
    business results of, 8–9
    concerns about, 8–13
    executive view of, 9–10
    lack of data about, reasons for, 11–12
    programs for. *See* Learning program(s)
    results of, 10–11, 11–12
Technology Learning Competency program,
      197–198
360-feedback evaluation, 46
Time
    for control group comparisons, 52
    data collection methods, 40
Transfer tools, 97, 99
Transoft Inc. case study, 177–194
Trend-line analysis, 53–54, 112

U
Udell, Chad, 8
Unstructured interviews, 42

V
Validity, 40
Video streaming, 5
Virtual classrooms, 5

W
WebCT, 5
Women, 3
Work engagement, 106–107, 119
Workbooks, 88

X
xMOOCs, 7

About the Authors

Tamar Elkeles, PhD, is the chief learning officer for Qualcomm. She is responsible for creating and implementing the overall learning and development strategy for the company. Her scope of leadership includes global learning, executive/leadership development, technical development, employee communications, organization development, learning technology and mobile learning for Qualcomm's 31,000 employees worldwide.

Elkeles created the Learning Center within Qualcomm in 1992 to meet the learning and development needs in a rapidly growing and changing high technology environment. Today, in addition to being a leader in mobile learning, the focus of her organization is to continually bridge the gap between learning and information to improve both individual and organizational performance. Since 2000, Qualcomm has consistently ranked in *Training* magazine's list of Top Training Organizations. In 2002, Qualcomm was ranked as "best in class" in telecommunications. In both 2000 and 1994, Qualcomm also earned the Organization of the Year Award from the American Society for Training & Development (ASTD) for exceptional employee development programs. Qualcomm has been an ASTD Award winner since 2005 and a *CLO* magazine "Learning Elite" Award winner since 2008.

Elkeles's extensive focus on alternative delivery methods for learning enabled Qualcomm to begin development of online learning in early 1995. As a result of these progressive efforts, Qualcomm was awarded the ASTD Best Practice Award for the Use of Technology for Learning in 1996 and in 1998 was honored with an ASTD Best Practice Award for Web-Based Learning. She has been featured in several publications including *Chief Learning Officer* magazine, *Training* magazine, and *T + D* magazine for her leadership and contributions to the learning profession. In 2007 she co-authored the first book on the CLO's role: *The Chief Learning Officer: Driving Value Within a Changing Organization Through Learning and Development* and in 2010 she was named "CLO of the Year" by *CLO* magazine.

Elkeles is a member of The Conference Board's Executive Council on Talent and Organizational Development as well a member of the CLO magazine Editorial Board. She also served on the ASTD Board of Directors. She holds both a MS and a PhD in organizational psychology.

Jack J. Phillips, PhD, is a world-renowned expert on account-ability, measurement, and evaluation. Phillips provides consulting services for Fortune 500 companies and major global organizations. The author or editor of more than 50 books, he conducts workshops and presents at conferences throughout the world.

Phillips has received several awards for his books and work. On three occasions, *Meeting News* named him one of the 25 Most Powerful People in the Meetings and Events Industry, based on his work on ROI. The Society for Human Resource Management presented him an award for one of his books and honored a Phillips ROI study with its highest award for creativity. The American Society for Training & Development gave him its highest award, Distinguished Contribution to Workplace Learning and Development for his work on ROI. His work has been featured in the *Wall Street Journal*, *BusinessWeek*, and *Fortune* magazine. He has been interviewed by several television programs, including CNN. Phillips served as President of the International Society for Performance Improvement from 2012 to 2013.

His expertise in measurement and evaluation is based on more than 27 years of corporate experience in the aerospace, textile, metals, construction materials, and banking industries. Phillips has served as training and development manager at two Fortune 500 firms, as senior human resource officer at two firms, as president of a regional bank, and as management professor at a major state university.

This background led Phillips to develop the ROI Methodology—a revolutionary process that provides bottom-line figures and accountability for all types of learning, performance improvement, human resource, technology, and public policy programs.

Phillips regularly consults with clients in manufacturing, service, and government organizations in 44 countries in North and South America, Europe, Africa, Australia, and Asia.

Phillips has undergraduate degrees in electrical engineering, physics, and mathematics; a master's degree in decision sciences from Georgia State University; and a PhD in human resource management from the University of Alabama. He has served on the boards of several private businesses—including two NASDAQ companies—and several nonprofits and associations, including the American Society for Training & Development and the National Management Association. He is chairman of the ROI Institute, and can be reached at 205.678.8101, or by email at jack@roiinstitute.net.

Patti Phillips, PhD, is president and CEO of the ROI Institute, the leading source of ROI competency building, implementation support, networking, and research. A renowned expert in measurement and evaluation, she helps organizations implement the ROI Methodology in 50 countries around the world.

Since 1997, following a 13-year career in the electric utility industry, Phillips has embraced the ROI Methodology by committing herself to ongoing research and practice. To this end, she has implemented ROI in private sector and public sector organizations. She has conducted ROI impact studies on programs such as leadership development, sales, new-hire orientation, human performance improvement, K-12 educator development, and educators' National Board Certification mentoring.

Phillips teaches others to implement the ROI Methodology through the ROI Certification process, as a facilitator for ASTD's ROI and Measuring and Evaluating Learning Workshops, and as professor of practice for The University of Southern Mississippi Gulf Coast Campus PhD in Human Capital Development program. She also serves as adjunct faculty for the UN System Staff College in Turin, Italy, where she teaches the ROI Methodology through their Evaluation and Impact Assessment Workshop and Measurement for Results-Based Management. She serves on numerous doctoral dissertation committees, assisting students as they develop their own research on measurement, evaluation, and ROI.

Phillips's academic accomplishments include a PhD in international development and a master's degree in public and private management. She is a certified in ROI evaluation and has been awarded the designations of Certified Professional in Learning and Performance and Certified Performance Technologist. She can be reached at patti@roiinstitute.net.

Jack and Patti Phillips contribute to a variety of journals and have authored a number of books on the subject of accountability and ROI, including: *Measuring the Success of Organization Development* (ASTD Press, 2013); *Survey Basics* (ASTD, 2013); *Measuring the Success of Sales Training* (ASTD Press, 2013); *Measuring ROI in Healthcare* (McGraw-Hill, 2012); *Measuring the Success of Coaching* (ASTD Press, 2012); *10 Steps to Successful Business Alignment* (ASTD, 2012); *The Bottomline on ROI*, 2nd ed. (HRDQ, 2012); *Measuring Leadership Development: Quantify Tour Program's Impact and ROI on Organizational Performance* (McGraw-Hill, 2012); *Measuring ROI in Learning and Development: Case Studies From Global Organizations* (ASTD , 2011); *The Green Scorecard: Measuring the ROI in Sustainability Initiatives* (Nicholas Brealey, 2011); *Return on Investment in Meetings and Events: Tools and Techniques to Measure the Success of All Types of Meetings and Events* (Elsevier, 2008); *Show Me the Money: How to Determine*

ROI in People, Projects, and Programs (Berrett-Koehler, 2007); *The Value of Learning* (Pfeiffer, 2007); *Return on Investment Basics* (ASTD, 2005); *Proving the Value of HR: How and Why to Measure ROI* (SHRM, 2005); *Make Training Evaluation Work* (ASTD, 2004); *The Bottom Line on ROI* (Center for Effective Performance, 2002), which won the 2003 ISPI Award of Excellence; *ROI at Work* (ASTD, 2005); the ASTD In Action casebooks *Measuring ROI in the Public Sector* (2002), *Retaining Your Best Employees* (2002), and *Measuring Return on Investment* Vol. III (2001); the ASTD *Infoline* series, including "Planning and Using Evaluation Data" (2003), "Managing Evaluation Shortcuts" (2001), and "Mastering ROI" (1998); and *The Human Resources Scorecard: Measuring Return on Investment* (Butterworth-Heinemann, 2001).